The Midwife: Or, The Old Woman's Magazine

Midwife, Christopher Smart

THE
MIDWIFE:
OR,
Old Woman's MAGAZINE.

VOL. II.

מ ש מ ת כ ש ם

Rumgoufius, Vol. 32. P. 6741.

Αιεν αριστευειν ϗ υπειροχον εμμεναι αλλων.

Hom.

——— *Non deficit alter*
Aureus & fimili frondefcit virga metallo.

Virg.

As for my Works in Verfe and Profe,
Perhaps I am no Judge of thofe,
Nor do I care what Critics thought 'em,
But this I know, all People bought 'em.

Swift.

LONDON:
Printed for Thomas Carnan, at J. Newbery's, the
Bible and *Sun*, in St. *Paul's Church-Yard.* 1751.

The MIDWIFE.

NUMBER I.

VOL. II.

The genuine Memoirs and most surprising Adventures of a very unfortunate TYE-WIG.

Communicated to Mrs. MIDNIGHT by the poor Sufferer.

HAVING some Business to transact with my good Friend Mr. NEWBERY, in St. *Paul's Church-Yard*, I was the other Day tempted by a fine Morning, to quit my House in St. *James's* Place, without my Chariot, and fairly tramp it for the Benefit of my Health. But before I had reach'd one third Part of my Way, I was overtaken by a Shower, which obliged me to take Shelter in a cover'd Alley; where I saw a Boy wiping a Gentleman's Shoes with a TYE-WIG, in order to prepare them for the Operations of the

Brufh. On this Sight, I cou'd not help contemplating what a Multitude and Variety of Circumftances this fame Wig had pafs'd thro' — and now, was I to follow the Example of the Writers of the laft Century, I fhou'd walk home peaceably, go to Bed, fleep foundly, and in the Morning write a *Vifion* upon this Occafion. But, as it happens, that I have a fuperlative Contempt for thofe old canting Vifionaries; I fhall fairly and fquarely, without Apology, Preface or Preamble, give my Reader the Memoirs of this TYE-WIG, which he very civilly and without Sollicitation deliver'd to me in the following Form of Words.

Madam,

" YOU fee before you one of the moft un-
" fortunate Pieces of Hair that ever poffef-
" fed the Capitol of the human Microcofm,"——
Here I cou'd not help interrupting his TYE-SHIP, and defired him to proceed in a more intelligible, and lefs pedantic Manner, which he thus did accordingly. " Madam, you wou'd have excufed
" my Stile had you known my Education, but
" for your more immediate Satisfaction, I fhall
" proceed with all the Simplicity imaginable. At
" my firft fetting out in the World I was the Pro-
" perty of a young Phyfician, who may with the
" ftricteft Propriety be faid to have *taken* his De-
" gree, becaufe it was *given* him by no Univerfi-
" ty in the World: From the Gravity which I
" lent him he got fome Repute, and being withal
" a very

" a very handfome Fellow, he was often con-
" fulted by Ladies of Diftinction. However,
" the little Credit he had with his Barber often
" threw me into very great and dangerous Dif-
" orders, and had not my Mafter been happily
" executed for poifoning an old Citizen, who
" ftood in the Way of a young *Blood*, my Me-
" moirs might have ended here. — I was fold by
" my Mafter's Executioner to an eminent fecond-
" hand Hair-Merchant in *Middle-Row, Holborn,*
" where I fpent the long Vacation in great Tran-
" quillity; but at the Beginning of the Term I
" was purchafed by a young *Irifh* Templar, and
" call'd to the Bar along with him. Had Na-
" ture furnifh'd the Infide of my Mafter's Head,
" as well as Art by my Means did the Outfide,
" he by this Time might have been a Judge. —
" But, alas! having nothing but me and Impu-
" dence on his Side, he was hifs'd out of the Court,
" laugh'd out of the Coffee-houfe, and finally
" kick'd out of the Kingdom. As for me, I
" I was left with other Effects in the Hands of
" Mr. ***, an eminent Pawnbroker, in *****
" *ftreet, Weftminfter,* from whom I was redeem'd
" by Mr. *Bullock* the Player, who fold me to the
" Wardrobe-Keeper of one of the Theatres.
" I may fay without Vanity, that I have acted
" the principal Parts both in Tragedy and Come-
" dy, to the Satisfaction of the Publick; and
" have often, with the Affiftance of fkilful Barbers,
" gain'd an Applaufe, in which the Actor that

" wore me, had no Share ; and from which I
" have sufficient Reason to be convinced, that a
" certain Quantity of Hair duly bedizen'd with
" perfumed Powder and Oil of sweet Almonds,
" will do more upon the Stage than Gracefulness
" of Action, Propriety of Pronunciation, or any
" other Theatrical Virtue whatsoever. You may
" judge, Madam, how long and how successfully
" I served the Patentee, when I assure you I was
" fifteen Times new mounted while I continued
" in his Majesty's Service. At length one *Garrick*
" came in Pow'r, the Pupil of Art, the Son of
" Nature, and the Cousin-German of *Shakespear*
" and the Passions ; Coats and Wigs which here-
" tofore were primary Qualities in acting, were
" now reduced to a secondary State. The Theatre
" rescued from Jargon, Rant, and senseless Show,
" now became the Temple of manly and ra-
" tional Mirth, and the Vehicle of good Sense
" and Morality. On this fatal Revolution I pru-
" dently abdicated, and was again sold to the
" Merchant of *Middle-Row*. My next Scene of
" Life was a Military one, for I was purchased by
" an Officer in the Welch Fuzileers, and expe-
" rienc'd all the Hardships of Wind and Weather,
" and served in the double Capacity of Caxon and
" Night-Cap. I went thro' a most surprising Di-
" versity of Accidents, there was hardly an Object
" in Nature that did not occur to me, except a
" Block, a Powder-puff, and a Comb ; at length
" in the fatal Action of *Fontenoy*, I lost Part of
                                                    " my

" my Fore-top and one of my Tails; upon which
" my Mafter prefented me to an old Serjeant,
" with whom I fhortly went Fellow-Penfioner to
" *Chelfea* Hofpital. Here I remain'd about Two
" Months, at length the Serjeant happening to be
" drinking a Pot of Porter at the World's End,
" a Perfon of a very fingular Character came in,
" and after tippling pretty freely, fwopt with my
" Mafter for a Brown-bob and Eighteen-pence.
" My prefent Poffeffor was a conftant Attendant
" at the *Temple-Exchange* Coffee-houfe, and his
" Profeffion was of a Nature very extraordinary.
" His Bufinefs was to affift the News-Writers in
" the Vacation, and other Times when there was
" a Dearth of Events; he wou'd make you a
" Plague at *Conftantinople* at a Minute's Warning,
" and for the Confideration of half a Crown
" wou'd dethrone the grand Signior, or kill you
" an hundred Thoufand *Tartars.* He was per-
" haps the only Man that knew the private Conver-
" fations of all the Foreign Minifters at the *Hague,*
" and wou'd publifh you a Letter in the *Daily-*
" *Advertifer,* in which he wou'd unlock the Ca-
" binets of all the crown'd Heads in *Chriftendom.*
" But one Night, chancing to fpeak difrefpect-
" fully of the grand Monarch, a *French* Dancing
" Mafter took him by the Nofe, and threw me
" into the Fire: From this lamentable Cataftro-
" phe, Madam, you may eafily account for my
" prefent Appearance. My Mafter never thought
" it worth his while to attempt my Refcue, and

B 3   " had

" had I not offended the Company with a dif-
" agreeable Stink, fhou'd have inevitably pe-
" rifh'd in the Flames, I was kickt about the
" Coffee-houfe, and trod upon by People of all
" Ranks and Degrees for upwards of a Week,
" when a Country Farmer, a great Œconomift,
" one of whofe Maxims it was, that every Thing
" had its Ufe, took me up by half of my only
" remaining Tail, and put me into his Pocket.
" As foon as I arrived in the Country I was fla-
" tioned on a Mop-ftick, to fright the Crows
" from a Pea-Field, in which Office I ferved for
" about a Fort-night, but a Beggar Man coming
" by one Day, who had Difcretion enough to
" think half a Loaf was better' than no Bread,
" and any Thing of a Wig better than a bald
" Pate, took me from my grand Poft, and placed
" me upon his own Idea-Pot; which, Madam,
" is a Philofophical Name for the Head. This is
" the worthy Gentleman, whom you now fee
" condefcending to amufe himfelf with cleaning
" the Shoes of Perfons of Quality, and who now
" employs me in the fervile Occupation of being
" the Harbinger of the Blacking-Ball, and Gentle-
" man Ufher to a Brufh.

A Letter from a Lady to a Maid Servant who had left her : In which is contained an useful Lesson for all Persons in that State of Life.

Dear SALLY,

I Had your Letter very safe, and tho' I have failed to answer it before, yet my daily Prayers, and best Wishes, have constantly attended you. I trust you have the good Fortune to please where you are, as I hear nothing to the contrary; I go by the old Saying, no News is good News. If you are so happy as to be in Favour with the good Family that you have the Honour to serve, I make no question of your continuing in it, by a constant Endeavour to deserve it.

I told you above, and I told you Truth, that I daily remember you in my Prayers; and, dear *Sally*, at the same Time I will not suppose that you forget to remember yourself. I fancy you lay with the other Maid, and know not that you have a Closet or retiring Place to yourself, but whether you have or not, I intreat you, let no Pretence whatever prevail on you to omit an indispensible Duty: Let no false Notion of Modesty suffer you to neglect an Action that is your utmost Glory to perform ; I hope your fellow Servant thinks as she ought on this Occasion, but if she be so unhappy as not to do it, endeavour to gain her over by your Example, but

B 4 beware

beware of being perverted by hers : To wake in a Morning, and without addreffing the Throne of Grace to commit ourfelf to the Hazards of the Day, is fuch a Degree of Impiety and Fool-hardinefs as fhocks one but to think on ; and furely it is equally the blackeft Ingratitude to clofe our Eyes at Night, without returning our unfeigned Thanks for the Dangers we have efcaped ; thofe Eyes, for ought we know, may never be again unclofed in this World————I was going to offer fome Advice of another Kind, but I recol-lect that, perform but your Duty to your Crea-tor, and all the reft is included.

Be fure in whatever you are about to do, think always on what is due to the Dignity of your Nature. Confider, that although you are placed by Providence in the Degree of a Ser-vant, yet your immortal Soul is of an equal Rank with that of an Emprefs. This Counfel at the firft Glance may appear to encourage Pride, but if duly attended to, it will be far otherwife, and prove the moft effectual Means to extinguifh it, for a proper Confideration on the feveral De-grees of Men in the Order the Wifdom of God has plac'd them with relation to this Life, will teach you to condefcend to your Superiors with-out Meannefs, and learn you to diftinguifh your-felf from thofe below you without Arrogance ; it will hinder Adverfity from oppreffing you ; and if Profperity be your Lot (as I heartily hope it will) it will find you worthy of it ; in a Word, it

will

will make you equal to good Fortune, and superior to ill.

Mr. *H——* joins me in best Respects to your Master and Lady, and Mr. ——; I desire you, whenever you are inclined to write to me, that you would chuse out half an Hour when you can best be spared, and ask Leave; this will save you the Confusion of equivocating, if you are demanded what has been your Employment, and prevent your turning an indifferent Action into a guilty one; for be sure never to forget your Time is not your own, but is entirely due to those you serve, and that you can never employ any of it on your own Occasions without leave without being unjust. Pray, good *Sally*, think of that.

I was concerned to find you had laid out so much Money in Play-things, &c. for the Children, however, acknowledge myself obliged to your good Nature; I shall take the Hint from you of sending this Free to *London*, and save half the Postage; observe my Method, and be not above being taught by any one, any thing that is worthy the Trouble of Learning, no Matter who it is teaches, provided the Instructions are good.

Adieu, dear *Sally*, do me the Justice to believe this Letter dictated from a Heart full of the warmest Wishes for your Welfare, from one who will always regard every Piece of Happiness that

B 5   befalls

befalls you as an additional one to herself, for I am

Your very sincere Friend,

M. ———.

———————————————

* *From the* RAMBLER.

Alternis igitur contendere Verſibus ambo
Cæpere: Alternos Muſæ meminiſſe volebant.

Virg.

AMONG the various Cenſures, which the unavoidable Compariſon of my Performances, with thoſe of my Predeceſſors has pro-
duced, there is none more general than that of
Uniformity, of the Want of thoſe Changes of
Colours which formerly fed the Attention with
unexhauſted Novelty, that Intermixture of Subjects, and Alternation of Manner, by which other
Writers relieved Wearineſs, and awakened Expectation.

I have, indeed, hitherto avoided the Practice
of uniting gay and ſolemn Subjects in the ſame
Paper, becauſe it ſeems abſurd for an Author to
counteract himſelf; to preſs at once with equal
Force upon both Parts of the intellectual Balance,
and give Medicines, which, like the double

* *A Paper publiſh'd every* Tueſday *and* Saturday,
price 2d.

Poiſon

Poifon of *Dryden*, deftroy the Force of one another. I have endeavoured fometimes to divert,
and fometimes to elevate, but have imagined
it an ufelefs Attempt to difturb Merriment by
Solemnity, or interrupt Serioufnefs by Drollery,
yet I fhall this Day publifh two Letters of very
different Tendency, which, I hope, like Tragi-
comedy, may chance to pleafe even when they are
not critically approved.

To the R A M B L E R.

Dear Sir,

THOUGH, as my Mamma tells me, I
am too young to talk at the Table, I have
great Pleafure in liftening to the Converfation of
learned Men, efpecially when they difcourfe of
Things which I do not underftand, and have,
therefore, been of late particularly delighted
with many Difputes about the *Alteration of the
Stile*, which, they fay, is to be done by Act of
Parliament.

One Day, when my Mamma was gone out
of the Room, I afked a very great Scholar what
the Stile was. He told me, he was afraid I
fhould hardly underftand him when he informed
me that it was the ftated and eftablifhed Method
of computing Time. It was not, indeed, likely
that I fhould underftand him; for, I never yet
knew Time computed in my Life, nor can imagine why we fhould be at fo much Trouble to
count what we cannot keep. He did not tell me

B 6 whether

whether we are to count the Time paft, or the Time to come ; but I have confidered them both by myfelf, and think it as foolifh to count Time that is gone, as Money that is fpent ; and as for the Time which is to come, it only feems farther off by counting, and therefore when any Pleafure is promifed me, I always think as little of the Time as I can.

I have fince liftened very attentively to every one that talked upon this Subject, of whom the greater Part feem not to underftand it better than myfelf ; for though they often hint how much the Nation has been miftaken, and rejoice that we are at laft growing wifer than our Anceftors, I have never been able to difcover from them, that any Body has died the fooner for counting Time wrong ; and, therefore, I began to fancy that there was great Buftle with little Confequence.

At laft two Friends of my Papa, Mr. *Cycle* and Mr. *Starlight*, being, it feems, both of high Learning, and able to make an Almanack, began to talk about the New Stile. Sweet Mr. *Starlight*——I am fure I fhall love his Name as long as I live, for he told *Cycle* roundly, with a fierce Look, that we fhould never be right without a *Year of Confufion*. Dear Mr. *Rambler*, did you ever hear any thing fo charming ? a whole Year of Confufion ! When there has been a Rout at Mamma's I have thought one Night of Confufion worth a thoufand Nights of Reft ; and

furely

furely if I can but fee a Year of Confufion, a whole Year, of Cards in one Room, and Dancings in another, here a Feaft, and there a Mafquerade, and Players, and Coaches, and Hurries, and Meffages, and Milleners, and Raps at the Door, and Vifits, and Frolicks, and new Fafhions, I fhall not care what they do with the reft of the Time, nor whether they count it by the old Stile or the new, for 1 am refolved to break loofe from the Nurfery in the Tumult, and plain my Part among the reft; and it will be ftrange if I cannot get a Husband and a Chariot in the Year of Confufion.

Cycle, who is neither fo young nor fo handfome as *Starlight*, very gravely maintained, that all the Perplexity may be avoided by leaping over eleven Days in the Reckoning; and indeed if it fhould come only to this I think the new Style is a delightful Thing, for my Mamma fays that I fhall go to court when I am Sixteen; and if they can but contrive often to leap over eleven Days together, the Months of Reftraint will foon be at an End. It is ftrange that with all the Plots that have been laid againft Time, they could never kill it by Act of Parliament before. Dear Sir, if you have any Vote or any Intereft get them but for once to deftroy eleven Months, and then I fhall be as old as fome married Ladies. But this is defired only if you think they will not comply with Mr. *Starlight*'s Scheme, for nothing furely could pleafe me like a Year of Confufion,

when

when I fhall no longer be fixed this Hour to my
Pen, and the next to my Needle, and wait at home
for the Dancing Mafter one Day, and the next for
the Mufick Mafter, but run from Ball to Ball,
and from Drum to Drum, and fpend all my
time without Tafks, and without Account, and
go out without telling whither, and come home
without regard to prefcribed Hours or family
Rules.

I am,

　　S I R,

　　　Your Humble Servant,

　　　　　　　Properantia.

Mr. Rambler,

I Was feized this Morning with an unufual Pen-
fivenefs, and finding that Books only ferved to
heighten it, took a Ramble into the Fields, in
Hopes of Relief and Invigoration from the Keen-
nefs of the Air and Brightnefs of the Sun.

As I wandered wrapped up in thought, my
Eyes were ftruck with the Hofpital for the Reception of deferted Infants, which I furveyed
with Pleafure, till by a natural Train of Sentiment, I began to reflect on the Fate of the Mothers ? for to what Shelter can they fly ? only to
the Arms of their Betrayer, which perhaps are
now no longer open to receive them ; and then
how quick muft be the Tranfition from deluded
Virtue to fhamelefs Guilt, and from fhamelefs
Guilt to hopelefs Wretchednefs ?

　　　　　　　　　　　The

The Anguiſh that I felt left me no Reſt till I had, by your Means, addreſſed myſelf to the Publick on Behalf of thoſe forlorn Creatures, the Women of the Town; whoſe Miſery here might ſurely induce us to endeavour, at leaſt, their Preſervation from eternal Puniſhment.

Theſe were all once, if not virtuous at leaſt innocent, and might ſtill have continued blame-leſs and eaſy, but for the Arts and Inſinuations of thoſe whoſe Rank, Fortune, or Education furniſhed them with Means to corrupt or to de-lude them. Let the Libertine reflect a Moment an the Situation of that Woman, who being for-ſaken by her Corrupter, is reduced to the Ne-ceſſity of turning Proſtitute for Bread, and judge of the Enormity of his Guilt by the Miſery which it produces.

It cannot be doubted but that Numbers fol-low this dreadful Courſe of Life, with Shame, Horror, and Regret; but, where can they hope for Refuge? " *The World is not their Friend, nor* " *the World's Law.*" Their Sighs, and Tears, and Groans, are criminal in the Eye of their Tyrants, the Bully and the Bawd, who fatten on their Miſery, and threaten them with Want or a Goal, if they ſhew the leaſt Deſign of eſcaping from their Bondage.

" To wipe the Tears from off all their Faces," is a Task too hard for Mortals; but to alleviate the Misfortunes of others is often within the moſt limited Power, yet the Opportunities which

every

every Day affords of relieving the most wretched of human Beings are overlooked and neglected with equal Disregard of Policy and Goodness.

There are Places indeed, set apart, to which these unhappy Creatures may resort when the Diseases of Incontinence seize upon them; but, if, they obtain a Cure, to what are they reduced? either to return with the small Remains of Beauty to their former Guilt, or perish in the Streets with complicated Want.

How frequently have the Gay and Thoughtless in their Evening Frolicks, seen a Band of these miserable Females, covered with Rags, shivering with Cold, and pining with Hunger; and, without either pitying their Calamities, or reflecting upon the Cruelty of those who perhaps, first seduced them by Caresses of Fondness, or Magnificence of Promises, go on to reduce others to the same Wretchedness by the same Means.

To stop the Increase of this deplorable Multitude, is undoubtedly the first and most pressing Consideration. To prevent Evil is the great End of Government, the End for which Vigilance and Severity are properly employed; but surely those whom Passion or Interest have already depraved, have some Claim to Compassion, from Beings equally frail and fallible with themselves. Nor will they long groan in their present Afflictions, if all those were to contribute to their Relief, that owe their Exemption from the

same

fame Diftrefs to fome other Caufe, than their Wifdom and their Virtue.

I am, &c.

A M I C U S.

A LETTER *from Mrs.* MIDNIGHT *to the College of* Phyficians, *in which is proved that* Old Women *and* Nature *are their greateft Enemies.* To *which is added, A modeft Propofal for extirpating the one, and for preventing the Operations of the other.*

Gentlemen,

THE World in general would be furprifed at my addreffing you in this affectionate Manner, and fpeaking at the fame time fo difrefpectfully as I am obliged to do of my own Sex, were I not to offer fome Reafons to prove the Rectitude of my Conduct. I am, Gentlemen (and I wou'd have every Body know it) under the greateft Obligations to your Fraternity; and if, as a certain Author fays, Ingratitude be worfe than the Sin of Witchcraft, fure Gratitude will be a fufficient Plea for my taking upon me the Defence of your Characters, and your Profeffion; Charaters that ftand full in the Front of Fame, and a Profeffion that has rais'd and fupported itfelf meerly by Art, has no Connection with, or De-

pendance

pendance on Nature, but is self-exiftent, and like a true Noun fubftantive ftands alone.

To prove this, and at the fame time to demonftrate the Ufefulnefs of your Science, we need only look back to the Days of Ignorance and Simplicity ; thofe Days when the People had no Means of getting genteely out of the World, but were obliged to wait till they were carried off by mere old Age ; and this did not happen to fome till they had lived feveral hundred Years ; nay, we have an Account of one old Fellow, *Methu-felah*, I think his Name was, who lived to the Age of Nine hundred and ninety nine. An evident Proof of their total Neglect of Phyfick ! Difeafes they had in thofe Days, that is certain ; but then, as they had no Practitioners in Phyfick to fupport them, they were foon rooted out. The Care of the Sick was the Province of the *Old Woman*, who, together with the Aid of one *Nature*, whom you may probably have heard of, foon cured their Patients : And fo ignorant were they of the true Principles of Phyfick, that they depended entirely upon Experience, confulted what they called the Symptoms, to diftinguifh one Difeafe from another, and when they had found out a Remedy that had cured nineteen Patients of any one Diftemper, they foolifhly fuppofed the fame Medicine would cure the twentieth. Thus they ignorantly went on, and in order to convey this their Experience to Pofterity, the Difeafes (with the Symptoms by which it might be known) the
Remedy,

Remedy, and the Succefs were engraven on Pillars, or written on the Walls of their Temples. So that then there was no more Art required to cure any Diforder, than there is now to walk over the New Bridge, *Weftminfter.* But when the Dawn of true medical Knowledge appeared, when we began to difcover the mechanical Operation of every Medicine, and to find out the latent Caufe of every Difeafe, Phyfick was no more that fimple filly Thing; for the true and invincible Heroes of the Science immediately called in the mechanical Laws, and an ingenious and ufeful Application was made of the Momenta of the Fluids, Cylinders, Triangles, Sines, Tangents and Secants, Levers, Ropes and Pullies. Millftones were brought into the Stomach, Flint and Steel into the Blood Veffels, and Hammer and Vice into the Lungs; and now People began to die in a reafonable Time, and the Son had fome hopes of enjoying his Father's Eftate before he himfelf was an old Man. Happy 'twould be for us, if Phyfick was to reft here! Happy would it be if all the Sick were committed to your Care, obliged to fwallow your Prefcriptions, and no Innovators permitted to break in upon your Practice. But fo it is, and I am forry to fay it, there are certain *old Women* who have had a Defcription of Difeafes and Remedies for them handed down from their foolifh Predeceffors, with which they cure Patients after they have been carried through the regular

Forms

Forms of Phyfick, and have been confign'd to Death by the moft knowing of ye all.

Mr. *Wilfon* t'other Day coming off a long Journey, was taken very ill, his Father immediately fent for a Gentleman of the Faculty, who order'd twenty Ounces of Blood to be taken from him, and then prefcrib'd him Sixteen Blifters and a Vomit. But his Grandmother (a mere old Woman) came in at that Inftant, and, upon examining the Patient, found that he had rode eighty Miles that Day, and, as he was well in the Morning when he fet out, fhe concluded that his Illnefs, and the fainting Fit he had, was occafion'd by the Fatigue of the Journey. She therefore fet afide the Prefcription; nor wou'd fhe fuffer him to be blooded; but order'd him to Bed, gave him fome warm Whey with Hartfhorn Drops in it, and lo in the Morning he was well. — Now here was a good Job fpoil'd by the Interpofition of an *old Woman*.

Mrs. *Mary Grove* was feiz'd with a Diforder which bereft her of her Senfes, fhe was abfolutely mad for fome Months, and attended by feveral of *our* Faculty, but the Difeafe was too obftinate to be removed till *Goody Curtis* was call'd in; who, when fhe had a lucid Interval, defired to fpeak to her. This old Woman afk'd her a Queftion, which was only proper to be put to a Woman, and upon Enquiry found out the Caufe of her Diforder, and with fome gentle Cathartics and Steel, the Lunatic was foon reftor'd. Now is not this provoking?

voking ? And if thefe old Jades are fuffered to go on in this Manner, true Phyfick will be turn'd topfey turvey, and all our valuable and effential *Greek* and *Latin* Terms will be laugh'd at.

Befides thefe fworn Enemies of yours, there is another combin'd with them, who is altogether as powerful and as much to be guarded againft, and that is NATURE; for fhe works in the Dark like a Mole under Ground, and ufes a thoufand little Tricks to baffle your Abilities.

Mr. *Johnfon* was feiz'd with a violent Diforder in his Head and Stomach, and, as he was a rich Man, they call'd in my worthy and learned Friends Dr. EMETIC, Dr. SUDORIFIC, Dr. CATHARTIC, and Dr. BLISTER. As the Gentleman was in imminent Danger they were defir'd to be fpeedy in their Conference. The firft Point to be fettled was who fhou'd write, which, after each had pleaded his Preeminence about an Hour, was agreed on; and Dr. EMETIC, after fhaking his Head a confiderable Time, obferv'd, *that it was an Exfoliation of the Glands; which, like the broken Wheels of a Watch, being unable to perform their Office, the unconcocted Matter had fallen upon the Membranous Coats of the Inteftines, and caufed a Laceration which muft be removed by a* VOMIT. Dr. SUDORIFIC faid, *it was a Pleurifie in the Thigh, which he was for fweating away.* In fhort, they were all four of fourteen different Opinions, and when Arguments fail'd, Arms were call'd in to their Aid; and the Room was foon ftrew'd with diflocat-

diflocated Canes, Tags of Wigs, and other Marks of a furious Engagement. During this Squabble, *Nature* excited in the Patient a powerful Purging, and he was so well recover'd before the Fray was over, that he fairly got up and run away, and by that Means preferved both his Life and his Money.

These, Gentlemen, are some of the fly Tricks of Nature, who is ever endeavouring to baffle your Art, and give the World a mean Opinion of your Learning, that fhe herfelf forfooth may be thought the chief Phyfician: And I believe from reading, confidering, and re-confidering what I have faid, you will find that *Old Women* and *Nature* are your greateft Enemies; and if after Deliberation and Confultation you find this to be true, I wou'd humbly propofe that the firft may be entirely extirpated, and the Operations of the laft may be as much as poffibly prevented: And how this may be moft effectually accomplifh'd, I fhall fignify to you in my next; for I have always your Welfare at Heart, and fhall upon every Occafion be ready to teftify with what Truth and Sincerity I am,

GENTLEMEN,

Your very affectionate Friend,

M. MIDNIGHT.

The

The ITCH *of* SCRIBBLING *proved to be catching.*

THAT this Diforder, like many of the cuta-
neous Kind is catching, may I think be proved from a Multitude of Cafes that have lately fallen
under my Cognizance ; and whoever confiders the
Nature, and bad Effects of it, will fee alfo the
Neceffity of this Invefigation. From a thoufand
Inftances that I have at hand, I fhall felect but a
few ; the firft I fhall introduce is the Cafe of
Mr. *J. Honeyfuckle*, who was originally a Barber
near the *Temple*, and a good honeft Man, that
had no more to fay for himfelf than other People,
till he became acquainted with the Mafter of
George's Coffee-houfe, and was called in to fhave
the WITS. There is fomething very powerful
and aftonifhing in the Nature and Action of the
Effluvia which afcends from certain Bodies, and I
doubt not but it was the Effluvia that afcended
from the Heads of thefe People while *John* was
fhaving them, that wrought this tickling Irri-
tation in his Fancy, and brought on him the Itch
of Scribbling. And perhaps it is alfo owing to the
Effluvia that dropped from the Brains of *John*,
which has affected many of the Members of that
Society with the terrible Degree of Dulnefs they
at prefent poffefs. When I look into my Book of
Mechanics, read over the Laws of Motion, and
find that all Bodies act reciprocally on each other,

that

that the Horse draws as much as the Log, and the Log as the Horse, I am confirmed in this Opinion: But what this Effluvia can be, or of what Sort of Materials it is compofed, no Man can tell, Doctor Puzzle, indeed, affirms, " That it is the Quin- " teffence of an Effence, which being. fpecifically " lighter than the heavier Parts, flies off one Bo- " dy, like *Alchohol,* and infinuates itfelf into ano- " ther Body fome how, and fomewhere, fo that that " Body is affected with it." But as the Doctor's Definition does not much affect or inftruct me, I muft beg Leave to retain my old Opinion, till I can find a better, and to conclude that this Efflu- via is a Sort of Animalcula, or Maggot, which infinuates itfelf through the Pores of the Skin ; and the only Difference between this Itch and the other is, that the Animalculæ in this are finer, and have the Power of infinuating themfelves through both the Skin and the Skull ; and this I think will plainly appear, when we confider the Manner and the dif- ferent Degrees of Infection. Mr. *Kenderico* was born of honeft Parents, who put him Apprentice to a Rule- maker, hoping thereby fo far to have provided for him, that he fhould have lived in the World, enjoyed a Cut from a hot Joint of Meat every *Sunday,* and have had a new Coat every *Eafter* in the Year: But, unfortunately for this poor Man, a Poet came in- to his Mafter's Shop, during his Apprenticefhip, and, while he was bargaining for a black-lead Pencil, receiv'd a Meffage from the Mufes, that precipitated him away without his Hat, which was

carry'd

carried after him by Mr. *Kenderico*, who, as it then rained, very inadvertently put it on his own Head, and, by that Means, contracted this terrible Diforder, which indeed has been the more fatal to him, on Account of his Trade; for the Effluvia of the Brafs ufed in the Joints of his Rules, has fo cafe-hardened his Face, that 'tis become abfolutely callous, and knows no more the Vermilion Tincture blufhed by the native Force of Modefty, than the Defarts of *Barca* do of the Bloom or Fragrancy of the Rofe: Befides the Effluvia from the Lead of his Pencils and other Inftruments, intermixing itfelf with the reft, preponderates all to the Bottom; every Thing he fcribbles finks into Oblivion, and yet the Incitation continues on the poor Wretch, and pufhes him on towards his own Deftruction.

STAMPERO, though a Boy of no Talents, Tafte, or Genius in the World, is afflicted with this Diforder; which Doctor *Rocko*, who attended him, affures me was caught only by packing up Magazines, the dulleft Things in the Univerfe; and this pitiful Creature is now in a deplorable State, ever attempting to do fomething, which always ends in nothing; for his Lines are as void of Meaning as his Advertifements are of Manners.

But if we leave thefe Wretches, who are the Drofs of Mankind, and afcend to a higher Sphere, we fhall fee the fame Traces, the fame wonderful Effects of the Effluvia. This is to be difcovered even in the inimitable Mr. SEDGLY; who,

C   though

though a Perſon incomparably above thoſe I have already quoted, and whoſe Pen, though infinitely ſuperior not only to them, but to moſt of our modern Scribblers, is neverthelefs indebted to the Effluvia evaporated from the Wits he has been almoſt continually in Company with : It was from them he imbibed this *Cacoethes* of Scribbling, and we may very well account for the Difference between his Writings and the Performances of the Perſons I have mentioned above, if we conſider that Nature has given him an extenſive Proportion of ſolid Underſtanding, and that he has long been a Companion not only for the Wits of the Times, but for the Men of Senſe. His Poem on Mr. *Worlidge*, the ingenious Painter over the *Little Piazza*, in *Covent-Garden*, is an evident Proof of his Genius, his Learning, and his Judgment in the Polite Arts ; and in his Pamphlet intitled, " Obſervations on Mr. *Fielding*'s Enquiry" there are uncommon Inſtances of his Knowledge of Mankind, as well as of his Sagacity and Penetration into the Laws and Polity of his Country.

But what more fully, and beyond all Contradiction, proves this Diſorder to be contagious, is the Caſe of this Gentleman's Dog *Colebrook*, who from only lying under the Table where the Wits uſually meet, and by walking out with his Friend *B———r*, is become one of the moſt eminent Writers of the Age, and has penned one Piece which has been receiv'd with Commendations even by the ingenious Authors

thors of the STUDENT, who have inferted it in their admirable Collection.

A few *Thoughts concerning* Elegy-Writing. *By Mrs.* MIDNIGHT.

WAS I difpofed to treat this Subject in a methodical Manner, I fhou'd be gravell'd at the firft fetting out, for the Inventor of this Kind of Writing is entirely unknown, and for this Affertion I have no lefs Authority than that of *Horace.*

> *Quis tamen* exiguos *elegos emifferit Author*
> *Grammatici certant & adhuc fub judice his eft.*

That is, *there is a great Conteft among the Critics, which is ftill undecided, who was the firft Inventer of* PIDDLING ELEGIES.

That *Horace* had a very mean Opinion of this Sort of Compofition, is clear from his contemptuous Manner in fpeaking of it. But what in the Name of *Phœbus* wou'd he fay, was he alive to perufe the Products of the prefent Monody-mongers. What miferable, infipid, unanimated Stuff are we pefter'd with ? It is a ftrange thing that People will not reflect, that though this is the meaneft Species of Poetry, 'tis ftill a Species of Poetry, and confequently requires very exalted Talents : No Matter for that—Away we go on,

Neck or Nothing, without either Senfe, Genius, or Learning——Gentle Reader, Do you chufe a little *Imagery* from one of thefe exquifite Bards ——Here it is for you.

> † Hard by a ftrange fantaftic Group appear,
>   Wan Cowardice, each Moment changing
>   Seat;
> Weak *Apprehenfion,* PRICKED IN THE Rear,
>   And fober Melancholy, Mother of Conceit.

And prefently after ————

> Look now where TIP-TOED Fear with fhiv'ring
>   Lips,
>   Has turn'd the Key, and wide her Portal
>   ftands;
> Quick Apprehenfion in before us trips,
>   And bids us follow with her beck'ning Hands.

If the Gentleman had fearch'd the whole Language for an Epithet for Fear, he cou'd not have found one fo unapplicable as TIP-TOED.

But poor APPREHENSION! fo inhumanly has he treated her, that fhe is exactly in the fame difaftrous Cafe as the *Dragon* of *Wantley,* in the old Ballad——PRICKED IN THE REAR——upon which he makes his Complaint to Mr. *More* in the following *Monody.*

† *Kenrick's Monody,* Page the 16th.

Oh

.Oh *More* of *More-Hall*
Thou fad Raf——call
 . I wifh I had feen thee never;
With the Thing in thy Foot,
Thou haft PRICKT MY A——I-GUT,
 And I am undone for ever.

It muft be acknowledged, in Juftice to Mr.
Kenrick, that his Piece is very equal, and tho'
he is an infufferable Poet, yet he's a very commendable Rule-maker, and underftands black
Lead Pencils.

N. B. Mrs. MIDNIGHT does not intend, by
what fhe has faid on Monodies and Elegies, to reflect upon Mr. *Rolt,* whom fhe efteems as a very
good Writer.

———————

Mrs. MIDNIGHT'S *Letter to the Ghoft of*
ALEXANDER the Great.

On the Subject of Glory.

HAD I been fo unfortunate, as to have lived, at
the fame Time with your Worfhip, I fhou'd
have waited upon you in Perfon, becaufe nothing is
more liable to Mifinterpretation than a Letter. But
as N———ers now ftand, Correfpondence muft fupply
the Place of Converfation; and Dr. *Brimftone* has
informed me, that an Epiftle, directed to *Alexander
the Great,* at his Chambers in Hell, will certainly

come

come fafe to Hand. I have confulted a good many Cafuifts on the Subject of Glory, but never received any tolerable Satisfaction from the moft expert of them. As you was the greateft Afpirer after it, I make no queftion but your Mafter *Ariftotle* gave you an accurate Definition of it, which I fhall take as a particular Favour, if you'll communicate to me; for my own Part was I not certified by the Writings of *Quintus Curtius* and others, I fhou'd have concluded, that you was begot by an *Hottentot*, born of a Tygrefs, and educated by a Butcher. If a Man murders his Neighbour, he is try'd, condemn'd, executed, and hung in Chains with a very little Ceremony: But if he murders Ten Thoufand Men, then it becomes *Glory*, and you have all the Poets, Painters, Printers, and Priefts to celebrate him for the GOOD he has done.— According to this Rule, I look upon you to be the beft Man that ever liv'd, but according to the Rule of Humanity and Common-Senfe, I believe you to be the greateft Scoundrel that ever exifted.

Your Servant,
M. MIDNIGHT.

A COUNTRY JUSTICE, *a True Story.*

BESET with Books, but little Law,
I once a Country Juftice faw,
A lighted Pipe regal'd his Nofe,
A Mug of Ale difpell'd his Woes;

His

His Face like Morning Sun appear'd,
An Elbow Chair his Body rear'd :
Before this Man of Law was brought,
A Girl, who in the Fact was caught :
Justice first took a Swig of Ale,
Then bid the Wench begin her Tale ;
Leer'd at the Girl, each Word she spoke,
Quite tickled at the smutty Joke ;
Made her the luscious Tale repeat,
And when, and how, was done the Feat :
Thus warm'd, he takes the Wench aside,
Tells her far worse will her betide ;
That *Bridewell* instant is her Lot,
Unless she'll let him —— you know what.

A very pretty Rascal ! A fine Fellow this to pre-
serve Peace, and protect Virtue and Modesty ; I
have a great Mind to put the Rogue's Name at full
length.

Lovely HARRIOTE.

A Crambo Song *by Mrs.* Midnight's *Nephew.*

I.

GREAT *Phœbus* in his vast Career,
Who forms the self-succeeding Year,
   Thron'd in his Amber Chariot,
Sees not an Object half so bright,
Nor gives such Joy, such Life, such Light,
   As dear delicious *Harriote.*

II.

Pedants of dull phlegmatic Turns,
Whose Pulse not beats, whose Blood not burns,
  Read *Malbranche*, *Boyle*, and *Marriote*,
I scorn their Philosophic Strife,
And study Nature from the Life,
  (Where most she shines) in *Harriote*.

III.

When she admits another Woer,
I rave like *Shakespear*'s jealous *Moor*,
  And am, as ranting *Barry* hot;
True, virtuous, lovely was his Dove,
But Virtue, Beauty, Truth, and Love,
  Are other Names for *Harriote*.

IV.

Ye honest Members, who oppose,
And fire both Houses with your Prose,
  Tho' never can ye carry ought;
You might command the Nations Sense,
And without Bribery convince,
  Had you the Voice of *Harriote*.

V.

You of the Musick common weal,
Who borrow, beg, compose, or steal
  Cantata, Air, or Ariet;
You'd burn your cumbrous Works in soote;
And sing, compose, and play no more,
  If once you heard my *Harriote*.

Were

VI.

Were there a Wretch, who durſt eſſay
Such wond'rous Sweetneſs to betray,
 I'd call him an *Iſcariot*;
But her ev'n Satyrs can't annoy,
So ſtrictly chaſte, tho' kindly coy,
 Is fair angelic *Harriote*.

VII.

While Sultans, Emperors, and Kings
(Mean Appetite of earthly Things)
 In all the Waſte of War-riot
Love's ſofter Duel be my Aim,
Praiſe, Honour, Glory, Conqueſt, Fame,
 Are center'd all in *Harriote*.

VIII.

I ſwear by *Hymen*, and the Pow'rs
That haunt Love's ever-bluſhing Bow'rs,
 So ſweet a Nymph to marry ought;
Then may I hug her ſilken Yoke,
And give the laſt, the final Stroke,
 T'accompliſh lovely *Harriote*.

On

On seeing Miss H—— P——t, *in an Apo-*
thecary's Shop.

FAllacious Nymph, who here by Stealth,
　　Would seem to be the Goddess Health!
Mask'd in that divine Disguise,
Think'st thou to 'scape Poetick Eyes?
Back, *Siren* — for I know thou'st stray'd,
From the harmonious Ambuscade;
Where many a Traveller, that took
The Invitation of thy Look,
Has felt the Coz'nage of thy Charms,
Tickled to Death within thy Arms.
Know, that I saw you Yester-Night,
At once with Horror and Delight,
Drag *Luna* from her heavenly Frame,
And out-shine her when she came.
Yes, Inchantress, I can tell
How by the Virtue of a Spell,
Cloath'd like Cherub-Innocence,
Here you fix your Residence;
That securely you may mix
Your Philters in the Streams of *Styx*;
And have at Hand, in every Part,
Materials for your magic Art,
Fossils, Fungus's, and Flow'rs,
With all the fascinating Pow'rs.
God of the prescribing Trade,
Doctor *Phœbus*, lend thine Aid;
If thou'lt some Antidote devise,
I'll call thee *Harvey* of the Skies;

Or

Or (for, at one Glance, thou can'ft fee
All that is, or that fhall be,
Intentions rip'ning into Act,
And Plans emerging up to Fact)
Look in her Eyes, and thence explain
All the Mifchief that they mean.
Say in what Grove, and near what Trees
Will fhe feek the *Hippomenes.*
There, there I'll meet her, — there I'll try
Th' affwafive Pow'r of Harmony.
I think I've got an Amulet,
That will her Rage awhile abate.
No — all Refiftance is in vain ——
Charmer I yield —— I hug my Chain :
Alas ! I fee 'tis to no End
With fuch Puiffance to contend ;
For finte continually you dwell
In that Apothecary's Cell ;
And while fo ftudioufly you pry
Into the fage Difpenfary,
And read fo many Doctors Bill,
You learn infallibly to kill.——

To *Mrs.* M I D N I G H T.

MADAM,

IT is an Affertion of Mr, *Voltaire's,* that *Hu-
dibras* cannot poffibly be tranflated into any
other Language, without lofing all the Drollery
and Spirit of the Original ; which perhaps you

C 6   will

will not fubfcribe to without fome Hefitation, when you perufe the following Lines, which were actually render'd extempore by a Gentleman of *Cambridge.*

So learned *Taliacotius,* from
The brawny Part of Porter's Bum,
Cut fupplemental Nofes, which
Shou'd laft as long as Parent Breech:
But foon as Date of *Knock* was out,
Off dropt the fupplemental Snout.

Sic *Taliacoti* ars amica
Victoris parte de poftîcâ,
Falfis invenit carnem nafis,
Quæ duret tamdiu, quam *Bafis:*
Sed roftrum patili ruinâ
Cum clune periit confobrinâ.

To Mifs A———n.

I.

LONG with undiftinguifh'd Flame
I lov'd each fair, each witty Dame;
My Heart the Belle-Affembly gain'd,
And all an equal Sway maintain'd.

II.

But when you came, you ftood confeft
Sole Sultana of my Breaft;

For

For you eclips'd, fupremely fair,
All the whole Seraglio there.

III.

In this her Mien, in that her Grace,
In a third I lov'd a Face;
But you in ev'ry Feature fhine,
Univerfally divine.

IV.

What can thofe tumid Paps excell,
Do they fink, or do they fwell?
While thofe lovely wanton Eyes
Sparkling meet them, as they rife.

V.

Thus in filver Cynthia feen
Glift'ning o'er the glaffy Green,
While attracted fwell the Waves,
Emerging from their inmoft Caves.

VI.

When to fweet Sounds your Steps you fuit
And weave the Minuet to the Lute,
Heav'ns! how you glide! — her Neck — her
    Cheft,
Does fhe move, or does fhe reft?

VII.

As thofe roguifh Eyes advance,
Let me catch their fide-long Glance,
Soon — or they'll elude my Sight,
Quick as Lightning and as bright.

VIII.

Thus the bafhful Pleiad peeps,
Charms her Moment, and retreats;

Then

Then peeps again,——then ſkulks unſeen,
Veil'd behind the azure Skreen.

IX.

Like the ever-toying Dove,
Smile Immenſity of Love;
Be *Venus* in each outward Part,
And wear the Veſtal in your Heart.

X.

When I aſk a Kiſs or ſo——
Grant it with a begging no,
And let each Roſe that decks your Face,
Bluſh aſſent to my Embrace.

The M I S E R *and the* M O U S E.

An E P I G R A M *from the* Greek,

By Mrs. M I D N I G H T.

TO a Mouſe, ſays a Miſer, "My dear Mr.
    Mouſe,
"Pray what may you pleaſe for to want in my
    Houſe?
Says the Mouſe, "Mr. Miſer, pray keep your-
    ſelf quiet,
"You are ſafe in your Perſon, your Purſe and
    your Diet,
"A Lodging I want, which ev'n you may afford,
"But none wou'd come here to beg, borrow,
    or board.

The

The MIDWIFE'S POLITICKS : Or, *Goſſip's Chro-nicle of the Affairs of Europe.*

SPAIN.

WE are ſtill informed of the Augmentation of the naval Force of this Country. The Bri-tiſh Miniſter has preſented another Remonſtrance a-gainſt the Spaniſh Privateers and Guarda Coſtas moleſt-ing the Navigation of the Britiſh Subjects in the Ame-rican Seas ; and alſo ſome Remarks relating to the Right of Navigation in the Bay of Honduras, which makes it reported that his Catholic Majeſty has ſent Orders for puniſhing with Death ſuch Commanders of Guarda Coſtas as have acted with Illegality to the Britiſh Mer-chants. There is a Rumour of another Negotiation car-rying on between Mr. Keene and the Spaniſh Miniſtry, which is conjectured to be another definitive Convention for explaining the laſt. But any old Woman, without the Spirit of Divination, may readily perceive that the ſagacious Spaniard will ſtill temporize with the Court of London, and perhaps make Don Benjamin an old Wo-man in good earneſt ; for the Spaniards are now relieved from the Load of Petticoat Government, and the Far-neſe Loquacity is vaniſhed from the Cabinet, where the natural Gravity of the Country is reſumed.

ITALY.

The holy Succeſſor of St. Peter intends to make a Promotion of nine Cardinals to the vacant Hats ; but Benedict XIV. has too great a Diſcernment to let any other old Woman into the Conclave, and give us another Pope Joan. Indolence and Luxury are the Foſt-erers of Pride, and this has occaſioned the ambitious Sons of the ſacerdotal Purple, to ſollicit the Catholic Powers to grant their Eminences the Precedency of Rank from

their

their Ambaſſadors where-ever they meet ; but his Sardinian Majeſty does not ſeem inclinable to gratify their Vanity, and it is expected they will be equally diſappointed at other Courts. The other Powers of Italy have nothing to incite our Curioſity at preſent ; but I cannot help obſerving, if theſe States were as unanimous in their political Intereſt as in their Religion, that a confederated Fleet may be ſpeedily equiped, which would awe the Inſolence of the Barbarian Rovers ; even this may be done without the Aſſiſtance of another Doria ; for an old Woman, at the Head of a formidable Squadron, would make theſe piratical Adventurers dread to ſail out of their Harbours.

T U R K E Y.

Beauty ſeems now diſregarded in the Seraglio of the Grand Seignior ; the favourite Sultana has loſt her Influence over the ductile Heart of Mahomet ; and a Spirit of War ſeems to be rekindled amongſt the Turks ; but to the Honour of the female Sex be it ſpoken, the Virgin Empreſs of Ruſſia, and the good Wife of the Emperor of Germany, can make the Ottomans tremble and repent their Temerity, if they ſhould endeavour to paſs either the Danube, the Neiſter, or the Don. The Turks very probably encourage the African Rovers, by aſſuring them of Aſſiſtance if attacked by the Chriſtian Powers ; which they ſeem apprehenſive will certainly happen ; but the Inhabitants of Algiers, Tunis, and Tripoli, appear to diſregard the Danger which has been long threatened them.

F R A N C E.

While this Power is ſecretly fomenting a Rupture between the Courts of Peterſburgh and Berlin, ſhe is making the neceſſary Preparations for aſſiſting his Pruſſian Majeſty on any Emergency ; with whom the Moſt Chriſtian

Chriftian King has lately concluded a Treaty, by which he is obliged to furnifh his Ally with 30000 Foot and 10000 Horfe. The French are alfo indefatigably increafing their Navy, from whence every old Woman may prognofticate what may happen in the Baltick, if Ruffia fhould be attacked by Sweden.

Terrible Hurricanes have happened in feveral Parts of France, particularly at Nantes in Britany, where, in the adjacent Road of Paimboeuf, out of 70 Ships at Anchor, only 4 rode out the Tempeft, the reft being either loft or driven to Sea ; by which 800 Seamen were drowned, and the Damages done within that Diftrict amoun to ten Millions of Livres. The Waters of the Seyne have overflowed a great Part of Paris ; and the Clergy are very fedulous in deprecating the divine Mercy ; in which I heartily concur, though, as an honeft old *Englifh* Woman, it is my Duty to wifh that France may be loaded with Adverfity.

NETHERLANDS.

Nothing has reached us from this Part of the Continent worthy of Attention. Prince Charles of Lorrain lives in great Magnificence at Bruffels, where, like a young Scipio, the Laurels of the Hero dignify the Man, and the Victories of War ferve only to augment the Serenity of Peace. The Dutch are now reftrained by their Stadtholder from that obftinate chattering, which diftinguifhed the greateft Part of their Deputies with the Appellation of old Women during the Courfe of the late War ; when, I may juftly infift upon it, they fhewed the Irrefolution and Cowardice of fo many female Goffips, together with all the cautionary Indolence of Age and Infirmity. The Stadtholder finds himfelf invefted with little lefs than a fovereign Authority over
thefe

thefe penurious Republicans, who are obliged to conceal their turbulent Difpofitions; while every thing is
conducted with Secrecy and Regularity in the Affembly
of the States.

GERMANY.

The King of Pruffia is ftill averfe to the Election of
a King of the Romans, to which he is incited by the
non-execution of the Treaty of Drefden, concluded
on the 14th of December, 1745; fuch as the guarantying Silefia by the Empire, and the Regulation of a
future Commerce, the former of which he has never
been able to procure, tho' by the 3d Article of the Treaty
of Hanover, made between his Majefty and the King of
Great Britain, this was exprefly ftipulated to be done;
and without the Affurance of which the Pruffian Monarch would not have concluded the Treaty of Drefden
in fo moderate a manner for the Queen of Hungary and
Elector of Saxony, at a time when his victorious Troops
had over-run that Electorate, and were in Poffeffion of
the capital City.

The Court of Vienna is apprehenfive of a Diftur-
bance from the Ottoman Forces affembling on the Confines of Hungary, in which Kingdom a Body of Impe-
rialifts are forming for its fecurity.

The Elector of Cologne has renounced his fubfidiary
Engagements with the Maritime Powers, and thrown
himfelf into the Arms of France, which is a very extraordinary Affair; becaufe this Prince cannot but remember the Devaftation that the French Troops, commanded by Marfhal Maillebois, committed in his Territories in the Year 1744, when his Dilection nobly
refufed them a Paffage, though in the Service of his
Brother the late Emperor. From this Inconfiftency, his

electo-

electoral Highneſs ſeems in his Dotage, and therefore ought to be inveſted with the Mantle of an old Woman, rather than with his eccleſiaſtical Habiliments, which, I am afraid, will contribute little to the Proſpect of Heaven for the Prince, if the Prieſt diſclaims the tender Tie of Conſcience, with the Virtues of a Patriot, and the Duty of a Sovereign.

DENMARK.

The Court is only attentive to the increaſe of Commerce, and the Proſperity of the Inhabitants. A Squadron of ten Ships, is ordered to convoy 600 regular Troops to the Coaſt of Africa, where they are intended to eſtabliſh a new Colony. The Danes and Swedes appear to have forgot all their former Animoſities; and, to corroborate this Harmony, a Marriage Contract has been reciprocally agreed to between the Prince Royal Guſtavus of Sweden, with the Princeſs Royal of Denmark, who are both in their Infancy : A Scheme, which if the young Princeſs was my Daughter, I ſhould not readily aſſent to; becauſe my natural Affection for a Child would over-ballance a Regard for the Community; but the admirable Queen her Mother was ſerved ſo herſelf.

SWEDEN.

A ſtrong Fleet is equipping at Carelſcroon, which has been conjectured to oppoſe the Ruſſians in the Baltick, in caſe of a Rupture between the Courts of Petersburgh and Berlin : However, all the Fears of a Commotion between Sweden and Ruſſia are extinguiſhed in the Death of his Swediſh Majeſty, who died lately at Stockholm, in the 75th Year of his Age. Adolphus Frederic, Duke of Holſtein, Biſhop of Lubeck, has now aſcended the Swediſh Throne, to which he was declared Prince Succeſſor by the Treaty of Abo, through the Influence o

the

the victorious Ruffians. It is true, that this Prince is at the Head of a potent Nation; but the regal Power in Sweden has been greatly abridged fince the Reign of Charles XII. on whofe Death the States were reftored to their ancient Rights and Liberties; fo that the legiflative and executive Power is now lodged in the States, and the Monarch finds his Authority fo much retrenched, that, like his Polifh Majefty, he has little more than the bare Name of Sovereignty.

Russia.

The Diffention between the Courts of Petersburgh and Berlin are rather aggravated than adjufted, notwithftanding the Interpofition of the Courts of Vienna and London: Both Powers are exerting their military Strength, and pouring down their Troops to their refpective Frontiers. The Ruffians are alfo in danger of an Attack from the Turks, but they have taken Care to defend the Ukrain: they have alfo fent a confiderable Body of Troops into the conquered Provinces, under the Command of General Lieven, it being currently reported that Marfhal Lacy was dead at Riga, though they have now little to apprehend from the Swedes, whofe new Monarch is Uncle to the Prince Succeffor of all the Ruffias. The Czarina has ordered the Herenhutters, or Moravians, to depart the Empire; and has publifhed an Edict for prohibiting the Importation of Books printed abroad.

Great-Britain.

Political Arcanums are lefs frequent in the Britifh Miniftry than in any other European Cabinet, and we are now acquainted that the Commiffaries affembled at Paris, for adjufting the Limits of the Poffeffions belonging to the Crowns of Great Britain and France, have come to fome Sort of an Agreement. The Britifh Miniftry has alfo acknowledged the Right of France to the Ifland of St. Martin's, one of the leffer Antilles, lying Eaft of Porto Rico, which is about 75 Miles in Circumference, and was firft planted by the French in 1645; though

Part

Part of the Island has been since inhabited by the English; and Mr. Hodge, the Deputy Governor of Anguilla, dispossessed the French entirely from the Island in the Year 1744; but now the whole Island is to be restored to the French, with a proper Indemnification for their Losses. However, this has too much the Air of an Old Woman's Story to gain any Credit with me; for how can it be expected that our Ministry will order the British Subjects to evacuate St. Martin's, before the French have come to a Determination concerning the Property of the neutral Islands?

The Gin Act is not yet passed, though it is to be hoped that some salutary Method will be speedily put into Execution to abolish the Use of this pernicious Liquor; and then we may expect to see the Revival of Health among the inferior Class of the Community, many of whom it is to be hoped will live long enough to be honour'd with the Appellation of Old Women. The Naturalization Bill was put off to this Day, when the Debates on that Affair will be resumed, and I can venture to prognosticate how it will be determined: As for the Alteration of the New Stile, I hope the good Earl of Macclesfield will succeed in a Scheme so visibly calculated for the Use of Posterity; especially as the Emperor has ordered a Conformity to the Gregorian Calendar to be observed in his Ducal Dominions of Tuscany, where the Julian Æra has been hitherto followed.

I am glad to hear that a Proposition is made to the Legislature for purchasing the Sovereignty of the Isle of Man, and annexing it to the Government; which will be extremely prejudicial to the clandestine Trade carried on with the Commodities of France; the Smugglers finding frequent Opportunities of running their Goods from this Island on the adjacent Coasts of Ireland, Scotland, England, and Wales.

Among the Acts of Parliament lately passed, there is one "For the better regulating of Trials by Juries." And I wish I could see an Amendment in it; "for
"pro-

" providing many of these sagacious Judges of Life and
" Property with a sufficient Share of Common Sense "
For it is not long ago that I attended a Trial at a certain
Court, on an Infamous Affair between a certain Beetle-
browed, squinting Sort of a Grocer, and his Apprentice,
who the Master had charged with Felony for taking
Five Shillings out of his Till, though he had at that
Time some Pounds belonging to the Apprentice in his
Possession; when the Foreman of the Jury imagin'd the
Fact amounted to a Felony, tho' it was actually no more
than a Breach of Trust, for which there can be no cor-
poral Punishment. If an Old Woman may venture to
give her Opinion, I think this requires the Legiflative
Attention, as much as any Thing in Mr. Fielding's Enquiry, or in Mr. Seegly's Observations on that Enquiry;
for how precarious is Life and Fortune when entrusted
to a weak and insensible Juror?

I had just sent all my Copy to the Printer's, and
thought of inserting no more in this Number, when I
accidentally called in at Mr. *Worlidge's*, the ingenious
Painter over the *Little-Piazza*, in *Covent-Garden*, to
gratify my Curiosity in seeing his valuable Collection of
Pictures, many of which, because they are the Offspring
of his own elegant Pencil, have been held in a contemptible Light in his own Apartments; but when removed to an Auction-Room, have been absolutely taken
for the Productions of a *Rembrandt*, a *Corregio*, and a
Vandyke; such is the pernicious Force of Prejudice to a
modern Artist, of Envy to a rival Genius, and of Partiality to a Man not yet mounted on the Wings of Fame.
As I have the Honour to be an intimate Acquaintance
with Mr. *Worlidge*, I have frequently taken an Opportunity of desiring him to expose some of his beautiful Performances in some Place where they may be more publickly seen than at his own Apartments; though these Re-
monstrances have been hitherto ineffectual, and all such En-
treaties disconcerted by a commendable, but an unseason-

able

able and unfashionable, Modesty: However, I hope that
Time will overcome this Bashfulness of honest Pride, this
Honesty of conscious Merit; or that Ingenuity may spare
her Blush by meeting with a proper Regard and Encouragement. This Gentleman took me into his Paint-
ing-Room, where he was putting the finishing Stroke to
a beautiful Portrait, which is executed in so very master-
ly a Manner, that I could not help exposing that Quality, so natural to an old Woman, of making a formal Enquiry into the Character of the Person it represented:
When Mr. *Worlidge* informed me that it was the Picture
of Mr. *Ben. Sedgly*, of *Temple-Bar*, who has lately made
himself so remarkable for his poetical and political Ac-
complishments. I recollected that I had seen several
Verses, and other Pieces of this Author, to which I had
given my Approbation, and particularly his Observations on Mr. *Fielding's Enquiry*, which are wrote with
an uncommon Spirit, and extraordinary Delicacy: I
therefore told Mr. *Worlidge*, that my Veneration for
every literary Genius, had excited an Inclination in me
to see Mr. *Sedgly*; but, as it wou'd be a Piece of Indecency for one of my Sex and Age, to go into a Publick-
House without a sober-looking Gentleman in Company,
I desired he wou'd attend me there, and introduce me
to *Ben*, which he readily agreed to, and very complai-
santly conducted me thither. I found Mr. *Sedgly*, to
be a good-natur'd Sort of a Man, though not so polite to
a Lady as I could have wish'd him at first; but this was
soon removed by Mr. *Worlidge's* acquainting him, that
he had taken the Liberty of introducing Mrs. *Midnight*
to his Acquaintance: upon which my Brother Author
gave me a very sagacious Look, an affable Smile, a low
Congee, and a civil Squeeze by the Hand. We had
half a Pint of Mountain, and were soon as great as two
Incle-makers; when Mr. *Sedgly* began to complain of
the censorious Reflections, and unmannerly Severities,
thrown upon every Man of Genius on his Appearance
in the literary World; concluding that he had been very

con-

contumeliously treated by a certain Player, who had made a low Criticism on his Performances, which he told me was genteely answered by one of his Customers, though without his Privity, He acquainted me that Mr. *Langham* of the *Blue Posts* had been set up as a Rival to him in Genius, as well as in Beer; but that Mr. *Langham* had submitted, and publickly acknowledged the Superiority of Genius to belong to Mr. *Sedgly*; which has occasioned a perfect Reconciliation between them, and made such a grateful Impression on the Heart of Mr. *Sedgly*, that he has given Way to the Muse in the following Lines, which, on my Approbation of them, he desired I would insert in my Magazine. I promised him I would; then took my Leave, with assuring him I would shortly dine at his House with honest *Beck the happy Cobler*; and have now performed one Part of my Promise, by inserting the following Verses.

To *Mr.* Solomon Langham, *an Author, at the* Blue Posts.

TO spare the Dart of Wit, the Pill of Jest,
    Langham, I own, thy Candour is confest.
Her Venom-crest let yelling *Envy* raise,
Genius commands, and *Truth* shall merit Praise;
What if, Muse-led, we seek *Aonia's* Bow'r,
Drink the rich Stream, or crop the beauteous Flow'r;
Shall this the Viper-sting of *Slander* rouze,
To blast the Laurels blooming on our Brows!
——Ye little Curs, still idly bay the Moon;
Try, with a Breath, to cool the Sun at Noon:
Langham and *Sedgly* shall, like Twins, combine;
Unblemish'd, undiminish'd, will we shine.
Oh, Friend! while *Comus* quaffs the nectar-Bowl,
Anacreon-like, we'll fire the drooping Soul;
Let Mirth and Song each happy Hour divide;
Friendship round us has now her *Cestus* tied.

Ship and *Anchor, Temple-Bar.* Ben. Sedgly.

The MIDWIFE.

NUMBER II.

VOL. II.

A certain Method by which a Man may engage the Fates in his Favour and procure himself GOOD LUCK.

Communicated to Mrs. MIDNIGHT, *as an* Arcanum: *By a Gentleman, who studied for it forty Years in the several Universities of* Europe.

Notwithstanding what the ancient and modern Authors have said concerning the Difference of Men's Opinions, there are two Points wherein I think we are all agreed, which are, first, to follicit *good Luck*; and, secondly, to avoid the *ill*. And as this is the Case, I think I cannot do a more acceptable Service to the Publick than to inform them in what Manner, and by what Means,

they may always, and at all Times, procure themfelves that which is good and agreeable, and avoid
the other, which is fo obnoxious : And I, with the
more pleafure, enter on this Subject, as it will, in
all probability, put an End to many of thofe Fears
and Anxieties which People poffefs themfelves with
on mere trifling Occafions.   Spilling a little Salt
fhall make a whole Family unhappy.   A fingle
Crow in the Road fhall turn a Man back, even
tho' he was going for the Midwife.   The Fall of a
Martin's Neft is a dreadful Symptom, and of more
Confequence than the Fall of a Star, or a Comet.
Ravens are the Harbingers of Death ; and the
Howling of a Dog has been thought fufficient to
call a Ghoft from the Grave.

For the valuable Secret, which I am about to
communicate to you to cure this Evil, I am obliged
to the learned and ingenious *Monfieur Bourgen-
derfis*, who affures me, from his own Experience,
that thefe, and all other Omens of ill Luck, may be
prevented by only placing the Body in a *proper Po-
fition* at the time of rifing.   As the abovemention'd
Gentleman has made this Affair his Study for forty
Years, and is a great Mafter of *Aftrology*, *Palmif-
try*, *Alchymy*, &c. he muft undoubtedly be a good
Judge of the Matter ; and I have his Authority to
fay, that every Thing has happen'd to his Wifh ever
fince he put this Method in Practice.   Befides this,
he has given me to underftand that feveral Great
Generals, who have been inftructed in this Myftery,

have

have practifed it with equal Succefs. The late
Duke of *M—lb——gh* made ufe of this Artifice,
when he obtain'd thofe glorious Battles for the *Englifh* Nation, at *Blenheim, Ramillies,* and *Mal-
plaquet.* The Sea Commanders did the fame twice
in the time of *Charles* II. when with fuch good Succefs
they engaged and defeated the *Dutch* Fleets. 'Twas
a Maxim with all our Admirals in the Days of
Queen *Elizabeth. Charles* XII. of *Sweden* fought
upon this very Principle, depended entirely upon
it, and perform'd Wonders, 'till he became fo
elated and puff'd up with Conqueft that he neglected this Rule, and then he was taken Prifoner,
and foon after kill'd by a Cannon Ball. In fhort,
fo wonderfully efficacious is this Method, that I
myfelf knew two Generals, engaged by different
Nations at War, who drew up their Armies, fought
a Battle, and both conquer'd, notwithftanding it
happen'd on a Childermas Day. But it would be
abfurd to fay more.——Thofe who confider how
many Gentlemen have advanc'd themfelves in the
Church and the State, in the Army and Navy, in
the Law and in Phyfick, meerly by this Means,
and without any Merit or Pretenfions to Merit
whatfoever, can no longer doubt that it is of the
utmoft Confequence for a Man TO RISE WITH
HIS BACKSIDE UPWARDS; —— for that is the
Noftrum, which I might have fold for an infinite
Sum — But I here give it you freely — there —
take it — and may the Obfervance of it make ye
all happy. M. MIDNIGHT.

Things to be laugh'd at :

O R,

A Collection of honeſt Prejudices. (continu'd)

NEXT unto *Arvi* there are two Rivers, *Atoica* and *Caora*, and on that Branch which is called *Caora* are a Nation of People whoſe Heads appear not above their Shoulders ; which, tho' it may be thought a meer Fable, yet for mine own Part I am reſolved it is true ; becauſe every CHILD in the Provinces of *Arramaia* and *Canuri* affirm the fame : They are called *Ewaipanoma* : They are reported to have their Eyes in their Shoulders, and their Mouths in the middle of their Breaſts ; and that a long Train of Hair groweth backward between their Shoulders.

Sir W. RALEIGH's *Works.* Page 209.

The Eighth Species of Earthquakes is, where over and above the riſing and ſinking the Parts of the Earth, there are a great Variety of other Accidents attending ; ſuch for Inſtance, as appears in that Relation which the learned *Camden* gives us, of a very famous Earthquake in *Herefordſhire,* where in the Year 1571, *Marclay Hill* in the Eaſt Part of the Shire, with a roaring Noiſe, removed itſelf from the Place where it ſtood, and for three Days together travelled from its old Seat.

It

It began firſt to take its Journey *February* 17th, being *Saturday* at Six of the Clock at Night, and by Seven the next Morning, it had gone forty Paces, carrying with it Sheep in their Cotes, Hedge-Rows and Trees, whereof, ſome were overturn'd; ſome that ſtood upon the Plain were firmly growing upon the Hill; thoſe that were Eaſt were turned Weſt; and thoſe in the Weſt were ſet in the Eaſt: In this Remove it overthrew *Kinaſton* Chapel, and turned two Highways near an hundred Yards from their old Paths. The Quantity of Ground thus removed was about twenty-ſix Acres, which opening itſelf with Rocks and all, bore the Earth before it for four hundred Yards ſpace, without any ſtay, leaving Paſturage in the Place of the Tillage, and the Tillage overſpread with Paſturage: Laſtly, overwhelming its lower Parts, it mounted to a Hill of twelve Fathoms high, and there reſted after *three Days travel.*

Diſſertation upon Earthquakes. Page 43.

Among the many People who have had Courage and Learning to lay *Spirits* and *Ghoſts*, G. W. SALOMINE may be reckon'd and eſteem'd the moſt conſiderable and knowing; for he made a Fortune and raiſed an Eſtate by this very Trade; and is ſaid to have laid 1379 Souls in the *Red Sea.* A Place which I know by Experience, and by Ex-amination have found all Ghoſts and Spirits are moſt afraid of; and this I think proves *Salomine's*

D 3 Power

Power to be very great, as it is a Place they wou'd not but by Force have went into.

It is to be remarked that *Salomine* was the seventh Son of his Father and Mother, who was a virtuous Woman; and he had also a wonderful Faculty of curing all Diseases *with a Touch*. Such surprising Power is there in some People. Yet this Gentleman was not more to be thought of than an Accquaintance of mine, an *Oxford* Scholar, who to my certain Knowledge and Belief hath cured many Disorders, and allayed the Ghosts of many disturbed People, when no other Person could do them. In a Village where I lived, I do know that there was a great House, a Mansion-House, haunted by a Spirit that turned itself into a thousand Shapes and Forms; but generally came in the Figure of a *boiled Scragg of Mutton*, and had baffled and defyed the learned Men of both Universities; but this being told to my Friend, who was a Descendant and Relation of the learned *Friar Bacon*, he undertook to lay it, and that even without his Books; and 'twas done in this Manner: He ordered some Water to be put into a clean Skellet that was new, and had never been on the Fire. When the Water boiled, he himself pulled off his Hat and Shoes, and then took seven Turnips, which he pared with a small Penknife that had been rubbed and whetted on a Loadstone, and put them into the Water. When they were boiled, he ordered some Butter to be melted in a new glaized earthen

earthen Pipkin, and then mashed the Turnips in it. Just as this was finished, I myself saw the Ghost, in the Form of a *boiled Scragg of Mutton*, peep in at the Window, which I gave him Notice of, and he stuck his Fork into him, and sowsed both him and the Turnips into a Pewter Dish, and eat both up : And the House was ever afterward quiet and still. Now this I should not have believed, or thought true, but I stood by and saw all the whole Ceremony performed.

JACKSON's *State of the Defunct.* Page 97.

A CERTIFICATE,

To satisfy the Publick, and prevent any farther Disputes concerning the Naturalization *Bill.*

I *Mary Midnight* of St. *James's, Westminster,* have, by Order of several noble Personages, examined a great Number of my own Countrymen promiscuously taken, and the same Number of Foreigners selected from all other Nations ; and I do, upon my Honour, hereby certify and declare, that I find the *English* are rather better qualify'd for the Business of the Ladies, and the Business of the Nation, than any other People : Wherefore I most humbly beg that the *Naturalization Bill* may be thrown out, and a Bill brought into the House, in lieu thereof, to oblige all our Batchelors to marry and get Children ; which would answer all the
Pur-

Purpofes of that Defign, and not fubject us to any
of the Inconveniencies generally attending thofe
Sort of Schemes.   Witnefs my Hand, *April* 20th
1751.

MARY MIDNIGHT.

VERSES *written in a* London Church-
yard.

MARIA now I'll ceafe to fing,
   And all the op'ning Sweets of Spring:
The *Chop-houfe* in my Verfe fhall ring,
   Where lives my lovely *Jenny*.

Where antient Cooks exert their Art ;
No youthful Damfel bears a Part :
Yet one has broil'd my very Heart,
   And that was lovely *Jenny*.

Brown as the Wallnut is her Hair,
Her Skin is like the Napkin fair,
More blooming than red Cabbage are
   The Cheeks of lovely *Jenny*.

Each fav'ry Difh to Cit and Fop
She bears, herfelf a nicer Chop ;
How far more elegant, to fop,
   And feaft on lovely *Jenny*.

More tempting than the fmoaking Stake,
Or fweeteft Tart her Fingers make !

                           I'd

I'd lofe my Dinner for the Sake,
  Of tafting lovely *Jenny*.

But when I pay for Stake or Tart,
I act a very Mifer's Part,
At once the Money and my Heart
  I give to lovely *Jenny*.

Let *Jove* his fam'd Ambrofia eat,
And youthful *Hebe* ever wait;
I envy not his Joy or State,
  While ferv'd by lovely *Jenny*.

While *Britifh* Herrings *Britons* love,
Or City Throats with Cuftard move,
While Nectar pleafes mighty *Jove*,
  So long fhall I love *Jenny*.

And when at length the Beauty dies,
Oh! cut her into little Pies!
Like Jelly-ftars fhe'll grace the Skies,
  So bright is lovely *Jenny*.

St *Clement's Church-yard*,
  May 1. 1751.

A Scheme for a Bill of Annihilation; *in a
Letter from Mrs.* Midnight, *to the Rt. Hon.
the E— of* C———.

My Lord,

AS the Troubles and Difcontents of Mankind,
  are daily increafing, and their Patience di-
minifhing in the fame Proportion; I humbly offer

to.

to your Lordſhip's Conſideration, a Scheme, which
will be a Catholicon againſt all Diſorders and Di-
ſturbances, which are, have been, or may be incident to human Nature. The whole Affair, my
Lord, is no more than this, to erect in ſome com-
modious Part of this opulent City, *an Office of An-*
nihilation, where all afflicted and diſcontented Perſons may come, in order to be Annihilated by one or
more of the auguſt College of Phyſicians, who there
muſt regularly attend for that Purpoſe.—— Half the
Work, my Lord, is done to our Hands; for I
can demonſtrate, that at leaſt one Moiety of the
People that *breathe*, cannot be ſaid to *exiſt* with
any Propriety of Language, *Cogito, ergo ſum, I*
think, therefore I am, is the great *Des Cartes*'s Definition of Exiſtence. If this be true, thoſe that
do not think, do not exiſt, which Obſervation
diſpatches ten Millions at a Blow———If the Naturalization Bill paſs into a Law, this will clear the
Way for it; for by Annihilating ſo many of our
Countrymen, we ſhall make more room for Foreigners, a Piece of Complaiſance, which is as amiable as it is neceſſary. It is almoſt incredible what
Advantages would redound from this Affair.——
All thoſe poor Objects, which, to the Scandal of
Humanity, are ſtarving and rotting in the Streets,
might be order'd to the Office.——In ſhort, every
Body that was weary of their Being, might apply
to the Phyſician in waiting; for this is a Diſeaſe
he'd never fail to Cure. I muſt take the Liberty
to add, that your Lordſhip is deeply intereſted in
this

this Affair, in refpect to fome Advantages that will more immediately happen to yourfelf.——You might fend fix or feven Cart Loads of thofe Block-heads to the Office, who have had the enormous Impudence to affix your Name to their *Grub-ftreet* Trafh, or, what is ftill worfe, to father upon your Lordfhip's manly Wit, the puny paltry Product of their own fumbling defpicable Dulnefs. There is not, my Lord, among all the Peft of Society, a more contemptible Sett of Men than your Pettyfogging Attorneys, your Haberdafhers of *fmall Ware* in the Law.——Thefe I wou'd have fent to the Office firft of all ; for the fooner Annihilation fhould happen to them, the fooner Mankind might expect the invaluable Bleffings of Peace and good Neigh-bourhood. In fhort, fince every Profeffion is too much crouded with its refpective Votaries, I wou'd, by this means, lop off all the redundant and ufelefs Members.——I wou'd finally have commanded to the Office—all Authors, who have no Qualifica-tion, but Vanity.——All Patrons, who give Merit nothing, but their *Word.*——All Pedants, Pyrates, and Pamphlet-Clubs, with every Thing that is of-fenfive and detrimental to good Learning, good Senfe, and good Manners. Which is all at pre-fent, from,

   My Lord,
    Your Lordfhip's
     moft obedient humble Servant,
      MARY MIDNIGHT.

          A Let-

A Letter from Mrs. MIDNIGHT, *to the Governors of the* Foundling-Hospital, *in which it will appear, why she does not apply to be of their Society.*

Worthy Sirs,

I Have been follicited by feveral Perfons of Diftinction, to offer myfelf as a Candidate for being a Governor of the *Foundling-Hofpital*, and find myfelf under fome fort of Neceffity of juftifying my Squeamifhnefs, in declining to make ufe of my Intereft in this Affair. No Perfon of common Senfe can doubt of my Impartiality in this Matter, for the Propagation of Mankind, which this *Charity* is peculiarly calculated to promote, is very delightful and lucrative to one of my Perfuafion and Profeffion.——In the firft Place you are guilty of a moft fcandalous Mifnommer, (as the *French* Phrafe is) for you call your Hofpital, an Hofpital for expofed and deferted Children, when expofed and deferted Children are abfolutely excluded by the Laws of your Houfe, and the whole of the Bufinefs is entirely left to Fortune, fo that the Baftard of a L—d, has an equal Chance with an helplefs Wretch, who, perhaps *was* (as *Shakefpear* has it) *Ditch-deliver'd by a Drab!* I know Gaming is very fafhionable, and in my Letter to Mr. *Hoyle*, I have proved it to be attended with many admirable Confequences.——But for your Black Balls and your White,—to play at *Roley-Poley* for the Bodies of your Fellow-Creatures, is carrying the Matter
somewhat

fomewhat too far. Extravagant Feafts, Mufick, Revelling and Dancing, are of that Species of Charity, which Pride and Gluttony are ever ready to beftow on themfelves and their Affociates.——But to *Faft* for a Friend in order to ferve him ;—to Pray for him in order to promote him ;—To undergo *Pain* to give him Pleafure, is Chriftian Charity.—All the reft is Oftentation, Nonfenfe, Noife, and fomething yet worfe than all of them, which I forbear at prefent to mention, becaufe I wou'd not give Offence to Perfons of Diftinction.

M. MIDNIGHT.

To the wife Inhabitants of TRING, *in* Hertfordfhire, *and the Towns and Villages adjacent.*

GENTLEMEN,

I Have receiv'd a very particular and impartial Account of your Behaviour to poor *Gaffer Ofborne* and his unhappy Wife ; and I am really fhock'd at your Inhumanity, and afham'd of your Stupidity. Don't you think the following Paragraph will make a pretty Figure in the Annals of *England*, and give Pofterity a fine Idea of your Wifdom, Sagacity, Humanity, and Religion ?

Letter from Tring *in* Hertfordfhire, April 24.
‘ On Monday laft a fhocking Affair happened
‘ here. One B—rf—d, who keeps a Publick-

Houfe,

' Houfe, from bafe and lucrative Views, had given
' out he was bewitched by one Ofborne and his
' Wife, (inoffenfive People of the Age of threefcore
' Years and upwards) and had it cry'd at feveral
' Market-Towns that they were to be try'd by
' Ducking the Day aforefaid; when about Noon
' a great Concourfe of People, to the Number of
' Five Thoufand at leaft, appeared in the Town.
' The Officers of the Parifh had privately re-
' moved the poor old Couple in the dead time of
' the Night into the Church, as a Place of Safety.
' The Mob demanded thefe unhappy Wretches at
' the Workhoufe, but on being acquainted they
' were not there, they pulled down the Pales and
' Walls, broke all the Windows, and demolifhed
' a Part of the Houfe : After fearching the Chim-
' nies and Cielings without Effect, they feized the
' Governor, hawled him down to the Stream, and
' declared they would drown him, and fire the
' whole Town, unlefs they delivered thefe poor
' Creatures into their Hands. The Mob ran up
' and down with Straw in their Hands, and were
' going to put their Threats into Execution, had
' they not been delivered up. Thefe miferable
' Creatures were now dragged two Miles, ftript
' ftark-naked, their Thumbs ty'd to their Toes,
' and in this fhameful manner were thrown into
' a muddy Stream. After much Ducking and ill
' Ufage, the poor old Woman was thrown quite
' naked on the Bank, almoft choaked with Mud,
' and expired in a few Minutes, being kick'd and
' beat

' beat with Sticks even after fhe was dead ; and
' the poor Man lies dangeroufly ill of the Bruifes
' he received. To add to their Barbarity, they
' put the dead Witch (as they called her) in Bed
' with her Hufband, and ty'd them together. The
' Coroner's Inqueft have brought in their Verdict,
' Wilful Murder. Several Perfons are apprehended
' on this account, and the Inhabitants are making
' diligent Search after others, being determined to
' bring them to condign Punifhment.'

Pray, (for God's Sake) if you have any Senfe at
all, if you are not meer Idiots and Lunaticks, let
me tell you a Story.

There was in the Weft of *England*, where I
lived feveral Years, a poor induftrious Woman,
who labour'd under the fame evil Report that the
above poor Wretches were ftigmatized with. E-
very Hog that died with the Murrain, every Cow
that flipt her Calf, fhe was accountable for. If a
Horfe had the Staggers, fhe was fuppofed to be in
his Head ; and whenever the Wind blew a little
harder than ordinary, *Goody Gilbert* was playing her
Tricks, and riding upon a Broomftick in the Air.
Thefe, and a thoufand other Phantafies, too ridiculous to recite, poffefs'd the Pates of the common People. Horfe-fhoes were nail'd with the
Heels upwards, and many Tricks were made ufe
of to intrap and mortify the poor Creature ; and
fuch was their Rage againft her, that they petition'd

E 2 Mr.

Mr. *Williams*, the Parfon of the Parifh, not to let her come to Church, and, at laft, even infifted upon it; but this he over-ruled, and allow'd the poor old Woman a Noke in one of the Ifles to herfelf, where fhe muttered over her Prayers in the beft Manner fhe could. The Parifh, thus difconcerted and enraged, withdrew the fmall Pittance they allow'd for her Support, and would have reduc'd her to the Neceffity of ftarving, had not fhe been ftill affifted by the benevolent Mr. *Williams*, who often fent her Bread and Meat, frequently procured her Spinning-Work from the next Market-Town; and fo provoked was he at their Behaviour to her, that he once apply'd to a neighbouring Juftice of Peace in her Behalf; but as there happen'd a Storm the Night before, which ftript Part of the Thatch off his Worfhip's Stable, that wife Haberdafher of the Law refufed her Relief. I was, one Afternoon, drinking Tea with Mrs. *Williams*, when a Meffage was brought that poor *Jane Gilbert* was extremely ill; upon which we all three went to fee her. As fhe was fick, I expected to have found her in Bed, and we open'd the Door foftly not to difturb her; but when we came into her little Hovel, poor *Jane* was fpinning by a fmall Peat Fire, which I could have cover'd with my Hand. As the poor old Creature was deaf, fhe did not hear us open the Door, and I had an Opportunity of taking a full Survey of her before fhe perceived us. A Picture of fuch Wretchednefs I never faw before or fince. Her Body was half

naked,

naked, infomuch that her wither'd Shoulders and
Part of her Breaft appear'd thro' her tatter'd Gown.
Her Head was bound round with an old blue Stock-
ing, that expofed her bald Crown and her Ears to
view. Her Hofe were compofed of two Haybands,
tyed round her Legs with a Packthread-ftring. She
fat in an old wooden Elbow-chair, and, by Fits,
dozed, and then again turn'd her Wheel; to the
Motion of which her Under Jaw kept exact Time.
When Mr. *Williams* call'd to her, fhe rais'd herfelf up, and, by the Support of the Chair made us
a Curtfey. The Manner of our coming in had a
little confus'd her, but fhe foon recover'd herfelf,
and, by our Defire, fat down. Mr. *Williams*
then enquired into the State of her Diforder, and
fhe told, him, that fhe believ'd her Illnefs was occafion'd by her eating that Food; (pointing to an
earthen Pan that ftood before us, in which were
mixed a little Barley Meal, Salt, and Water) and
added, that fhe had not had any Bread or Meat
for feven Days. At this he was furpris'd, and
afk'd what became of the Victuals he fent her the
Beginning of that Week? She thank'd him for it,
and reply'd, that two Fellows in the Neighbourhood, whofe Names fhe mention'd, had taken it
from her; and that one of them had ftruck her
feveral Blows. Mr. *Williams* feemed angry that
fhe did not inform him of it; but fhe defired he would not be difpleafed, and faid, fhe
was loth to be too troublefome. Mrs. *Williams*
(who is a mighty good Woman) was greatly af-

E 3   fected

fected with this Circumftance, and fhed Tears,
which were indeed accompany'd with my own:
She then warm'd a little Sack-whey, fhe had
brought in her Pocket, and gave it the poor
Creature to drink. This *Jane* fwallow'd eagerly,
and was fo chearful after it, that fhe talked to us
above two Hours, entertained us with her whole
Story, and the Hiftory of her Time, which was
frequently interrupted with the warmeft Expreffions
of Gratitude to Mr. and Mrs. *Williams.* When I
exprefs'd my Surprife at her Memory and good
Senfe, fhe told me that fhe was once a young Gentlewoman's Waiting-maid, with whom fhe had a
good Education, and could, even now, read and
write very well, but that the Neighbours would
not fuffer her to have a Pen and Ink, and had fto-
len her Bible and her Spectacles. Juft as we were
coming away, I put two Half-Crowns into her
Hand, which fhe return'd me again, and begg'd I
would oblige her with fome Halfpence in their
Stead; for the People, fays fhe, in the Neighbourhood are poffefs'd with a Notion that I can turn
Lead into Silver and Gold, but that by and by it
will become Lead again, and therefore none of the
Shops will change my Money. When we parted
with the old Woman, fhe cryed, and whifpered to
Mr. *Williams* to come again and give her the
Sacrament, for that fhe did not think fhe
fhould live long. —— I could recite many
other Circumftances in *Jane*, or (as they by
way of Reproach called her) *Joan Gilbert*'s

Be-

Behaviour, which I think prov'd that fhe was not a Witch, but a pious and good Chriftian; unlefs you fuppofe Witchcraft to confift in true Wifdom, Morality and Religion, and that wou'd be too abfurd even for you yourfelves to fuppofe. But I now haften to the Sequel of my Story, in which you will find that the true Source from whence Witchcraft is reputed to fpring, is *Poverty, Age*, and *Ignorance*; and that it is impoffible for a Woman to pafs for a Witch, unlefs fhe is *very Poor, Aged,* and lives in a Neighbourhood where the People are *void of common Senfe.*

Sometime after we had this Interview with *Jane Gilbert,* a Brother of hers died in *London,* who, tho' like a truly adopted Son of Care, would not part with a Farthing while he lived, at his Death was obliged to leave her Five-thoufand Pounds; Money that he could not carry in the Coffin with him. ——This alter'd the Face of *Jane's* Affairs prodigioufly: She was no longer *Jane,* alias *Joan Gilbert* the ugly old Witch, but *Madam Gilbert*; Her old ragged Garb was exchanged for one that was New and Genteel: Her greateft Enemies made their Court to her, even the Juftice himfelf came to wifh her Joy; and tho' feveral Hogs and Horfes died, and the Wind frequently blew after that, yet *Madam Gilbert* was never fuppos'd to have a Hand in it: And from hence it is plain, as I obferved before, that a Woman muft be *very Poor, very Old,* and live in a Neighbourhood where the People are

very

very stupid, before she can possibly pass for a Witch.

> *Yours,*
>
> MARY MIDNIGHT.

P. S. 'Twas a Saying of Mr. *Williams*, who wou'd sometimes be jocose, and had the Art of making even Satire agreeable; that if ever *Jane* deserved the Character of a Witch, 'twas after this Money was left her; for that with her five thousand Pounds, she did more Acts of Charity and friendly Offices, than all the People of Fortune within fifty Miles of the Place. Many Thousands of my Readers know this to be true, but as some may be ignorant of it, I must inform them, that she gave Bibles and Common-Prayer Books to all the People in the Neighbourhood, and she paid for the Schooling of Forty Boys and Girls. She boil'd a large Copper twice a Week, and made Broth and Dumplings for all her Neighbours who were old or sick: She lent 500 *l.* in small Sums to poor Tradesmen and Farmers, without Interest, for ever, and appointed Trustees to take the best Security they cou'd, so that the Principal might not be lost, and to remove the Sums, occasionally, from one Family to another, when the one cou'd spare it, and the other wanted Assistance. She settled Twenty-five Pounds per Annum for a skillful Apothecary or Surgeon to attend poor People who were Sick; and Twenty-five Pounds per Annum on the Minister of the Parish, to visit and pray by
them,

them, and teach the Children their Catechifm; and to each Child that came to Church to learn the Catechifm, fhe order'd a Plumb-Cake every Sunday. Among her Donations, fhe did not forget her Friends Mr. and Mrs. *Williams,* but gave their Son and Daughter Five-hundred Pounds a-piece in her Life-time. As to her own Part, fhe allow'd herfelf but Eighteen Pounds a Year to live on, and that at her Death fhe bequeathed to an old Woman who attended her. And this is a Woman they were about to deftroy for Witchcraft and Sorcery! But the People are now afhamed of their Behaviour, and therefore I have concealed the Name of the Place.

An E P I G R A M.

The PHYSICIAN *and the* MONKEY.

A Lady fent lately to one Doctor *Drug,*
 To come in an Inftant and clyfter poor Pug—
As the Fair one commanded, he came at the Word,
And did the Grand-Office in Tie-Wig and Sword:
 The Affair being ended, fo fweet and fo nice!
He held out his Hand with—" You know Ma'm
  my Price."
Your Price! fays the Lady —Why, Sir, he's a
  Brother,
And Doctors muft never take Fees of each other.

W

We insert the following SPEECH *to let the World see with what Candour, Good-Nature, and Intrepidity, a Gentleman, a Poet, and a Philosopher can bear the Disappointments of Life.*

The SPEECH *of Mr.* RICHARD GLOVER, *to the Court of* Aldermen, *the* Sheriffs, *and worthy* Livery *of the City of* LONDON, *as it was spoken from the Hustings on Tuesday last, upon his declining the Poll for* Chamberlain *of this* City.

GENTLEMEN,

AFTER the Trouble which I have had so large a Share in giving you, by my Application for your Favour to succeed Sir JOHN BOSWORTH in the Office of Chamberlain, this Day so worthily supplied, I should deem myself inexcusable in quitting this Place, before I rendered my Thanks to those in particular, who so generously have espoused my Interest; to your new-elected Chamberlain himself, and Numbers of his Friends, whose Expressions and Actions have done me peculiar Honour, amidst the Warmth of their Attachment to him; to the two deserving Magistrates, who have presided among us with Impartiality, Humanity, and Justice; and lastly, to all in general, for their Candour, Decency, and Indulgence.

Gentlemen,

Gentlemen,

Heretofore I have frequently had Occasion of addressing the Livery of *London* in Public, but at this Time I find myself at an unusual Loss, being under all the Difficulties which a Want of Matter, deserving your Notice, can create. Had I now your Rights and Privileges to vindicate; had I the Cause of your suffering Trade to defend; or were I now called forth to recommend and enforce the Parliamentary Service of the most virtuous and illustrious Citizen, my Tongue would be free from Constraint, and expatiating at large, would endeavour to merit your Attention, which now must be solely confined to so narrow a Subject as myself. On those Occasions, the Importance of the Matter, and my known Zeal to serve you, however ineffectual my Attempts might prove, were always sufficient to secure me the Honour of a kind Reception and unmerited Regard. Your Countenance, Gentlemen, first drew me from the Retirement of a studious Life; your repeated Marks of Distinction first pointed me out to that great Body, the Merchants of *London*, who, pursuing your Example, condescended to intrust me, unequal and unworthy as I was, with the most important Cause; a Cause, where your Interest was as nearly concerned as theirs. In Consequence of that Deference which has ever been paid to the Sentiments and Choice of the Citizens and Traders of *London*, it was impossible but some faint Lustre must have glanced on one, whom, weak as he was,

they

they were pleafed to appoint the Inftrument on their Behalf: And if from thefe Tranfactions I accidentally acquired the fmalleft Share of Reputation, it was to you Gentlemen of the Livery, that my Gratitude afcribes it; and I joyfully embrace this Public Opportunity of declaring, that whatever Part of a Public Character I may prefume to claim, I owe primarily to you. To this I might add the Favour, the Twenty Years Countenance and Patronage of one, whom a fupreme Degree of Refpect fhall prevent me from naming; and though under the Temptation of ufing that Name, as a certain Means of obviating fome Mifconftructions, I fhall however avoid to dwell on the Memory of a Lofs fo recent, fo juftly and fo univerfally lamented.

Permit me now to remind you, that when placed by thefe Means in a Light not altogether unfavourable, no lucrative Reward was then the Object of my Purfuit; nor ever did the Promifes or Offers of private Emolument induce me to quit my Independence, or vary from the leaft of my former Profeffions, which always were, and remain ftill founded on the Principles of univerfal Liberty; Principles which I affume the Glory to have eftablifhed on your Records. Your Senfe, Liverymen of *London*, the Senfe of your great Corporation, fo repeatedly recommended to your Reprefentatives in Parliament, were my Senfe, and the principal Boaft of all my Compofitions, containing Matter imbibed in my earlieft Education, to which I have

always

always adhered, by which I ftill abide, and which
I will endeavour to bear down with me to the
Grave; and even at that gloomy Period, when deferted by my good Fortune, and under the fevereft
Trials, even then, by the fame Confiftency of Opinions and Uniformity of Conduct, I ftill preferved
that Part of Reputation, which I originally derived
from your Favour, whatever I might pretend to
call a Public Character, unfhaken and unblemifhed;
nor once, in the Hour of Affliction, did I banifh
from my Thoughts the moft fincere and confcientious
Intention of acquitting every private Obligation,
as foon as my good Fortune fhould pleafe to return;
a diftant Appearance of which feemed to invite me,
and awakened fome flattering Expectations on the
rumoured Vacancy of the Chamberlain's Office;
but always apprehending the Imputation of Prefump-
tion, and that a higher Degree of Delicacy and
Caution would be requifite in me, than in any
other Candidate, I forbore, 'till late, to prefent
myfelf once more to your Notice, and then, for the
firft Time, abftracted from a Public Confideration,
follicited your Favour for my own private Advantage. My Want of Succefs fhall not prevent my
chearfully congratulating this Gentleman on his
Election, and you on your Choice of fo worthy a
Magiftrate; and if I may indulge a Hope of de-
parting this Place with a Share of your Approbation
and Efteem, I folemnly from my Heart declare,
That I fhall not bear away with me the leaft Trace
of Difappointment.

F

Som

Some Reflections on the State of the Stage.

AMONG the Multiplicity of theatrical Performances, we have a Scarcity of thofe rational Productions, that either animate the Heart,
warm the Soul, place Virtue in her Orb, or give
Vice her Dungeon, I have been thinking what
this ought principally to be attributed to; and am
of Opinion, it is more to the prevailing Taftes of
the different Ages, than to a Sterility of Invention
in our Writers, or the natural Depravity of our
Cotemporary Auditors: However, I am extremely
enraged to fee a Play, intrinfically good, affaffi-
nated, and barbaroufly murdered, by an injudi-
cious Performer, which has been too frequently the
Cafe. The Audience never fails to be offended at
fuch a Difappointment; they at firft vent their
Diffatisfaction on the Player, and afterwards load
the Conduct of the Managers with innumerable
Invectives: Though this Refentment is mifapplied
both to the one and the other. What can a Manager do, if a tyrannical Sultan of a Player will fhew
his arbitrary Difpofition; if the ambitious Hero
ftruts with Infolence behind the Scenes, and abfolutely refufes to play that Character which is adapted
to his Abilities? How is a Manager to blame, if
fuch a Performer fhou'd violently difdain the Lega-
lity of his folemn Engagements, and refufe one
Night to play becaufe he has an Appointment with
a fa-

a favourite Actress, and a succeeding Night because his Head has been disordered with the Intemperance of his *Bacchanalian* Companions? Perhaps there is such a Person: Nay, perhaps there are some Women who have equally disappointed the Town; because, forsooth, the Pride of one Lady, is put in Opposition against the Vanity of another.

The Stage is a little Republic, whose Constitution is very mysterious: It has not yet been confidently asserted, whether it is a democratical, or an oligarchical Government: Sometimes indeed it has a Resemblance of the *Venetian* Legislature, where the judicial Authority concentres in the Nobility; and at others it seems like the *Genoese*, where the Populace are predominant: One while it has an Appearance of the *Swedish* Constitution, where the Monarch is invested with all the Apparatus of Royalty, without the Power; At another time it approaches to a Similitude of the political System of our own Nation, where the Sovereign and the Subject act with a concurrent Zeal for the Promotion of their mutual Felicity, and the Preservation of national Liberty: It has once or twice been like the Prerogative of the *French* Monarch; but it has never yet been similar to the arbitrary Power of *Russia*, or any of the oriental Empires: Though for sometime past it has been extremely correspondent to the *Polish* Constitution, where the proud Subject not only aspires to outvie the Magnificence of his Prince, but endeavours to obstruct the general Welfare of the Community,

F 2

to gratify his own ambitious and unruly Paſſions : And it has alſo been ſomewhat ſynonimous to the *Dutch* Commonwealth, where every Deputy endeavours to accompliſh his own Buſineſs, and then deſerts the Intereſt of the Public.

Hence the Managers of our Theatres are obliged to deface a beautiful Character, by a Miſapplication of the Performers ; and the Performer is obliged to expoſe his own Inability in a Part for which he was never adapted, though he might have attracted Applauſe in thoſe Characters which were peculiarly his own. We are not redundantly ſtocked in what is generally called the uſeful Player, that is the univerſal one : Mr. *Rich* has been long happy in ſuch a Perſon, by the Attachment of Mr. *Ryan* to the New Houſe; and the Managers of the Old Houſe are now equally happy in Mr. *Berry,* who is meritorious of Praiſe in every thing he undertakes ; but I am particularly delighted with this Performer in every Scene, where he has an Opportunity of exerting the Force of aged Grief, or the Sentiments of a grateful Friend : I was indeed aſtoniſh'd at his late Performance in the Character of *Horatio* in *the Fair Penitent*, where his noble Deportment in the Scene between him and *Lothario,* ſo ſenſibly ſtruck the Audience, that every judicious Spectator was now conſcious that a Gem may be long undiſtinguiſhed, and an excellent Player be long prevented from obtaining that Applauſe, which the pleaſed Heart ſhou'd fondly beſtow on the Promoter of its Felicity. I have obſerved, that this

Performer

Performer is equally remarkable for a Readiness to serve his Fellow Players, in acting any Character for their Benefit, and this is a Point of Integrity as seldom to be found on the Stage, as Honesty is on the Change of *Amsterdam :* Though I must observe in Justice to the Character of Mr. *Garrick*, that his most inveterate Enemies cannot help confessing, that his Alacrity and Diligence in promoting and attending to the Interest of his Performers, has been singularly great, and uncommonly generous : This Gentleman has constantly performed in almost every Play since the Commencement of the Benefits; out of 170 Plays, since the beginning of the Season, he has acted more than Ninety Nights, and where he did not perform in any Benefit, it was by the Choice of that Person who was intitled to it. Indeed this Manager has so laboriously endeavoured to promote the Interest of every Individual belonging to his House, that I believe he has been extremely concerned to perceive those Jealousies and Animosities so natural among the many Competitors for theatrical Fame, and the envious Beholders of a crouded Benefit : For I heard him, as I was the other Night behind the Scenes, publickly declare to two or three grumbling Performers, who had been disappointed of full Houses at their Benefits, that he was ready to oblige them all as far as his Ability extended, without any Partiality; for, while they were endeavouring to distress one another, by their unseasonable Negligence or Resentment, he was de-

termined

termined to affift them all, without any Diftinction, from his beft to the moft inferior Performer: at the fame time kindly recommending it to them all, awhile to forget the Pleafures of the Country, and confult the Intereft of thofe whofe Benefits were ap-proaching.

I muft acknowledge myfelf to be fo great an Admirer of Mr. *Garrick*'s Dramatic Excellencies, that I am much chagrined if I cannot be prefent whenever he performs; and when I am fo hap-py to fee him in any of his principal Characters, my old Blood flows with a vivifying Swiftnefs thro' my icy Veins, I am reanimated with all the Spirit of Youth, and am fure to clap him moft heartily on every beautiful Excurfion with which he capti-vates the Soul: nay, I have been fo extraordinary fervent fometimes upon thefe Occafions, that I have attracted the Obfervation of a confiderable Part of the Audience, and at one time even of Mr. *Garrick* himfelf; upon which Account feveral of my Ac-quaintance have entertained different Opinions of me, and my known Impartiality has not efca-ped uncenfured; for Lady *Boxlove*, of *Red-Lion-Square*, has confidently affirmed to the rich Apo-thecary's Wife, that I muft pofitively have fome particular Regard for Mr. *Garrick* more extraordi-nary than what was to be difcerned from his Perform-ances on the Stage: which Regard my good *Shrop-shire* Friend, an elderly Lady, who lives in *Panton-Square*, violently infifts is the Affection or Love of an old doating Woman for a fprightly handfome

young

young Gentleman; and if I was to be in Love with him, she does not so much wonder at it, because she says she once fell in Love with a Man only for the Delicacy of his Voice : but Mrs. *Vainbrew,* the young Widow of *Conduit-Street,* will have it, that it is impossible a Woman of my Years and Discretion shou'd have a Heart susceptible of the Power of Man ; and, with the greatest Assurance, reports, that Mr. *Garrick* was really brought into the World under my Care ; which occasions me so strenuously to vindicate whatever he does in Preference to Mr. *Barry,* who she says is a fine tall proper Man, and has a sweet Voice, only such old Women as I am are too obstinate to praise any Thing that other People are fond of commending. I cannot really say I ever took a very particular Notice of Mr. *Barry,* and therefore won't deny that he may be a handsome Man : but the last Time I saw Mr. *Garrick* in the Character of *Lothario,* I could not help recollecting what the Author of the *Rosciad* says of him, with which, as I think it is no strained Compliment, I shall conclude these Observations :

———— though no martial Port,
No Stride majestic, and no Front august,
His Person grac'd ; yet *Nature* in his Eye,
Roll'd beauteous, on his Visage stampt the Seal
Of rich Perfection dignify'd by *Art,*
And from his Soul beam'd forth the brightest Ray
That

That with Meridian Luftre e'er illum'd
The *Mufes'* confecrated Dome.

Rofciad v : 252.

EPIGRAM.

On two fine Gentlemen difputing on Religion.

ON Grace, Freewill, and Myft'ries high,
    Two Wits harangu'd the Table;
B——y believes he knows not why,
    N——b fwears 'tis all a Fable.
Peace, Idiots, Peace —— and both agree,
    N——fh kifs thy empty Brother;
Religion laughs at *Foes* like thee,
    But dreads a *Friend* like t'other.

To the little Elevators in Poetry who love to Surprife.

Gentlemen,

THE following fublime Defcription of a Storm
    was wrote, in Manner of a certain *Great*
Author, from which I hope you will receive a *great*
deal of Pleafure and Benefit, as it is in all Refpects
greatly worthy your Imitation.

As when in bluftring, thund'ring, wintry Days,
The Bully *Boreas* on his Bagpipe plays;

When

When old *Aquarius* ducks this earthly Ball,
And empties on our Heads his Urinal;
When rumbling Clouds on grumbling Clouds *do* dafh,
And 'midft the flafhing Lightnings Lightnings flafh;
Hogs, Dogs, and Men, perceive the troubled Sky,
Hogs, Dogs, and Men, away for Shelter fly;
While all around, the black, dark, gloomy Scene
Looks grey, looks white, looks red, looks blue,
    looks green;
So green, fo blue, fo red, fo grey, fo white,
Look'd Don *Grimalchio,* when he faw the Spright.

          Gentlemen,
               Your Servant, and fo forth,
                  M. MIDNIGHT.

---

* *From the* RAMBLER.

Redditum Cyri *folio* Phraaten,
Diffidens Plebi, *Numero beatorum,*
Eximit virtus: Polumque falfis.
               Dedocet uti
Vocibus.   HOR.

IN the Reign of *Jenghiz Can,* Conqueror of the East, in the City of *Samarcand,* lived *Notradin* the Merchant, renowned throughout all the

---

* *A Paper publifh'd every* Tuefday *and* Saturday, *price* 2d. *which really merits the utmoft Attention and Encouragement of the Publick.*

                       Re-

Regions of *India* for the Extent of his Commerce and the Integrity of his Manners. His Warehouses were filled with all the Commodities of the remoteſt Nations; every Rarity of Nature, every Curioſity of Art, whatever was valuable, whatever was uſeful, haſted to his Hand. The Streets were crouded with his Carriages, the Sea was covered with his Ships, the Streams of *Oxus* were wearied with Conveyance, and every Breeze of the Sky wafted Wealth to *Nouradin*.

At length *Nouradin* felt himſelf ſeized with a ſlow Malady, which he firſt endeavoured to divert by Application, and afterwards to relieve by Luxury and Indulgence; but finding his Strength every Day leſs, he was at laſt terrified, and called for Help upon the Sages of Phyſick; they filled his Apartments with Alexipharmicks, Reſtoratives, and eſſential Virtues; the Pearls of the Ocean were diſſolved, the Spices of Arabia were diſtilled, and all the Powers of Nature were employed to give new Spirits to his Nerves, and new Balſam to his Blood. *Nouradin* was for ſome time amuſed with Promiſes, invigorated with Cordials, or ſoothed with Anodynes; but the Diſeaſe preyed upon his Vitals, and he ſoon diſcovered with Indignation, that Health was not to be bought. He was confined to his Chamber, deſerted by his Phyſicians, and rarely viſited by his Friends; but his Unwillingneſs to die flattered him long with Hopes of Life.

                                        At

At length, having paſſed the Night in tedious
Languor, he called to him *Almamoulin*, his only
Son, and having diſmiſſed his Attendants, " My
" Son," ſays he, " behold here the Weakneſs and
" Fragility of Man ; look backward a few Days;
" thy Father was great and happy, freſh as the
" vernal Roſe, and ſtrong as the Cedar of the
" Mountain ; the Nations of the Eaſt drank his
" Dews, and Art and Commerce delighted in his
" Shade. Malevolence beheld me, and ſighed;
" his Root, ſhe cried, is fixed in the Depths ; it is
" watered by the Fountains of *Oxus* ; it ſends out
" Branches afar, and bids Defiance to the Blaſt;
" Prudence reclines againſt his Trunk, and Pro-
" ſperity dances on his Top. Now, *Almamoulin*,
" look upon me withering and proſtrate; look
" upon me, and attend. I have trafficked, I have
" proſpered, I have rioted in Gain, my Houſe is
" ſplendid, my Servants are numerous; yet I diſ-
" played only a ſmall Part of my Riches; the reſt,
" which I was hindered from enjoying by the
" Fear of raiſing Envy or tempting Rapacity,
" I have piled in Towers, I have buried in Ca-
" verns, I have hidden in ſecret Repoſitories,
" which this Scroll will diſcover. My Purpoſe
" was, after ten Months more ſpent in Commerce,
" to have withdrawn my Wealth to a ſafer Coun-
" try; to have given ſeven Years to Delight and
" Feſtivity, and the remaining Part of my Days to
" Solitude and Repentance; but the Hand of
" Death is upon me; a frigorifick Torpor en-
                                            " croaches

" croaches upon my Veins; I am now leaving the
" Produce of my Toil, which it muſt be thy Buſi--
" neſs to enjoy with Wiſdom." The Thought of
leaving his Wealth filled *Nouradin* with ſuch Grief,
that he fell into Convulſions, became delirious,
and expired.

Almamoulin, who loved his Father, was touched
a while with honeſt Sorrow, and ſat two Hours in,
profound Meditation, without peruſing the Paper
which he held in his Hand. He then retired to his
own Chamber, as overborn with Affliction, and
there read the Inventory of his new Poſſeſſions,
which ſwelled his Heart with ſuch Tranſports, that
he no longer lamented his Father's Death. He
was now ſufficiently compoſed to order a Funeral
of modeſt Magnificence, ſuitable at once to the
Rank of *Nouradin*'s Profeſſion, and the Reputation of his Wealth. The two next Nights he ſpent
in viſiting the Tower and the Caverns, and found
the Treaſures greater to his Eye than to his Imagination.

Almamoulin had been bred to the Practice of
exact Frugality, and had often looked with Envy
on the Finery and Expences of other young Men;
he therefore believed that Happineſs was now in his
Power, ſince he could obtain all of which he had
hitherto been accuſtomed to regret the Want. He
reſolved to give a Looſe to his Deſires, to revel in
Enjoyment, and feel Pain or Uneaſineſs no more.

He immediately procured a ſplendid Equipage,
dreſſed his Servants in rich Embroidery, and covered

vered his Horſes with golden Capariſons. He ſhowered down Silver on the Populace, and ſuffered their Acclamations to ſwell him with Inſolence. The Nobles ſaw him with Anger, the wiſe Men of the State combined againſt him, the Leaders of Armies threatened his Deſtruction. *Almamoulin* was informed of his Danger, he put on the Robe of Mourning in the Preſence of his Enemies, and appeaſed them with Gold, and Gems, and Supplication.

He then ſought to ſtrengthen himſelf by an Alliance with the Princes of *Tartary*, and offered the Price of Kingdoms for a Wife of noble Birth. His Suit was generally rejected and his Preſents refuſed ; but a Princeſs of *Aſtracan* once condeſcended to admit him to her Preſence. She received him ſitting on a Throne, attired in the Robe of Royalty, and ſhining with the Jewels of *Goncolda* ; Command ſparkled in her Eyes, and Dignity towered on her Forehead. *Almamoulin* approached and trembled. She ſaw his Confuſion and diſdained him ; how, ſays ſhe, dares the Wretch hope my Obedience, who thus ſhrinks at my Glance ; retire, and enjoy thy Riches in ſordid Oſtentation ; thou waſt born to be wealthy, but never to be great.

He then contracted his Deſires to more private and domeſtick Pleaſures. He built Palaces, he laid out Gardens, he changed the Face of the Land, he tranſplanted Foreſts, he levelled Mountains, opened Proſpects into diſtant Regions, poured Rivers

G   from

from the Tops of Turrets, and rolled their Waters through new Channels.

Thefe Amufements pleafed him for a Time, but Languor and Wearinefs foon invaded him. His Bowers loft their Fragrance, and the Waters murmered without Notice. He purchafed large Tracts of Land in diftant Provinces, adorned them with Houfes of Pleafure, and diverfified them with Accommodations for different Seafons. Change of Place at firft relieved his Satiety, but all the Novelties of Situation were foon exhaufted ; he found his Heart vacant, and his Defires, for want of external Objects, ravaging himfelf.

He therefore returned to *Samarcand*, and fet open his Doors to all thofe whom Idlenefs fends out in Search of Pleafure. His Tables were always covered with Delicacies ; Wines of every Vintage fparkled in his Bowls, and his Lamps fcattered Perfumes. The found of the Lute, and the Voice of the Singer chafed away Sadnefs ; every Hour was crouded with Pleafure, and the Day ended and began with Feafts and Dances, and Revelry and Merriment .*Almamoulin* cried out, " I have at laft found " the Ufe of Riches ; I am furrounded by Friends " who view my Greatnefs without Envy, and I " enjoy at once the Raptures of Popularity, and " the Safety of an obfcure Station. What Trou- " ble can he feel whom all are ftudious to pleafe, " that they may be repaid with Pleafure ? What " Danger can he dread to whom every Man is a " Friend ?"

Such

Such were the Thoughts of *Almamoulin*, as he looked down from a Gallery upon the gay Affembly regaling at his Expence ; but in the Midft of this Soliloquy, an Officer of Juftice entered the Houfe, and in the Form of legal Citation, fummoned *Almamoulin* to appear before the Emperor. The Guefts ftood a while aghaft, then ftole imperceptibly away, and he was led off without a Friend to witnefs his Integrity. He now found one of his moft frequent Vifitants accufing him of Treafon in Hopes of fharing his Confifcation ; yet, unpatronifed and unfupported, he cleared himfelf by the Opennefs of Innocence and the Confiftence of Truth ; he was difmiffed with Honour, and his Accufer perifhed in Prifon.

Almamoulin now perceived with how little Reafon he had hoped for Juftice or Fidelity from thofe who live only to gratify their Senfes, and having wearied himfelf with vain Experiments upon Life, and fruitlefs Searches after · Felicity, he had Recourfe to a Sage, who, after fpending his Youth in Travel and Obfervation, had retired from all human Cares, to a fmall Habitation on the Banks of *Oxus*, where he converfed only with fuch as folicited his Counfel. " Brother," faid the Philofopher, " thou haft fuffered thy Reafon to be de-
" luded by idle Hopes, and fallacious Appearances.
" Having long looked with Defire upon Riches,
" thou hadft taught thyfelf to think them more
" valuable than Nature defigned them, and to ex-
" pect from them what Experience has taught thee

" they

" they cannot give. That they do not confer
" Wifdom thou mayft be convinced by confider-
" ing at how dear a Price they tempted thee upon
" thy firft Entrance into the World, to purchafe
" the empty Sound of vulgar Acclamation. That
" they cannot beftow Fortitude or Magnanimity,
" that Man may be certain, who ftood trembling
" at *Aftracan* before a Being not naturally fuperior
" to himfelf. That they will not fupply unex-
" haufted Pleafure, the Recollection of forfaken
" Palaces and neglected Gardens will eafily inform
" thee. That they cannot purchafe Friends, thou
" didft foon difcover when thou wert left to ftand
" thy Trial uncountenanced and alone. Yet think
" not Riches ufelefs; there are Purpofes to which
" a wife Man may be delighted to apply them;
" they may, by a rational Diftribution, eafe the
" Pains of helplefs Difeafe, ftill the Throbs of
" reftlefs Anxiety, relieve Innocence from Op-
" preffion, and raife Impotence to Cheerfulnefs and
" Vigour. This they will enable thee to perform,
" and this will afford the only Happinefs ordained
" for our prefent State, the Confidence of divine
" Favour, and the Hope of future Rewards."

The MIDWIFE's POLITICKS : Or, *Goßip's Chronicle of the Affairs of Europe.*

PORTUGAL *and* SPAIN.

THE Dominions of his moſt faithful Majeſty afford no material Intelligence ; though this young Monarch is endeavouring to encourage the maritime Intereſt of his Country, to aboliſh the Rigour of thoſe inhuman Directors of the Inquiſition, and to promote the general Felicity of his Subjects. His moſt Catholic Majeſty is vigilantly attempting to re-eſtabliſh his Marine, which was almoſt totally ruined during the late War : He alſo applies himſelf diligently to whatever may contribute to the Happineſs of his Subjects, and the Proſperity of his Kingdom ; to accompliſh which, ſuch prudent Meaſures are taken, as already indicate their Utility, by the Progreſs which has been ſo quickly made in the Manufactures and Cultivation of Land in the Kingdom : —Whatever the Spaniards are, I cannot help aſking, if ſome People are not highly culpable in ſuffering Engliſh Workmen to quit their own Country, and carry their Improvements in Manufactures among the Natives of Spain. Mr. Keen has preſented a Memorial concerning the Navigation of the Engliſh in the Weſt-Indies, ſo as to prevent, by means of ſome fixed Regulation, the irregularities which they ſtill complain of, eſpecially in regard to the Right they pretend to have of trading to the Bay of Honduras : The Spaniſh Council has been employed for ſome Days in examining this Memorial ; but I will venture to pronounce, that the Spaniards will never acknowledge this Right, and will ſtill procraſtinate every Meaſure which Don Benjamin can undertake to remove their Inflexibility. A Rumour is ſpread, that the Spaniards have inveſted Gibraltar ; but if they have,

I

I shall call them a Parcel of Old Women, for they ought to remember the Destruction of their Quixotic Army when they besieged this formidable Fortress in the Year 1727; and they may be assured that this Place will be impregnable to the Spaniards, till such time as they can get an Admiral and a Fleet, with the Bravery of Sir George Rook, and the Resolution of British Sailors, in which they may be the more readily convinced by reflecting on what happened to them in the Year 1704, when Admiral Leake defeated the united Squadrons of France and Spain, and raised the Siege of Gibraltar, after they had besieged it by Sea and Land for upwards of five Months.

ITALY.

His Sicilian Majesty has settled a Fund of 800,000 Crowns to carry a Scheme into Execution for establishing an Assurance Office, upon the same Plan with those that have been erected long since in other European Countries relative to Commerce. It is also currently reported, that a maritime Academy will shortly be established, for the more expeditious Instruction of the Neapolitan Sailors in the Art of Navigation. Such a Conduct as this, is a corroborating Instance; that though Sir Robert Walpole was old Woman enough to establish Don Carlos in his regal Dominions, the Monarch is not Child enough to value the royal Gewgaw of the Sicilian Crown, and takes the most prudential Steps for making it Hereditary in the Bourbon-Family; the Promotion of which in so extraordinary a Manner, on the Ruins of the House of *Austria*, we are now convinced, was entirely owing to the Councils of some blundering old Woman on this Side the Water.

The Corsairs of Barbary continue to molest the Trade upon the Coast of the Ecclesiastic State more than ever,

upon

upon which Orders have been sent to Civita Vecchia, to fit out the Pope's Galleys as soon as possible. These Rovers daily commit great Depredations in the Mediterranean, and are become so formidable, that in the beginning of last Month, there sailed from Algiers 28 armed Vessels, to cruize against the Christian Powers, who took their Rout towards Sicily and the Adriatic Sea. The Tunisians and Tripolines have several Vessels at Sea, who render Navigation perillous, and greatly prejudice Commerce: But as the Court of Naples, the Religion of Malta, and the Genoese, are preparing to go in Pursuit of these Pirates, it is expected they will be able to give them a Check, especially as it is reported that the Court of Spain has ordered several Men of War and Xebecks from Alicant and other Ports, to sail in quest of these free-booting Barbarians.

The Republic of Venice has settled the Differences with the Court of Vienna, concerning the Patriarchship of Aquileia, and has also concluded a Convention with the same Court for five Years; by Virtue of which they are reciprocally to deliver up all Deserters, Malefactors, Bankrupts, &c. At the same time they have agreed, that the Conferences began between their respective Commissaries for settling the Limits of the Tyroleze, and the Confines of the Republic, shall be continued at Roveredo, till the Business be finally concluded: They likewise talk of a Defensive Alliance between the Imperial Court and the Venetians, against the Turks, who are assembled in Dalmatia.—So excellent a Determiner of Differences is Danger!

FRANCE.

The French Ministry discover at present no Inclination to foment Differences among their Neighbours, but rather

rather to cultivate the general Peace; from whence it is highly probable their Syftem is broken in the North; and that they are now at a ftand where elfe to blow up the Coals of Diffention: However, they are extremely vigilant in augmenting their naval Force, which is a Matter that deferves the Attention of Mother *Britannica*; for the French have lately launched a Ship of 80 Guns at Toulon, and there are now upon the Stocks two of 74 Guns, two of 64, a Frigate of 36 Guns, and feveral Xebecks. M. Orry de Tulvy, Counfellor of State, and Superintendant of the Finances, died lately, in the 48th Year of his Age; and Cardinal Tencin has obtain'd Permiffion to retire to his Diocefe, with this Mark of royal Efteem, that he may come and attend the Council of State whenever he pleafes. It is now reported that the Forces of the Great Mogul, who had invefted Pondicherry, have been obliged to abandon the Siege.

N E T H E R L A N D S.

Inteftine Commotions feem ftill to threaten the Dutch Republic, where the Death of the Countefs of Portland very much embarraffes the Party which is in the true Intereft of the Country: So that Meffieurs Pagel, Catwyck, and Larrey, who are the principal Perfons attached to the Prince Stadholder, it's apprehended will not be in a Condition of refifting the Torrent of his Serene Highnefs's Enemies, who are inceffantly traverfing his Projects, though they are apparently calculated for the good of the Republic. The natural Confequence of thefe civil Difcords among the States, is the gradual Decay of their Importance with the neighbouring Powers, which becomes more and more vifible every Day: Even the Court of France will hear no talk of renewing the Treaty of Commerce concluded in 1739, which it has entirely

changed,

changed, confiftent with its own particular intereft, without favouring the the Dutch in the leaft ; who, like good-natured eafy old Women, were contented to hear his moft Chriftian Majefty declare them his good Friends, while he was bombarding their barrier Towns about their Ears. Baron d'Imhoff, who fo cruelly maffacred the Chinefe in Batavia, died there on the 1ft of November laft, and is fucceeded by M. Mofell, firft Counfellor and Director-General, in the Government of all the Dutch Settlements in the Eaft-Indies.

G E R M A N Y.

The Court of Vienna has not yet been able to accomplifh its grand Defign in electing the young Archduke Jofeph to the Dignity of King of the Romans; in which it is principally oppofed by his Pruffian Majefty, who feems to be the moft vigilant and cautious of all the Princes of Europe, as perhaps he has more to fear from his Neighbour than any other Prince of Germany : The Power he has lately acquired by the Conqueft of Silefia, and its Dependencies, has alarmed thofe who before regarded him only as upon a Level with the other Electors; and his Alliance with France, which he finds neceffary to preferve his Weight, adds to their Jealoufy. The Elector of Cologn has at laft convinced us that he is little better than an old Woman, by entering into a Treaty with France, whereby his Electoral Highnefs engages to entertain a Body of 6000 Troops for the Service of his moft Chriftian Majefty, who engages on his Part to pay that Prince a Subfidy of 270,000 German Florins. However, the Court of Vienna feems to aim at difuniting the Bourbon Family, for the Marriages are now talked of between the Infant Don Lewis of Spain and the eldeft Archduchefs of Auftria, and the Archduke Jofeph with a Princefs of the Two Sicilies.

D E N-

DENMARK.

His Danish Majesty has published an Edict relating to the Greenland Trade, whereby he enlarges the Grant to the Company of Commerce trading to the Colonies of Greenland ; ordering that the Penalty of Seizure and Confiscation shall take Place with Respect to all and every one, whether Natives or Foreigners, who shall attempt to trade there: declaring that the Limits shall extend 15 Miles on both Sides of each Colony, including all the Places lying between the Western Isles, and Blackbird's Bay.

SWEDEN.

At length, by the Death of the old King of Sweden, that Crown is descended upon the Head of Adolphus Frederic, Duke of Holstein, and Bishop of Entin. This Prince is the Founder of the second Royal Family, derived from the Counts of Oldenburgh ; and when his Nephew, the Grand Duke of Russia, comes to succeed her present Czarian Majesty, the Three Northern Crowns will be all vested in Princes of the same House, which will then be no less formidable in the North, than the House of Bourbon is in the South of Europe. The Accession of this Monarch to the Swedish Throne, promises to produce no Alteration in the System of Government, which was the Point so much contended for by Russia ; his Majesty, by his Coronation Oath, having solemnly engaged to observe the present Form of Government, which has given the Swedes such an additional Scene of Liberty since the Death of Charles XII. The King has wrote a Letter to the Czarina, giving her the strongest Assurances of his sincere Desire to maintain a perfect Friendship with her Imperial Majesty.

RUSSIA.

The Court of Petersburg seems entirely satisfied with the Declarations of his Swedish Majesty, wherein he

pro-

promises that his first Care shall be to confirm, as King, the Engagements he contracted as Prince Successor. There are above 100,000 Troops in the conquer'd Provinces, to guard against any Attempts from the Side of Prussia ; nor are the Russians at all intimidated at the Approach of the Turks towards the Frontiers. Every Thing seems to go on prosperously under the Direction of the Czarina, who is herself a very sensible Lady, and I dare say has many worthy old Women in her Cabinet ; tho' some of the young ones belonging to her Court, have acted in a most surprizing Manner, by impeaching their own Father, Count Douglas, of treasonable Practices ; but this is apprehended to be only the Effects of Love ; an Instance that this subtle Flame is more predominant in these frozen Regions of the North than filial Duty.

DOMESTIC OCCURRENCES.

Last Week an Express arrived from Commodore Holborn, with an Account that the French had entirely evacuated the Islands of Tobago, St. Lucia, and St. Vincent :——— if this be true, all the old Women in Barbadoes may sing Oh be joyful, because they will now have a Supply of Timber for Crutches, which their own Island is entirely destitute of.

16. There was a Call of the House of Commons, when upwards of 400 Members were present, to attend on the Bill for naturalizing foreign Protestants, which has been happily rejected, to the great Joy of the Inhabitants of Bristol, whose Corporation had presented a Petition to the House in Favour of the Bill, though there were no more than 40 who took upon them to represent the general Voice of the People, which was speedily opposed by a Counter-petition, signed by almost 2000 of the principal Inhabitants.

MARY

MARY MIDNIGHT, to all Potentates, Prime Ministers, Politicians, Heads of Houses, Fellows of Colleges, Counsellors and Physicians, whether *Male* or *Female*, GREETING.

Dearly beloved,

AS we are fully perfuaded that you have, all and every of you, our Intereft greatly at Heart, we take this Opportunity to gratify you with the good Tidings, that we have now compleated the *Firft* Volume of our MIDWIFE, Or, *Old Woman's Magazine,* which has obtained the Sanction, Imprimatur and Encouragement of the Literati of all Nations. And this you are defired to fignify to all your Friends, Allies, and Dependents, that they may compleat their Books accordingly; and poffefs themfelves of a Work, for the Conclufion of which PUBLIUS OVIDIUS NASO wrote the following Lines in the Golden Age of AUGUSTUS.

Jamque opus exegi, quod nec Jovis Ira nec ignis,
Nec poterit ferrum, nec edax abolere Vetuftas.

Which in plain English runs thus:

Now I have accomplifhed a Work, which neither the Wrath of Jove, nor Fire, nor Sword, nor the Tooth of Time fhall be able to abolifh.

Dearly Beloved,
Yours with great Truth,
MARY MIDNIGHT.

N. B. We fhould have informed you, that many of the Numbers contained in that Work, have flew with the Impetuofity of a Whirlwind through *fourteen Editions,* maugre all the Oppofitions, Thefts, and artful Contrivances of the Enemies of Wit, found Senfe, and good Learning; but as fuch Information might have looked like a Puff, we purpofely avoided it.

*** No fingle Numbers of the *Firft* Volume will be fold after the 25th of June next, and from that Period of Time, that Volume which now fells for *Two Shillings,* will be advanced to Two Shillings and Six pence.

Sold by my Publifher, *T. Carnan,* at Mr. *Newbery's,* at the Bible and Sun in St. Paul's Church-Yard.

The MIDWIFE.

NUMBER III.

VOL. II.

Mrs. MIDNIGHT's *Differtation on* the Perpetual Notion.

THE Prejudice, that the Publick has imbibed in Favour of all my Performances, induces me to believe, that my Readers, at the firft Glance on the Title of this Differtation, will precipitately conclude, that there is a Typographical Error, and that I am actually about to communicate to the Woild the wonderful Difcovery of the *Perpetual Motion*. However, I proteft at prefent, I have no fuch Defign ; not that I will abfolutely promife to conceal that Secret from Mankind much longer ; but my prefent Bufinefs is to treat on the *Perpetual Notion,* which I define to be an inherent Opinion (I will not fay an innate one, for fear of being haunted by the Ghoft of *John Locke*)

VOL. II.　　　　　H　　　　　I fay,

I fay, an inherent Opinion every Individual has, that he either now is, or at fome Time, will be a Perfon of great Confequence. This is the *Perpetual Notion*, and, I will be bold to fay, is of more Service to the Happinefs and Well-being of Man, than any Mechanick Art, that ever was invented. What makes the 'Prentice chearfully plod thro' a feven Year's Servitude, but the *Perpetual Notion* he will one Day be a Mafter? What makes the Lover go thro' a ten Year's Siege, but a *Perpetual Notion* that the fair Obftinate will at length furrender? What makes the Toadeater to a State-Mountebank think there is Mufick in his Chains, and Dignity in his Difgrace, but the *Perpetual Notion* of his fome time being raifed on that very Pedeftal, which is at prefent the Support of his Idol? By Means of the *Perpetual Notion* every Body has always a *Profpect*, and a *Profpect* is a very good Thing at a very great Diftance; thofe therefore who have the leaft Expectations have the fineft *Profpect*, the Objects of their Defires being moft remote, which muft be a great Confolation to the Poor and the Unfortunate. But fee more of this in the fourteenth Volume of my Treatife on Perfpective, which was lately publifhed at *Amfterdam*.

Hope, that Paffion, which was given to amufe us from the Confideration of real Mifery, by deluding us with vifionary Happinefs, is founded on the *Perpetual Notion*, which nothing can deftroy but Self-Contempt and Defpair; Difeafes of the Mind not incident to one Man in ten Million.

Every

Every Perfon is fond of Exiftence, every Perfon wou'd fain be *Somebody*, a *Perpetual Notion* highly cheriflhed by many a Man, who, in Fact, is *Nobody*.

The brifk Minor that pants for Twenty-one, the brifker Damfel that pants for a Hufband, the Culprit that wants to go abroad, and the Exile that fighs to come home, have no Peace, no Life, but in the *Perpetual Notion*. Even I myfelf, even MARY MIDNIGHT, who is writing this Differtation, wou'd want Spirits to comfort herfelf in her old Age, was it not for the *Perpetual Notion*, that tho' the Works of her Hands bring nothing but frail Mortals into the World, yet the Works of her Head fhall triumph in Immortality.

REFLECTIONS *on* MATRIMONY.

By Mrs. MIDNIGHT.

MAtrimony is of fuch Confequence to the Increafe and Well-being of Mankind, and fo connected both with my Perfuafion and Profeffion, that no lefs than two Millions of my Readers have pefter'd me with Letters to defire or rather demand my Sentiments on the Subject. 'Tis remarkable, that Sir *Thomas More*, in his * UTOPIA, treats of

---

* *A beautiful Edition in* Englifh *of this Work will fhortly be publifh'd by Mr.* Newbery.

this State under the Article of Servitude: I fay,
'tis remarkable, and I am afraid that I muft be
obliged to own 'tis judicious. Not that I wou'd
be underftood to caft any Reflections on· my own
Sex by this Expreffion; for, in the Circle of my Experience, I have met with more Male Tyrants than
Female ones; but I have ftill found in moft Houfes
an *Emperor*, or *Emprefs*, whereas the Dominion,
I apprehend, ought to be divided; or, to ufe a
Phrafe of *Shakefpear*, There fhou'd be fuch an
Union in the Partition, fuch a reciprocal Conformity, that the moft difcerning Eye fhou'd never
know who has the Predominancy. It is fingular
and fomewhat lamentable, that there is more of
Chance in Engagements of this Nature than in almoft any other. This Confideration made *Butler*
extreamly witty.

    —— There are no Bargains driven
Nor Marriages made up in Heaven;
Which is the Reafon, as fome guefs,
There is no Heaven in Marriages.
                       HUDIBRAS.

The fingle Life is, to be fure, a very imperfect
and a very nonfenfical one; and, in my Senfe,
Cælibacy is as great a Crime as Polygamy; but yet
I wou'd not have our Youth too precipitate in their
Choice. — They are too apt (in the Language of
Mr. *Locke*) to know but little, prefume a great
deal, and *jump* to a Conclufion. The moft obvi-
                             ous

ous Affair, the very Introduction to Marriage is the Perfon; if that be eligible, the next Requifite for Peace and Happinefs is the Temper and Difpofition of the Mind; if that be mild, agreeable, and engaging, proceed we in the next Place to examine the Furniture of the Head; if Wit has fet up herfelf there on the Bafis of Good Senfe, there can be no Objection, but I cry out with old *Weftern* in TOM JONES, " That's it my little Honies," and will fend for the Parfon To-morrow. Such was my Choice in my late dear Mr. MIDNIGHT, to whom I bore fix and twenty Children, and with whom, for the Space of fix and fifty Years, I never had the leaft Shadow of a Quarrel. If we ever had any Difpute, it was not who *fhou'd*, but who *fhou'd not* have the Sway and the Afcendancy; and I fhall never forget an Expreffion he once made ufe of to me, when I infifted upon relieving a poor Family out of my own private Purfe. — " My Dear, fays " he, how can you be fo unfair as to monopolize " Good-nature, and be fuch a *Niggard*, that you " will infift upon doing all the generous Things " yourfelf," ————— I intend, fhortly, to publifh the whole Hiftory of my Amours with that beft of Men, from which my fair Readers may extract an hundred Recipes to make and keep them happy in their Conjugal State, which Squeamifhnefs itfelf muft own to be the moft perfect here below. ——— Such is the Opinion of *Salomon*, fuch of *Socrates*, fuch of Sir *Thomas More*, and fuch of *Mary Midnight*, four Perfons, (*Swift* wou'd fay) to which all the

H 3 Ages

Ages in the World fhall never be able to add a
fifth.

Mr. Juftice B U N D L E'S *Charge to the Grand
Jury.*

ALL Laws are Laws, and every Law is a
Law, and Laws are Things made by the
Lawyers to make Men live according to Law,
without any Refpect to the Gofpel, for that is another Affair, and to be confidered at another Opportunity, and by another Sort of Men, and in another Manner. *Vide Coke upon Littleton*, Chap. X.
Page 15. But as to the Law. —— Now there are
fome Men that are good Men, and fome Men that
are bad Men; and the bad Men are not the good
Men, and the good Men are not the bad Men : ——
But the bad Men and the good Men, and the good
Men and the bad Men are two different Sorts of
Men, and this we gather from *Magna Charta,*
an old Man that lived in the Reign of King *John*
the Great. Now if all Men were good Men there
wou'd be no need of Law ; therefore, *Ergo,* The
Laws were made for the bad Men, and the good
Men have no Bufinefs therewith, nor no Advantage
to receive therefrom. *Ergo,* therefore, thofe that
receive Advantage from the Law muft be bad Men ;
And fo, Gentlemen, call up the Prifoners, and
difpatch them as foon as poffible, for I muft go out
of Town To-morrow.

* *From*

* From *the* R A M B L E R.

—— Tacitum filvas inter reptare falubres
Curantem quicquid dignum fapiente bonoque eft.

HOR.

THE Seafon of the Year is now come in which the Theatres are fhut, the Card Tables forfaken, the Regions of Luxury are for a while unpeopled, and Pleafure leads out her Votaries to Groves and Gardens, to ftill Scenes and erratick Gratifications. Thofe who have paffed many Months in a continual Tumult of Diverfion, who have never opened their Eyes in the Morning but upon fome new Appointment, nor flept at Night without a Dream of Dances, Mufick and good Hands, or of foft Sighs, languifhing Looks, and humble Supplications, muft now retire to diftant Provinces where the Syrens of Flattery are fcarcely to be heard, where Beauty fparkles without Praife or Envy, and Wit is repeated only by the Echo.

As I think it one of the moft important Duties of focial Benevolence, to give warning of the Approach of Calamity when by timely Prevention it may be turned afide, or by preparatory Meafures be more

---

* A Paper publifh'd every *Tuefday* and *Saturday*, price 2d.

eafily endured, I cannot feel the encreafing Warmth, or obferve the lengthening Days, without confidering the Condition of my fair Readers, who are now preparing to leave all that has fo long filled up their Hours, all from which they have been accuftomed to hope for Delight, and who, till Fafhion proclaims the Liberty of returning to the Seats of Mirth and Elegance, muft endure the rugged Squire, the fober Houfewife, the loud Huntfman, or the formal Parfon; the Roar of obftreperous Jollity, or the Dulnefs of prudential Inftruction, without any Retreat but to the Gloom of Solitude, where they will yet find greater Inconveniences, and muft learn, however unwillingly, to endure themfelves.

In Winter the Life of the Polite and Gay may be faid to roll on with a ftrong and rapid Current; they float along from Pleafure to Pleafure without the Trouble of regulating their own Motions, and purfue the Courfe of the Stream in all the Felicity of Inattention; content that they find themfelves in Progreffion, and carelefs whither they are going. But the Months of Summer are a Kind of fleeping Stagnation without Wind or Tide, where they are left to force themfelves forward by their own Labour, and to direct their Paffage by their own Skill; and where, if they have not fome internal Principle of Activity, they muft be ftranded upon Shallows, or be torpid in a perpetual Calm.

There are, indeed, fome to whom this univerfal Diffolution of gay Societies affords a welcome Opportunity

portunity of quitting without Difgrace the Poft which they have found themfelves unable to maintain, and of feeming to retreat only at the Call of Nature from Affemblies where, after a fhort Triumph of unconteſted Superiority, they are overpowered by fome new Intruder of fofter Elegance or brighter Vivacity. By thefe, hopelefs of Victory and yet afhamed to confefs a Conqueſt, the Summer is regarded as a Releafe from the fatiguing Service of Celebrity, a Difmiſſion to more certain Joys and a fafer Empire. They folace themfelves with the Influence which they fhall obtain where they have no Rival to fear, and with the Luſtre which they fhall effufe, when nothing can be feen of brighter Splendour. They image, while they are preparing for their Journey, the Admiration with which the Ruſticks will croud about them, plan the Laws of a new Affembly, or contrive to delude their Ignorance with a fictitious Mode. A thoufand pleafing Expectations fwarm in the Fancy, and all the approaching Weeks are filled with Diſtinctions, Honours, and Authority.

But others, who have lately entered the World, or have yet had no Proofs of its Inconſtancy and Defertion, are cut off by this cruel Interruption from the Enjoyment of their Prerogatives, and doomed to lofe four Months in unactive Obfcurity. Many Complaints do Vexation and Terrour extort from thefe exiled Tyrants of the Town, againſt the inexorable Sun, who purfues his Courfe without any Regard to Love or Beauty, and vifits
either

either Tropick at the stated Time whet'er shunned
or courted, deprecated or implored.

To those who leave the Places of publick Re-
fort in the full Bloom of Reputation, who with-
draw from Admiration, Courtship, Submission,
and Applause, a rural Triumph can give nothing
equivalent. The Praise of Ignorance, and the
Subjection of Weakness, are little regarded by
those who have been accustomed to more important
Conquests, and more valuable Panegyricks. Nor
indeed should the Powers which have made Havock
in the Theatres, or born down Rivalry in Courts,
be degraded to a mean Attack upon the untravelled
Heir, or ignoble Contest with the ruddy Milkmaid.

How then must four long Months be worn away ?
Four Months, in which there will be no Routs,
no Shews, no Ridottos ; in which Visits must be
regulated by the Weather, and Assemblies will
depend upon the Moon! The Platonists imagine
that the future Punishment of those who have in
this Life debased their Reason by Subjection to their
Senses, and have preferred the gross Gratifications
of Lewdness and Luxury to the pure and sublime
Felicity of Virtue and Contemplation, will arise
from the Predominance and Solicitations of the
same Appetites, in a State which can furnish no
means of appeasing them. I cannot but suspect
that this Month, bright with Sunshine, and fragrant with Perfumes ; this Month, which covers
the Meadow with Verdure, and decks the Gardens
with

with all the Mixtures of colorifick Radiations ; this Month, from which the Student expects new Infufions of Imagery, and the Naturalift new Scenes of Obfervation ; this Month will chain down Multitudes to the Platonick Penance of Defire without Enjoyment, and hurry them from the higheft Satisfactions which they have yet learned to conceive, into a State of hopelefs Wifhes and pining Recollection, where the Eye of Vanity will look round for Admiration to no Purpofe, and the Hand of Avarice fhuffle Cards in a Bower with ineffectual Dexterity.

From the Tedioufnefs of this melancholy Sufpenfion of Life, I would willingly preferve thofe who are expofed to it only by Inexperience, who want not Inclinations to Wifdom or Virtue, though they have been diffipated by Negligence, or mifled by Example, and who would gladly find the Way to rational Happinefs, though it fhould be neceffary to ftruggle with Habit and abandon Fafhion. To thefe many Arts of fpending Time might be recommended, which would neither fadden the prefent Hour with Wearinefs, nor the future with Repentance.

It would feem impoffible to a folitary Speculatift, that a human Being can want Employment. To be born in Ignorance with a Capacity of Knowledge, and to be placed in the Midft of a World filled with Variety, perpetually preffing upon Senfe and irritating Curiofity, is furely a fufficient Security againft the Languifhment of Inattention,

Novelty

Novelty is indeed neceſſary to preſerve Eagerneſs and Alacrity; but Art and Nature have Stores inexhauſtible by human Intellects, and every Moment produces ſomething new to him who has quickened his Faculties by diligent Obſervation.

Some Studies for which the Country and the Summer afford peculiar Opportunities, I ſhall perhaps endeavour to recommend in ſome future Eſſay; but if there be any Apprehenſion not apt to admit unaccuſtomed Ideas, or any Attention ſo ſtubborn and inflexible as not eaſily to comply with new Directions, even theſe Obſtructions cannot exclude the Pleaſure of Application; for there is a higher and a nobler Employment to which all Faculties are adapted by him who gave them. The Duties of Religion ſincerely and regularly performed will always be ſufficient to exalt the meaneſt, and to exerciſe the higheſt Underſtanding. That Mind will never be vacant which is frequently recalled by ſtated Duties to Meditations on eternal Intereſts, nor can any Hour be long which is ſpent in obtaining ſome new Qualification for celeſtial Happineſs.

CRAMBO SONG, *on Miſs* SCOTT,
A beautiful Lady whom the Author ſaw at Ruckholt-Houſe, *Eſſex, attended by a very ugly Sea Captain.*

I.

Come one of ye Laſſes,
Who dwell in *Parnaſſus*,
To *London* on *Pegaſus* trot;

And

And bring me some Verse
That I may rehearse
    The Praises of pretty Miss *Scott*.

II.

When I saw the fair Maid
First in *Ruckholt*'s gay Shade,
    I wish'd —but I dare not say what;
If I had her alone,
With a Sigh and a Groan
    I'd whisper it all to Miss *Scott*.

III.

Full close by her Side,
By way of a Guide,
    A damn'd ugly Fellow she'd got,
The Dog did appear,
Like the Dev'l at *Eve*'s Ear,
    He's so foul, and so fair is Miss *Scott*.

IV.

He'd a traiterous Face,
And a Jesuit's Grace,
    Yet you'd swear he'd no Hand in the Plot;
He was fitter to go
With a Drum at a Show,
    Than to follow the charming Miss *Scott*.

V.

Oh had I a Part
In the Heav'n of her Heart,
    Contented I'd dwell in a Cot;
What are Titles but Toys,
What is Fame but a Noise,
    When compar'd with the Charms of Miss *Scott?*

VI.

The Pain of dull Pleasure,
The Poorness of Treasure,
    Are the Rake's and the Miser's sad Lot;
But Riches immense
And Pleasure intense
    Can come from no Fund but Miss *Scott.*

VII.

Whoe're in this Dearth
Of Enjoyments on Earth
    Thinks of Bliss, is a Fool and a Sot:
But we that are wise,
Know that Happiness lies
    In Heav'n, or pretty Miss *Scott.*

VIII.

The Scholar in Books,
The Glutton in Cooks,
    The Drunkard delights in his Pot;
But what is dull thinking,
Or eating, or drinking,
    To the feasting on pretty Miss *Scott?*

IX.

Some greatly desire
Wisdom to acquire,
    Some after Religion are hot;
But Wisdom's a Fool,
And Zeal it is cool,
    If compar'd with my Flame for Miss *Scott.*

X.

Oh! she's all that is rare,
Engaging and fair,
    A good Husband alone she has not.

And

And that, if I might,
I'd give her to-night,
   T'accomplifh the charming Mifs *Scott*.

The Power of INNOCENCE.
A SONG. *By Mrs.* MIDNIGHT.

I.

THE blooming Damfel, whofe Defence
   Is adamantine Innocence,
Requires no Guardian to attend
Her Steps, for Modefty's her Friend.
Tho' her fair Arms are weak to wield,
The glitt'ring Spear, and maffy Shield ;
Yet fafe from Force and Fraud combin'd,
She is an *Amazon* in Mind.

II.

With this Artillery fhe goes,
Not only 'mongft the harmlefs Beaux,
But ev'n unhurt and undifmay'd,
Views the long Sword and fierce Cockade.
Tho' all a Syren as fhe talks,
And all a Goddefs as fhe walks,
Yet Decency each Motion guides,
And Wifdom o'er her Tongue prefides.

III.

Place her in *Ruffias'* fhowery Plains,
Where a perpetual Winter reigns ;
The Elements may rave and range,
Yet her fix'd Mind will never change.

Place

Place her, Ambition, in thy Towers,
'Mongſt the more dangerous golden Showr's;
Ev'n there ſhe'd ſpurn the venal Tribe,
And fold her Arms againſt the Bribe.

IV.

Leave her defenceleſs and alone,
A Pris'ner in the torrid Zone,
The Sunſhine there might vainly vie
With the bright Luſtre of her Eye:
But *Phœbus* ſelf with all his Fire,
Cou'd ne'er one unchaſte Thought inſpire,
But Virtue's Path ſhe'd ſtill purſue,
And ſtill ye Fair, wou'd copy you.

---

*Upon the Lady's Garter, dropt in St. Paul's,
at the Rehearſal of the Muſick for the Sons
of the Clergy.*

By the GENTLEMAN *who found it.*

*Tentanda via eſt, qua ut quoque poſſim
Tollere* ———
　　　　　　　　VIR. GEORG.

Mox magis alta canam. ———
　　　　　　　　SIL. ITAL.

THIS Ribband, which was wont to be
　　The Cincture of my *Celia's* Knee,
Blind Chance to me has giv'n, and how
Shall I, what Chance has giv'n, beſtow?

In

In Man prefumptuous it were
To keep what has belong'd to her.
Some Deity from *Celia*'s Slave
The rare Oblation fhall receive.

Should I this confecrated Wreath
To Father *Jupiter* bequeath,
With Honours how the God would heap it!
In fragrant Nectar firft he'd fteep it:
(And yet when it has touch'd the Maid
What need of fragrant Nectar's Aid)
'Mid Garniture of Lightnings fork'd
In Gold a Motto on it work'd,
Shall ftyle the Fires lefs fierce, which fly
From *Jove*'s Right Hand than *Celia*'s Eye.
Forthwith a Diadem divine
On his ambrofial Locks 'twou'd fhine.

Yet muft not I an Off'ring make it
To *Jove*; for how would *Juno* take it?
Soon as fhe knew from whence it came,
For whom 'twas worn, the jealous Dame,
Wou'd bounce and fly, and rage and riot,
Nor give her Spoufe one Moment's Quiet.
But threaten for his Brows to find
An Ornament of diff'rent Kind.

Wou'd I to any Goddefs give it,
There's not one Goddefs would receive it.
Jealous on *Celia* they lour,
Each fears to lofe her Paramour.
But why, fair Rulers of the Skies,
Should ye her Garter thus defpife?

I 3

Oh

Oh rather, think, you've light upon
Another Love-exciting Zone,
Whofe magic Virtue is the fame
With that which to *Jove*'s royal Dame
Fair *Venus* lent.   Its Efficacy
(In *Homer* this averr'd you may fee)
Was fuch that on a Lady's Waift,
As foon as ever it was brac'd,
Who faw her would fuch Charms difcover,
He'd inftantly to Madnefs love her.
   I well imagine what wou'd follow
In Cafe 'twas given to *Apollo*.
Soon as that youthful am'rous God
Gay fprightly *Phœbus* underftood,
That what was offer'd had a Share,
I'th Drefs of that tranfcendent Fair,
On whom he us'd fo long to gaze,
We wonder'd at the Length of Days;
Pleas'd fuch a Token to poffefs
He'd oft the facred Texture kifs.
And now no more perfift to wear
The Laurel Chaplet on his Hair :
But clean forgetting *Perfeus*' Daughter,
He'd bind his Brows with *Celia*'s Garter.
The fweet Remembrance whence it came
Adding new Fuel to his Flame.
Thee, *Celia*, *thee*, he'd doat upon,
To Clofe of Day from early Dawn :
His tuneful Voice and golden Lyre
To praife my *Celia* would confpire.

In

In fine, at ſuch a Sacrifice
What heav'nly Power wou'd not rejoice?
Each gratefully wou'd me endow,
With the beſt Gift he could beſtow.
Hermes would teach me better far
Than any Lawyer at the Bar,
His Arts to be alert and quick in,
Speaking, to wit, and Pocket-picking.
Mars teach me to deal out my Blows,
And draw my Sword on Friends and Foes;
Vulcan wou'd forge me Armour for it,
And *Bacchus* give me Store of Claret,
 This votive Fillet might beſure
Wond'rous Advantages procure;
But 'tis reſolv'd, I'll nought receive
Unleſs the Gods can *Celia* give:
There's nought below is worth my Care
But that bright beauteous heav'nly Fair.
 What ſtrange Abſurdities a Lover
In Hopes and Wiſhes will diſcover!
A love-diſtracted Swain can hope
The rival Gods will render up,
And be ſo much o'erſeen to barter
The Lady for the Lady's Garter.
Therefore no more of *Jove* or *Phœbus*,
Or *Mars* or *Hermes* ſhall eſcape us.
'Twere greater Prudence to diſmiſs
Theſe idle uſeleſs Reveries,
My Suit in Perſon to prefer,
And urge without Delay the Fair.

If she my proffer'd Love refuses,
The Garter still may have its Uses;
It's friendly Noose shall me suspend;
A mournful Load some Bough shall bend;
And I be sung in doleful Ballad,
'Till *Bateman*'s Fame in mine is swallow'd.

A JACKBOOT.

Being an *Essay in the Manner of the Moderns,*

On Times, Persons, *and* Things.

A JACKBOOT is a Discourse, which will suit any Subject whatsoever, as its Namesake will fit any Leg. It requires no Title, yet is capable of all. You may preach it as a Sermon, declame it as an Oration, say it as a Prayer, or sing it as a Song. It will finally answer all Intents and Purposes, tho' in itself it is to no Intent or Purpose; such is the whimsical, ænigmatical Nature of the JACKBOOT. For these twenty Years last past we have had little else publish'd but JACKBOOTS. One Man prints a Sermon, which may as well be called a Satire, another comes out with a *Monody* with three or four Interlocutors in it. Our Poetry is all Prose, and our Prose is false English. And shall not *Mary Midnight*

night club her JACKBOOT amongft the reſt ? Yea verily ſhe ſhall. ———— Here therefore begins a JACKBOOT upon *Times, Perſons* and *Things*. And firſt for the Times. I think we are all pretty unanimous with reſpect to the Times. That is, there is almoſt an univerſal Conſent to rail at them. There has been a perpetual Prejudice in Behalf of the Times paſt, tho' God knows, we have but littl: to do with them, and we are daily grumbling and *abuſing* the preſent, when we ought to make uſe of it, and be thankful. *O Tempora ! O Mores !* is an Exclamation that has been made uſe of long before the *Roman* Orator. Nevertheleſs one of the wiſeſt tells us, " that the former Times were not better than theſe," —— And now I'll quote you a Bit of *Greek,*

'Οιη μεν φυλλων γενεη τοινδε κỳ ανδρων.　HOMER.

The Generation of Man is even as the Generation of Leaves. One Winter demoliſhes a whole Tribe, and in the Spring you have a Succeſſion of the ſame wavering, weak, inconſtant Trifles. —— And now I'll quote you a Piece of *Latin:*

————— *Elapſum ſemel*
Non ipſe poſſit Jupiter reprehendere.

PHOEDRUS.

That is, When old Time has once turn'd Tail upon you, the Devil himſelf can't get hold of his Forelock. Which brings me (where I was before-
hand

hand determin'd to go) to my fecond and third
Particulars, *viz.* *Perfons* and *Things* : —— Now,
as every Perfon is a Thing, tho' every Thing is
not a Perfon, I fhall jumble thefe two Articles
together in the true JACKBOOT Tafte. Now it
would require the united Wit of *Fielding, Lucian,
Swift, Butler,* and *Erafmus,* to treat of this
Head with any tolerable Adroitnefs, fo (as Mr.
Bays fays) in fine, I'll fay no more about it, and
if any body afks me, where lies the Jeft of all
this? I anfwer with Mr. *Johnfon,* Why, In the
BOOT; where fhou'd the Jeft lie?

E P I G R A M.

On a certain Scribbler.

WORD-valiant Wight, thou great He-
  Shrew,
  That wrangles to no End;
Since Nonfence is nor falfe nor true
  Thou'rt no Man's Foe or Friend.

Mrs. MIDNIGHT'S Laws *of* Converfation.

ONE of the higheft Enjoyments we are capable of on this Side the Grave, is manly
and rational Converfation, which in thefe Days,
exclufive of its intrinfick Value, has the Merit of
                                          being

being a very great Rarity. If one goes amongſt
what is called the ſober Part of Mankind, downright Dulneſs uſurps the Title of ſerious Senſe, and
Sleepineſs that of Decency and Tranquillity. If
we mix ourſelves with the Joys of the Young,
and grow giddy with the gay Head-ach of Pleaſure,
we ſhall find Baudry, and even Blaſphemy paſſing
for Wit and Humour, or the low nonſenſical in-
ſipid HUMBUG, that worthy Succeſſor to *Biting*
and *Selling of Bargains.* In order, to remedy,
in ſome Meaſure, theſe Evils, I humbly beg Leave
to lay down the following Rules of Converſation,
which are ſubmitted to the Conſideration, Cor-
rection and Improvement of the Publick.

1ſt. Never to converſe on what we don't underſtand.

2dly. Let there be always certain Intervals, to
give Room for any Perſon to make an Objection,
a Reply, or a Rejoinder.

3dly. Let the Subject be on Things, rather
than Perſons.

4thly. Let the Subject be on hiſtorical Matters,
rather than of the preſent Age.

5thly. Let the Subject be on Things diſtant
and remote, rather than at home, and ſo of your
Neighbours.

6thly.

6thly. Blazon all the Good, and conceal all the Faults of both Friend and Enemy.

7thly. Let nothing ever be said which good Senfe may difapprove, Good-nature diflike, or found Judgment condemn.

As fome late unhappy Events have made Duelling *a very popular Topic, the following Letter which I can warrant to be genuine, will, I apprehend, be deem'd not unfeafonable.*

A Letter from Alexander Robinfon, *Efq; to Mr.* Walter Smyth.

S I R,

I Muft abfolutely decline accepting the Challenge you fent me Yefterday by *Robin,* and frankly acknowledge I *dare not* fight you. I am very fenfible the World in general will call this Cowardice, and that the odious Appellation of Scoundrel will be given me in every Coffee-houfe. But, I hope, you'll not judge with the Multitude, becaufe you have been an Eye-witnefs to my Behaviour, in no lefs than feven Engagements with the common Enemy. I then had the Reputation of being a brave Man, and am confcious I am fo ftill, even when I once more tell you I *dare not* fight you. The Reafons of my Conduct in this Affair, Sir, are very valid, tho' but very few. To be brief,

Sir,

Sir, I had rather endure the Contempt of Man, than the Anger of my Maker, a temporal Evil rather than an eternal one. In one of the wifest States of the World, there was no Law against Parricide, becaufe they thought it a Crime, which the worft of Villains would be incapable of. Perhaps the Silence of our Legiflature, with Regard to Duelling, is owing to fome fuch Reafon. What can be more enormous than for Men, not to fay *Chriftians* and Friends, to thirft for the Blood of each other —— nay more, —— to aim the Blow with a true *Italian* Vengeance at once, both at the Body and the Soul. I hope in the Coolnefs of Reflexion you'll think as I do —— If otherwife, I am determined to give you up to the Tyranny of your Paffions, as I am to remain Mafter of my own.

Yours, &c.

A genuine Letter from an amorous Cantab. *to a* Chandler's *Daughter, being a Specimen of Academic Gallantry.*

MADAM,

THE very firft Moment I faw you, I conceived an inexpreffible Paffion for you, which at length has rifen to fuch an Height, that I fhould not difcharge the firft Duty of Self-

vation, were I to conceal it any longer. I
am convinced by the charming engaging Softnefs,
which is perpetually in your Looks, that it is impoffible you fhould be ill-natur'd, and that you
would free any Animal from Pain, when you could
do it without Danger or Detriment to yourfelf.
I here therefore offer you an Opportunity of exer-
cifing your Humanity, by condefcending to a Re-
queft I am about to make. The Favour I would
beg, Madam, is, that you would contrive fome
Means, by which I may have the Pleafure, the
exquifite Pleafure of converfing with you. Then,
Madam, I fhall be able more at large to explain
my Sentiments, declare that vehement Love, with
which you have infpired me, and make an Apology
for my Pretenfions, which if you don't approve,
I promife, never to trouble you with 'em any
more. If there is, Madam, any Impertinence in
this Addrefs, it muft be placed to the Account of
your Beauty, and you muft confider, that 'tis the
fame Nature, which both lavifh'd all thofe Charms
upon you, and raifed in me a proper Regard for
'em, and the Defire of the Poffeffion of 'em.
My Intentions, Madam, are honeft, my Love is
pure and unfeigned, and like thofe Excellencies
in you that occafioned it, too great to be defcribed.
I am confcious you'll have fome Objections to the
favouring me with an Interview; but upon more
mature Deliberation you will, I believe, acknowledge, that no Lady need be afhamed of converfing with any Gentleman, unlefs fhe knows him

                                                        not

not to be a Man of Honour; and 'tis the Privilege of every Englishman to plead for Love as well as for Life, but I shall plead for both at the same Time, since I hardly think the latter worth holding without the former. The Uncertainty I am in, (and a cruel Uncertainty it is) how you'll receive this, hinders my discovering to you my Name and my College: But tho' I don't tell you what I am, I'll tell you what I am not: I am not quite three and twenty, not in bad Circumstances, not a Freshman, not Fellow of the College, not in Orders.

If you'll please to appoint any Place of meeting, you'll make me the happiest of Men. My Love is so impatient that I shall perpetually plague you with Letters till you give me some Answer or other. On Wednesday Night at Eight o'Clock, a Person shall come to the Apothecary's Shop which you frequent, under Pretence of buying some Tamarinds; by him you may send a Note, and my dear sweet Angel, I beg you will not fail being there.

A modern Love Letter, copied from the W * r-Office: Being a Specimen of Martial Gallantry.

Damme Madam,

WHAT because *Cupid* basks in your Eyes, and the Graces perch on your Bubbies,

and

and I have no Beard, you think to treat me as you pleafe, and to make a *Tom Shuttlecock* of me, do you? You little, impertinent, plaguy, audacious Devil! Have not I beftowed all the Plunder I got in the laft War upon you, and pawn'd even my Honour to maintain you? And am I now to be rivall'd, and you to be run away with by a Templar, a Lawyer's Clerk, a Fellow that lives by fcratching of Parchment? Blood, I can't bear it! I'll make Parchment of his Skin, and burn you into a Pumice Stone to pounce it with, before I'll be plagued in this Manner. Is this all the Refpect you have for a Red Coat, and a Cockade, and a fine Gentleman? 'Tis mighty well —— but I fwear by the united Powers of Gun, Blunderbufs, and Thunder, that I fhall not hereafter vifit you with Sighs, as the God * *Cuper* did *Phyfic*, but in Storms of Lightning, as the God *Jopiter* did *Simile*.

I am d——mme you, Madam, Yours;

BEN. BAGONETT.

---

* I fuppofe Capt. *Bagonett* means to refer to the Stories of *Cupid* and *Pfyche*; and *Jupiter* and *Semele*, tho' he is a little out in his Orthography.

A

A modern Love Letter, composed of such Materials as may serve for any other Love Letter whatever, and with a little Variation will suit every Circumstance where Love is the Subject.

Being a Specimen of Universal Gallantry.

Oh my dear angelick Angel!

EVERY Minute is an Hour, and every Hour is a Day, and every Day is a Year since I had the Happiness to fall at your Feet, and warm myself at the Sunshine of your Beauty. Oh my little *Cherub,* I was yesterday flying with all the Wings of Fervency to offer myself at thy Shrine, but the angry Heavens threatned me with their forked Lightning, which darted round me, and the big black Thunder roar'd horrid o'er my Head, as much as to say, Wilt thou, oh rash Youth, who art but mortal, assume a Goddess? Can'st thou sustain her refulgent ineffable Bright'ness? Can'st thou mount the golden flaming Car of *Phœbus,* and give genial Warmth to the World? I trembled at this chiding of the Elements, and stood wrapt up in Fear and Amazement, till the Clouds in downright Compassion (perceiving me weep) wept themselves also, till with our joint Tears I was wet from Top to Toe, and all the Rivers swell'd and overflow'd with my Sorrows; so that I was this Morning obliged to swim thro' a whole Flood of my own Griefs to procure from thy bright Eyes one Dawn of Comfort. Oh, come my fweet Angel, and fave me from myfelf, or I fhall hang myfelf, or drown myfelf, or make away with myfelf, and all for the Love of thee. I am now at the Sign of the Lamb in a freezing burning Fever. Oh come to me! melt down my Ificles with the Beams of thy Eyes, and cool and comfort me with the Balm of thy Lips, that I may live till I die.

> *My dear Angel,*
> *Your moft obfequious Slave,*
> T. TAWDERY.

A Defcription of the Vacation, to a Friend in the Country.

Dear CHARLES, *Camb.* July 9, 1745.

AT length arrives the dull Vacation,
And all around is Defolation ;
At Noon one meets unapron'd Cooks,
And leifure Gyps with downcaft Looks.
The Barber's Coat from white is turning,
And blacken's by Degrees to Mourning ;
The Cobler's Hands fo clean are grown,
He does not know them for his own ;
The Sciences neglected fnore,
And all our Bogs are cobweb'd o'er ;
The Whores crawl home with Limbs infirm
To falivate againft the Term ;

Each

Each Coffee-honfe, left in the Lurch,
Is *full* as *empty* — as a Church —
The Widow cleans her unus'd Delph,
And's forc'd to read the News herfelf;
Now Boys for bitten Apples fquabble,
Where Geefe fophiftic us'd to gabble;
Of hoary Owls a reverend Band
Have at St. *Mary*'s took their Stand,
Where each in folemn Gibberifh howls,
And gentle *Athens* owns her Fowls.
To *Johnian* Hogs obferve, fucceed
Hogs that are real Hogs indeed;
And pretty Mafter *Pert* of *Trinity*,
Who in lac'd Waiftcoat woes Divinity,
Revifits, having doft his Gown,
His gay Acquaintance in the Town:
The Barbers, Butlers, Taylors, Panders,
Are prefs'd and gone to ferve in *Flanders*;
Or to the Realms of *Ireland* fail,
Or elfe (for Cheapnefs) go to Goal. —
Alone the penfive Black-Gowns ftray
Like Ravens on a rainy Day.
Some faunter on the drowfy Dam,
Surrounded by the Hum-drum Cam,
Who ever, and anon, awakes,
And grumbles at the Mud he makes,
Oh how much finer than the Mall
At Night to traverfe thro' *Clare-Hall!*
And view our Nymphs, like beauteous Geefe,
Cackling and waddling on the Piece;

Or

Or near the Gutters, Lakes, and Ponds
That ftagnate round ferene St. *John's,*
Under the Trees to take my Station,
And envy them their Vegetation.

* * * * * * * * * * * * *

* * * * * * * * * * * *

Cætera defiderantur.

Mrs. M I D N I G H T's *Account of her own Abilities. In Imitation of feveral Authors.*

THE Reputation I have acquired by my Wit
and Humour in my younger Days, and the
Candour I have difcover'd fince I commenced Critic,
added to the Judgment which I have fhewn in my
maternal Profeffion, have given all People a prodigious Opinion of my Abilities. And really, if I
may be allow'd to do myfelf Juftice, and to fpeak
myfelf for myfelf, I don't believe that the whole
Race of Lawyers, Divines, or even Phyficians
themfelves can produce a greater old Woman than
I am. People flock to me from every Quarter,
and I find, tho' too late, that a fuperb and exalted
Reputation is but an Incumbrance, a Sort of Rub,
in the Road to Happinefs ; for befides my own Bufinefs (I mean that of my Profeffion) and the Care
of my Magazine, I am continually pefter'd with
Cafes and Queftions from the Literati of all Nations.

tions. No Cafuiſt ever had ſo many Cafes of Conſcience as I when Conſciences were in Vogue;
indeed ſince the Uſe of Doubts and Scruples have
been dropt by the better Sort, and conſider'd as old
faſhion'd Furniture, I have been eas'd in that Reſpect. For when once my Lord puts off all Senſe
of Religion, of Conſcience, of Honour, and of
Honeſty, his Steward, his Gentleman, his Valet de
Chambre, and indeed all his Family, will do the
ſame. And, Pray where is the Wonder?———
Wou'd not any complaiſant Man, any Servant of
good Breeding, readily throw off a Garb which he
ſaw had render'd itſelf ſo obnoxious to his Maſter.
But this is a Digreſſion which I make by way of
Digreſſion, to ſhew People the Uſe of Digreſſions,
and now let us return to our Subject.———I ſay,
notwithſtanding the total Neglect of Religion and
Conſcience, of Honour and Honeſty among the
Great, and of Conſequence among the Small, I
am as much as ever harraſs'd with Cafes and Queſtions, tho' of another Nature. Religion and Conſcience, while in Vogue, were a Sort of ſtimula-
ting Plaiſters to the Paſſions, and braced them up
within their proper Cells; but when the Uſe of thoſe
became unfaſhionable, the Paſſions obtain'd their
wiſh'd for Elaſticity and acted without Reſtraint;
ſo that Drinking and Whoring, and Theft and
Murder advanced, as Religion and Virtue, Honour
and Honeſty declin'd; and conſequently there was
no Buſineſs for the Caſuiſt, Fortune, by eſtabliſhing
a diſſolute Courſe of Life, had thrown all her Fa-
vours

vours into the Laps of the Lawyer and the Physician; those are the People to be apply'd to, and as those People are continually applying to me, I find myself obliged to publish the following Advertisement.

MARY MIDNIGHT,

Author of the *Old Woman's Magazine,* and of many other celebrated Pieces, which can never be enough admired, proposes *(for the Benefit of the Publick)* to open at the Sign of the Mop-Handle in ~~*Shoe-Lane,*~~

An Office for the IGNORANT,

OR,

A Warehouse of Intelligence.

Where Physicians may learn the true Practice of Physic, Divines the true Practice of Piety, and Lawyers the true Practice of the Law. In a Word, Fumblers of all Faculties will be corroborated without Loss of Time.

VIVAT REX.

An

An Essay on LOVE.

Solid Love, whose Root is Virtue, can no more die
than Virtue itself. ERASMUS.

SINCE Love is a Paſſion deeply implanted
in the Nature of Human Kind, and productive
of as much Miſery as Happineſs, ſince Emperors,
Kings and Princes are oblig'd to ſubmit to its
Power; and we may every Day obſerve more pine
away with ſecret Anguiſh, for the Unkindneſs of
thoſe upon whom they have fix'd their Affections,
than for any other Calamity in Life; it cannot be
foreign to our Deſign to point out thoſe Soils in
which this *amphibious* Plant is moſt likely to grow
and proſper: But that we may not be thought too
rigid in Principle, or to advance any new *Hypotheſis*,
repugnant to the known Laws of Nature and Religion, let us firſt lay before you the Sentiments of
a *gay* and great Genius, as well read in *this Science*
as any of his Predeceſſors were, or any of his Suc-
ceſſors ought to be.

Love the moſt generous Paſſion of the Mind,
The ſofteſt Refuge Innocence can find;
The ſafe Director of unguided Youth,
Fraught with kind Wiſhes, and ſecur'd by Truth;
The cordial Drop Heav'n in our Cup has thrown,
To make the nauſeous Draught of Life go down;
On which one only Bleſſing God might raiſe,
In Lands of Atheiſts Subſidies of Praiſe;

For

For none did e'er so dull and stupid prove,
But felt a God, and bless'd his Pow'r, in Love.

Thus far we agree with him, for the wise Author of our Motto informs us, that if we would keep *Love* from withering, and preserve its Verdure, we should plant it in Truth and Virtue, prune off all the luxuriant Branches, which weaken the Stock, and depreciate the Fruit: How careful therefore should we be in the Choice of this happy Spot, in which, should we mistake, we are sure to entail Sorrow and Anxiety upon ourselves and Posterity.

To anticipate Success in this important Affair, be careful not to make too much Haste to be happy, any more than to be rich, to avoid Strangers, and to let your Eyes and Inclination keep Pace with your Reason and Understanding. Laugh at the old Miser who covets you for a Nurse, and despise the vain young Butterfly, who bristles with gaudy Plumes, squanders away his Wealth and Patrimony, and tosses about his empty Noddle to no other Purpose, than to get Possession of a Mistress altogether as trifling and vicious as himself. Then turn your Eyes upon the gay World, and behold it made up for the most Part of a Set of conceited, fluttering, emaciated Animals, worn out in hunting after their own Pleasures; Wretches who confess, condemn and lament, but continue to pursue their own Infelicity! These are Scenes of Sorrow, and Objects of Misery! Vultures that prey upon the Vitals of
the

the Imprudent, and hope to repair their fhatter'd Fortunes from the Spoils of Innocence and Credulity!

There is another fatal Mifchief incident to virtuous Love, which calls aloud for Redrefs; in the Courfe of my Life I have more than once or twice been prefent at the Bargain and Sale of Children and Orphans of both Sexes, to the beft Bidder: Nay, not long ago I was by when a young Gentleman of no inconfiderable Fortune was fent for from * * * * to *London,* and in lefs than three Hours after his Arrival, obliged to marry a young Lady he had never before fet his Eyes on, or perhaps heard of. What Love, Harmony, Conftancy or *Friendfhip* (the Bands of conjugal Happinefs) can poffibly be expected from fuch Precipitancy? If indeed a large *Premium* given to the principal *Marriage Broker,* or the laying together large Eftates could purchafe Felicity as it does Hufbands and Wives, the Contract might be deem'd laudable; but when we daily obferve Controverfies, Animofities, Elopements, and Divorces, the Confequences of fuch Junctions, it is an evident Act of Inhumanity and Barbarity.

It has often amazed me to obferve how nice and anxious Gentlemen are in keeping up and improving the Breed of their irrational Stocks, whether Horfes, Sheep, Poultry, &c. and how carelefs and indolent in that of their own Progeny. Oh fhocking Cuftom! the Height of Cruelty, the Scandal of Chriftianity!

VOL. II. L 'Tis

'Tis well known there are Gentlemen and Ladies enough in the Kingdom of Rank, Quality, and Affluence with perfonal Endowments fuitable to any Degree of Life; why then fhould we chufe to couple them fo unequally? Old Age with Youth; Difeafe with Health; Debauchery with Modefty; and all Vices with the contrary Virtues.

Let the prudent Lady chufe for a Partner, a Gentleman fraught with Religion, Virtue, and good Manners; of a free, open, generous Difpofition; of a Soul fincere and fufceptible; one who can fee and feel the Misfortunes of others, and is ready to lend his friendly Advice and timely Affiftance to thofe who are in Diftrefs. He who is not poffefs'd of a warm generous Heart, will make but a cold, friendlefs Companion; you are therefore to find the Way to that, and not precipitately take a Man becaufe he wears a Smile on his Cheek, and a fine Coat on his Back, which perhaps may difguife and cloak a thoufand Rogueries, and vile Intentions. You muft learn to diftinguifh between Reality and Appearance, which is not to be done without being intimately acquainted with the Object. And from hence arifes the Neceffity of a formal Courtfhip, for in the Courfe of Time, however artful the Perfon may be, fome unguarded Sallies will be made, fufficient to give you a *Cue* to the whole Character, provided Paffion does not eclipfe the Sun Beams of Reafon, and prevent your laying hold of the Opportunity.

But

But that our *Britiſh* Ladies may be the better enabled to engage Gentlemen with theſe Endowments 'twill be neceſſary for them to imitate the following Character of *Antiope.*

' *Antiope* is gentle, plain hearted, prudent;
' her Hands deſpiſe not Labour; ſhe foreſees Things
' at a great Diſtance; ſhe provides againſt Contin-
' gencies; ſhe knows how to be ſilent; ſhe acts
' regularly without a Hurry; ſhe is for ever
' employ'd, but never embarras'd, becauſe ſhe
' does every Thing in due Seaſon; the good Order
' of her Father's Houſe is her Glory; it adds a
' greater Luſtre to her than her very Beauty. Tho'
' the Care of all lies upon her, and ſhe is charg'd
' with the Burden of reproving, refuſing, ſparing,
' (Things that make all other Women hated) ſhe
' has acquir'd the Love of all the Houſhold; and
' this, becauſe they find not in her either Paſſion,
' Conceitedneſs, Levity, or Humour, as in other
' Women. With the ſingle Glance of her Eye they
' know her Meaning, and are afraid to diſpleaſe
' her. The Orders ſhe gives are plain; ſhe com-
' mands nothing but what may be perform'd; ſhe
' reproves with Kindneſs, and even amidſt her Re-
' prehenſions ſhe finds Room to give Encourage-
' ment to do better. Her Father's Heart repoſes
' itſelf upon her, as a Traveller, fainting under
' the Sun's ſultry Rays, repoſes himſelf upon the
' tender Graſs, beneath a ſhady Tree.

' *Antiope,* O *Telemachus,* is a Treaſure worthy
' to be ſought for, even in the moſt remote Re-

' gions: Her Mind is never trimm'd, any more
' than her Body, with vain gaudy Ornaments;
' her Fancy, though full of Life, is reftrain'd by
' her Difcretion; fhe never fpeaks but when there
' is an abfolute Occafion; and when fhe opens her
' Mouth, foft Perfuafion and genuine Graces flow
' from her Lips. The Moment fhe begins every
' Body is filent, which throws a bafhful Confufion
' into her Face; fhe could find in her Heart to fup-
' prefs what fhe was about to fay, when fhe per-
' ceives fhe is fo attentively liften'd to.

' You may remember, O *Telemachus*, when
' her Father one Day made her come in, how fhe
' appear'd with Eyes caft down, cover'd with a
' large Veil, and fpoke no more than juft enough
' to moderate the Anger of *Idomeneus*, who was
' juft going to inflict a rigorous Punifhment on
' one of his Slaves. At firft fhe took part with
' him in his Troubles, then fhe calm'd him; at laft
' fhe intimated to him what might be alledg'd in
' Excufe of the poor Wretch, and without letting
' the King know that he was tranfported beyond
' due Bounds, fhe infpir'd into him Sentiments of
' Juftice and Compaffion. *Thetis*, when fhe fooths
' old *Nereus*, does not appeafe with more Sweetnefs
' the raging Billows.

' Thus, *Antiope*, without affuming any Autho-
' rity, and without taking any Advantage of her
' Charms, will one Day manage the Heart of a
' Hufband, as fhe now touches the Lute, when fhe
' would draw from it the moft melting Sounds.
Once

' Once again, I tell you, *Telemachus*, your Love
' for her is well grounded ; the Gods defign her for
' you ; you love her with a rational Affection, but
' you muft wait 'till *Ulyffes* grants her to you. I
' commend you for not having difcover'd your
' Sentiments to her; but know, that if you had
' taken any By-methods to let her know your
' Defigns, fhe would have rejected them, and
' ceas'd to have a Value for you ; fhe will never
' promife herfelf to any one, but will leave herfelf
' to be difpofed of by her Father. She will never
' take for her Spoufe a Man that does not fear the
' Gods, and who does not quit himfelf of all the
' Duties that are incumbent upon him.

The MIDWIFE's POLITICKS : Or, *Goffip's Chro-nicle of the Affairs of Europe.*

PORTUGAL *and* SPAIN.

THOUGH his moft faithful Majefty has rejected
the Miniftry of his Predeceffor ; he, however,
has purfued his Example in publifhing a Procla-
mation for the Prevention of Luxury ; in which the Ufe
of gilt Coaches and Chariots is allow'd, provided they
are made in Portugal. This occafions me to make an
old Woman's Obfervation, that either the Portugueze
Miniftry have lefs Pride, or more Frugality, than are to
be generally found in other Countries ; particularly my
own dear native Kingdom of old England, where,
whilft my poor fellow Subjects are moft grievoufly op-
preffed with publick Debts and Taxes, yet a Spirit of

Luxury

Luxury prevails, when our firſt rate Quality ſhould follow my Example, and go clad in plain home-ſpun and grey, if they have half that Love for their Poſterity, as I have for the whole Community.

The Spaniards have ſatisfied us, that we were all old Women, to imagine they had any Deſign on Gibraltar: They, indeed, make Don Benjamin more remarkable for this Character than all the reſt of his Countrymen; for while he is continually preferring Memorial after Memorial, in hopes of the Procuration of ſuch Conceſſions in America, which the Spaniards have hitherto obſtinately diſregarded, in what other Light m uſt ſuch a Negotiation be held ! And as for his Remonſtrance to obtain the Return of ſuch Britiſh Manufacturers as have been invited over to Spain ; in the Name of good Luck, what muſt the Spaniards think of ſuch a Demand, when we but lately had it in our Power, to encourage theſe Artizans at home, inſtead of letting their Neceſſity, and our onerous Taxes, drive them to ſeek Employments in other Countries ? I am afraid, if they give us no worſe an Appellation than that of old Women, they will deal very candidly by us. —— The Infant Don Lewis is to reſign all his eccleſiaſtical Employments, to marry a Daughter of France, and aſcend the Throne of Corſica ; if the termagant old Woman at St. Ildefonſo can get Poſſeſſion of it.

ITALY.

From the Reſolution which the King of Sardinia has taken to reform his Troops, as well as ſeveral other Diſpoſitions, no Troubles are apprehended in Italy ; even the Barbary Corſairs are check'd in their Piratical Excurſions, by the Vigilance of ſome Malteſe and Neapolitan Veſſels. The poor Republick of Genoa is ſtill

ſtruggling

ftruggling with thofe Difficulties, which her Senators, like
a Parcel of filly old Women, entailed upon their Country by affociating with France in the Year 1746 : Their
Regality of Corfica evinces what the Duke of Wir-
temberg formerly told their Doge, that the whole Ifland
is not worth Poffeffion : So that we are in Expectation
of feeing this Saracen Crown inclofe the Head of another Prince of the Bourbonian Line ; while, miferable
Theodore, their late acknowledged Sovereign, is a ne-
ceffitous Prifoner within the Confines of an Englifh
Goal. The Genoefe Bills belonging to the Bank of
St. George, are ftill 45 per Cent. under Par ; and the
Senate intend to have an annual Lottery, of 600,000
Livres, for reviving the Credit of the Bank.

F R A N C E.

While the poor acceding Parties to the definitive
Treaty of Aix la Chapelle have been quietly amufing
themfelves with the Thoughts of enjoying the Product
of their own Vintages ; the vigilant French have been
extending their Commerce on the Coafts of Africa, and
repairing their ruin'd Marine ; which they have done
fo expeditioufly, as to be now able to boaft of 96 Men of
War and Frigates ready for Service, exclufive of the
Ships built in Canada, and thofe on the Stocks in the
feveral Ports of France —— But this muft needs be
falfe ; for we are told by the *beft Authority*, no longer
ago than January laft, that *all* the contracting Powers
in the *definitive* Treaty, had given the *fulleft* and *cleareft*
Declarations of their Refolution to *preferve* the general
Peace. Befides this, the French have juft erected a new
Manufactory of Cottons and Linnens, plain, ftriped,
and flower'd : — All rare News for England ! Hey ho !
Old Women and Aix la Chapelle, for ever ? huzza ! for

my

my Lord S——, huzza, huzza!——But if Mr. Perrier should fail from Breft, or the Veffels from Toulon should get out, before Commodore Rodney departs from Portfmouth, what is to come of our new difcovered Ifland?

GERMANY.

The Imperial Diet have come to the Refolution of guarantying the Treaty of Drefden in its utmoft Extent, and which it is expected his Imperial Majefty will ratify from Hungary, where his royal Confort is making frefh Work for her Midwife. The Election of the King of the Romans is ftill oppofed by the King of Pruffia; while France, who has already made an old Woman of the Elector of Cologne, is endeavouring to clap the filly Petticoat over the facerdotal Habiliments of the Electors of Mentz and Cologne.

DENMARK and SWEDEN.

The old Tranquility is predominant at the Court of Copenhagen. The Court of Stockholm has fent fatisfactory Accounts of its Proceedings to the Czarina, and every Thing feems to promife a durable Harmony between the two Courts, at the fame Time that they are both putting their Frontiers in the moft defenfible Condition; and they are both to be commended; for the Ruffian Miniftry are well apprized that Count Teffin has the Afcendency over the new Swedifh Sovereign, who may probably imbibe the ambitious and defpotick Sentiments for which that Minifter is fo remarkably diftinguifhed in all the different Courts of Europe.

RUSSIA.

The Court of Peterfburgh does not feem to entertain any dangerous Attempts from the Ottoman Forces; the Grand Vizir has affured the Ruffian Minifter that his

Sub-

Sublime Highnefs is defirous of contributing to the Peace of Europe; the Swedes, notwithftanding their Tranfportation of 8000 Men into Finland, occafion no Apprehenfions that his Swedifh Majefty will difregard his Coronation Oath, or not fulfil his Affurances he has made to the Czarina, of preferving the prefent Form of Eftablifhment in Sweden: So that the Czarina is entirely eafy; but, notwithftanding, fhe keeps up a numerous Army in the Ukraine.

The Czarina is an Honour to her Sex; for while fhe maintains the Poffeffions of her illuftrious Father by the Sword; fhe alfo follows his excellent Example in refining their Inhabitants by the Introduction of Commerce: For it appears, by the Cuftom-houfe Books of Peterfburgh, that the foreign Ships arrived there, within this Year, have traded with the Ruffians to the Value of 5 Millions of Rubles, in fuch Commodities only as are produced in the Ruffian Territories; and it is generally conjectured that the Englifh have taken off no lefs than 3 of the 5 Millions, for the Commerce with Ruffia has greatly increafed within this laft ten Years.

PERSIA.

This Country is now in a more calamitous Condition than ever, principally owing to the Intrigues of the Ottoman Miniftry, to divide and weaken the Perfians by different Factions caufing the Deftruction of one another. For this politic Purpofe, the Turks have infpirited Heraclius, Prince of Georgia, to make an Invafion upon that diftracted Empire; who has ingratiated himfelf into the Affections of the Aghuans, a bold People, continually at War with the Perfians; with whofe Affiftance he has marched from Candahar, at the Head of a numerous Army, into the Perfian Provinces, where he lays all wafte before him, to deprive the other contending

Com-

Competitors for the Throne, of Provisions, and at the same Time strike such a Terror into the Persians as may accelerate their Submission to him.

TURKEY.

The Pestilence has again broke out in the Neighbourhood of Constantinople, particularly in the Suburbs of Pera; the foreign Ministers have retired into the Country on this Account.

PLANTATION NEWS.

From Maryland, we hear, that a Convict Servant lately went into his Master's House, with an Axe in his Hand, determined to kill his Mistress; but changing his Purpose, thro' the Innocence of her Countenance, he laid his Left Hand on a Block, cut it off, and threw it at her, saying, *Now make me work if you can*; which to be sure manifested a noble Spirit of Industry.

We have Advice from Rhode-Island, that their last Assembly at Providence, passed an Act for emitting 200,000 l. old Tenor, on Loan, for ten Years; both Principal and Interest to be paid at that Period. They have ascertained the Value at eight for one, fixing Dollars at 48 per Bill of Exchange at 1200, that is 1100 Advance; enforcing the Observance of this Law with the like Penalties as those in New-England, and making the Punishment for Counterfeiting, Death. The Interest is Six per Cent, to be paid annually, and to be employed in encouraging Industry, and giving a Bounty on Linnen and Woollen Manufactures of the Colony, as also on the Whale and Cod Fishery.

A very barbarous Murder was lately committed at Elkridge, in New-York, by Jeremiah Swift, a Convict Servant belonging to Mr. John Hatherley, about 21 Years of Age; who took an Opportunity, while Mr.

Ha

Hatherley and his Wife were attending a Funeral, to knock out the Brains of their two Sons with a Hoe, and to kill their Daughter with an Axe.

DOMESTIC OCCURRENCES.

To encourage the Crew of each Buſs belonging to the Britiſh Herring Fiſhery to do their Duty, a Premium of 30 l. will be given to the Company of that Veſſel who ſhall catch the moſt Herrings during the Seaſon, and cure them beſt; 20 l. to the ſecond, and 15 l. to the third; to be diſtributed among them in Proportion to their Wages.

The Chamber of Campbel-Town have ſubſcribed 10,000 l. into the Society of the free Britiſh Fiſhery.

The Dutch have 450 Buſſes ready for the Herring Fiſhery; but we, alas! have no more than ten.

The iniquitous Cuſtom of Duelling has been lately very prevalent. Capt. Sole and Mr. Paſcal, upon a Quarrel ariſing from a Diſpute at Gaming, quitted the Tavern, with an Intent to terminate their Difference in Hyde-Park: But Mr. Paſcal was either too much in Liquor, or too little in Reaſon, to ſtay till they got to the appointed Place, and drew his Sword upon his Antagoniſt in the Street, who with much Reluctance alſo drew his Weapon, and after a little Trial of Skill very prettily pink'd his drunken Enemy thro' the Body, the Sword entering below the Navel, and coming out at the Back-bone. Mr. Paſcal was afterwards ſo ſenſible of the Provocation he had given Capt. Sole, that he freely forgave him; and the Coroner's Inqueſt brought in their Verdict Manſlaughter.

But the moſt remarkable Accident of this Nature happened between Mr. Dalton and Mr. Paul, two young Gentlemen of Fortune, and very intimate Friends. Mr. Paul had paid his Addreſſes to a young Lady, but Mr.
Dalton

Dalton had met with a more favourable Reception, and
the Lady gave him a Promife of Marriage. Mr. Paul
and Mr. Dalton paid a Vifit to the young Gentlewoman
in Company with Mr. Paul's Sifters; when the young
Lady told the Company, Mr. Dalton had detained
her Snuff-box; which Mr. Paul, on her Intreaty
procured from Mr. Dalton, and did not return it
him, which made Mr. Dalton fomewhat angry; a few
Words arofe; the Gentlemen parted; and the Ladies
were in the utmoft Confufion on this Occafion. Mr.
Paul conduƈted his Sifters home, put on his Sword, and
went to Mr. Dalton's Lodgings; fent him a Challenge
while he was in Company at the Braund's Head Tavern,
which the other accepted, and went to meet Mr. Paul.
They went up into Mr. Dalton's Room, who feemed
to retain his Anger, and propofed fighting in the Room;
which the other agreed to. They firft propofed firing
off Piftols, but retraƈted that Propofal, and meafured
Swords. They then embraced, and invok'd Heaven
for Mercy, Forgivenefs, and Succefs, and made feveral
violent Paffes, in which the Candles were knock'd
down. Mr. Dalton went out and lighted the Candles; on his Return they repeated their Embrace; and
renewed the Encounter; Mr. Dalton received a Wound
on his Left-hand, but difregarding that he preffed home
on his Antagonift, and received a Wound in the Breaft,
of which he immediately expired. Mr. Paul, on this
fatal Accident threw down his Sword, and ran with all
poffible Expedition to two eminent Surgeons, who came
direƈtly, but in vain, for the unhappy Gentleman was
dead. ——— How terrible is this inhuman Proceeding
of Duelling! in this melancholy Affair Mr. Paul has depriv'd himfelf of a Friend, a young Lady of a valuable
Lover, the King of a Subjeƈt, a diftreffed Parent of a
Son, and the World of a fine Gentleman.

The MIDWIFE.

NUMBER IV.

VOL. II.

*A Remarkable Prediction of an Author, who
shall write an History of* England *in the
Year* 1931, *with Part of the Contents of his*
23d *Chapter. By Mrs.* MIDNIGHT.

'TIS now near two Centuries since the Inhabitants of this Island contracted a mis-
chievous Habit of drinking Gin, which
has been fatal to all their Race, and is the Reason
why we are now the most diminutive Creatures
upon Earth. By what I can learn from the Historians of that Time, and by what we gather from
the Door-Posts of their Buildings, it plainly appears
that the *Britons* were then as big as the *French*,
Spaniards, or any other People; and this also agrees
with what Old *Poplin* hath often told me: This
old Man saw the Tower of *London* before it was

deftroy'd, and affured me, that by the Armour ~~there, the Inhabitants of that Time~~ muft have been between five and fix Feet high. And this is farther proved and confirm'd by Mr. *Caxall*, the Antiquarian, who hath now by him a Walking-Staff, dug out of the Ruins of *Canbury-Houfe*, near *Iflington*, which is four Foot long, and on it are engraved the Letters *N E W B E R Y*. Probably the fame *Newbery* who wrote the Heroic Poem entitled *The Benefit of eating Beef*,* a Sort of Food much in Repute in thofe Days, tho' now not digeftible by our puny Stomachs; and if the fame, he was not ~~a very tall Man, if we may believe the Biographer~~ who wrote his Life, which is prefix'd to the Poem. —Thefe Things confidered, have we not Reafon to curfe the People who entail'd fuch Mifery on their own Race, and brought us to this State of Deftruction. At that Time we made a glorious Figure in Hiftory, we were refpected by other Nations; and it was no Wonder then to fee an *Englifhman* fix Feet high and his Hat cock'd, whereas the mightieft of us now is not above two Feet and a half, and we hang down our Heads and are defpifed by all the People in the World.

Thus much by Way of Introduction, or Proem, or Reflection; for in thofe Days Hiftorians will make their Reflections at the Beginning of their Chapters.

---

* Of which there now (fays the Author) remain fome Fragments, with the Commentary of one *Smart*, who tho' but four Feet high would now be efteem'd a Giant.

He

He then proceeds to his History, from which I shall
select a few Paragraphs.

At this Time there was a War between our
Nation and the *French* and the *Spaniards*, wherein
we were assisted, or at least ought-to have been
assisted, by the *Dutch*; A People who at that
Time inhabited the Low Countries, which are now
called *Frenchalia*. There was nothing very remarkable effected by our Land Forces; but Admiral *Anson* and Admiral *Hawk* beat the *French* and
Spaniards by Sea damnably *(this Phrase may seem*
rather too rough for the Ladies, but I am oblig'd to
keep literally to my Author) He proceeds———I
cannot quit this Period without taking Notice of
one of the Authors of that Time, namely, Madam
Mary Midnight : She wrote that celebrated Book
entitled The M I D W I F E : Or, *Old Woman's Ma-*
gazine, which is now translated into all the modern
Languages, and read in all the *European* Universities and Schools as a Classic. She was a Woman
of prodigious Vivacity, of fine fertile Fancy, of
profound Learning, of good found solid substantial
Sense, and had more Wit and Humour than all the
Writers of that Age or any other Age whatever.
She had a most superb * * * * * * * * * * *
*. * * * * * * * * * * * * *
* . * * * * * * * * * * * *
* * * * * * * * * * * * * *
* * * * * * * * * * * * * *

My Modesty will not permit me to transcribe any

far-

farther; the Encomium is fo great 'twou'd be Vanity in me to own it. But as he will be an Author of great Veracity, I cannot quit his Hiftory without giving you the Copy of a Letter from his 54th Chapter. He is there got down to the Year 1915. The Reflections on this Chapter are at the Beginning like the former, and the Subject of them the Parliaments of Britain.

The Parliaments in former Ages were of fome Ufe, but now the only Figure they make is a Cypher: They talk of this and that and t'other and do nothing, or at leaft what they do is to no Purpofe; and this has generally been the Cafe fince the Eftablifhment of Bribery and Corruption, which began in the Reign of King *Jonathan* the Third. —— Mark what a Letter a Member at that Time wrote to a Prime Minifter who had offer'd him Money for his Vote.

Honrd. Sir,

The Money you bid me is too little, I really can't afford to take lefs than I afk'd you, and if you will not give me my Price I am determin'd to vote according to my Confcience.

I am, Honrd. Sir,
Your moft obfequious humble Servant,
P. H. Truckle.

Turnagain-Street,
Aug. 12, 1901.

P. S. Confider I have ten Years of my Time to come.

N. B

. *N. B.* In order to underſtand this Poſtſcript, it will be neceſſary for me to inform you, that the Parliaments will then ſit fourteen Years; but as that is a terrible Proſpect to look at, let us drop the Veil of Fate, and hide the other Parts of this Hiſtory 'till the Time be expired, and the Author has wrote them.

M. MIDNIGHT.

The Hiſtory of the Birth and Adventures of Meſſ. INCLINATION *and* ABILITY.

MRS. *Virginia Virtue,* an ancient Maiden, who about a Century and a half ago reſided in this Kingdom, after refuſing a great many Offers, at length gave her Hand to one Sir *David Deſire.* But ſhe did not long enjoy the Comforts of Matrimony, for *Deſire* ſoon expired after Poſſeſſion, and left Lady *Virtue* a Widow, as ſhe had been before an Orphan. Lady *Virtue* having a Fortune of her own, which neither Time nor Chance cou'd diveſt her of, did not deſpair of a ſecond Huſband; but finding herſelf pregnant, ſhe thought proper to wait till ſhe was deliver'd, and in due time ſhe brought forth a brave ſhopping Boy, whom ſhe call'd *Hercules Ability,* who in Proceſs of Time became remarkably diſtinguiſhed for all the Accompliſhments both of Body and Mind. In about a Year after the Deceaſe of Sir
M 5   *David*

David Defire, Lady *Virtue* liften'd to the Vows of Sir *Surface Smatter*, by whom in ten Years Time, and with the help of Medicines, fhe had a little ricketty Brat, whom they agreed fhou'd have the Name of *Ifgrim Inclination*. *Ability* had the beft Mafters in all the Arts and Sciences, and profited by them all; *Inclination* had the fame Advantages, and profited by none. The younger Brother had a perpetual Affectation of mimicking the Elder, but he did it in fo uncouth a Manner, that he appeared beyond Meafure abfurd and ridiculous. *Ifgrim* was extravagantly fond of his Brother *Hercules*, but he (tho' otherwife a Lad of fingular Humanity) cou'd not help both pitying and contemning poor *Ifgrim*. At the Age of thirteen *Ability* fhew'd fome Signs of a Genius for Poetry, and has fince wrote feveral excellent Pieces, which he publifhed under the Names *Collins*, *Warton*, *Mafon*, and others. This fet *Ifgrim* agog, and to fay the Truth, moft of the modern Compofitions are in Fact his, tho' they pafs under the Names of others. But I can favour the Publick with a little Piece of Poetry which he wrote at Eighteen, and which he valued himfelf upon above all his other Compofitions.

> *The little Bee into the Garden hies,*
> *To fearch out various Flow'rs of various Dies;*
> *The Rofe and Lilly fweetly fucketh he,*
> *Then goeth Home again the little Bee.*

Thus

> *Thus little i away to charming* Phyllis,
> *To* Sylvia, Daphne, *or to* Amaryllis,
>   *Clasp'd in their Arms I sweetly taste and try,*
> *Then full of Rapture home comes little i.*

The Conceit of expressing himself with a little i instead of a Capital, he acknowledges to be the greatest Stroke of Genius he ever hit off in his Life. —— It is remarkable * Lady *Virtue* gave her Children no Fortune, so they were obliged to earn a Livelyhood in the best Manner they were able. *Ability* took to the Stage at one House, and *Isgrim,* who always imitated his Brother, chose the same Profession at another. Their different Reception in this and other Occupations in Life will be recounted in the next Number.

––––––––––––––––––––

To the Keeper of the Curiosities at Gresham-College.

SIR,

IN the Month of *December*, 1709, Capt. *Lemuel Gulliver* deposited several Curiosities in your Repository, as appears by a Memorandum in his Red-leather Pocket-Book, which I have

––––––––––––––––––––

* We hope no Person of Distinction will take it amiss that *Virtue* is made a Lady of Quality.

now in my Poſſeſſion, and by a Paſſage in the 3d Chapter of his Voyage to Brobdingnag. As the Articles are not ſpecified in the Pocket-Book, I am at a Loſs to know exactly what and how many they are; but the following Quotation from the Chapter abovementioned will ſet us right in one Particular.

Extract from the Voyage to Brobdingnag, *Chap.* III.

" I remember one Morning when *Glumdalclitch*
" had ſet me in a Box upon a Window, as ſhe
" uſually did in fair Days to give me Air, (for
" I durſt not venture to let the Box be hung on a
" Nail out of the Window, as we do with Cages
" in *England*) after I had lifted up one of the
" Saſhes, and ſat down at my Table to eat a
" Piece of ſweet Cake for my Breakfaſt, above
" twenty *Waſps* allured by the Smell came flying
" round the Room, humming louder than the
" Drones of as many Bagpipes. Some of them
" ſeized my Cake, and carried it piece-meal away,
" others flew about my Head and Face, and con-
" founded me with their Noiſe, and put me in the
" utmoſt Terror of their Stings. However I had
" the Courage to riſe and draw my Hanger, and
" attack them in the Air. I diſpatch'd four of
" them, but the reſt got away, and I preſently
" ſhut my Window. Theſe Creatures were as
" large as *Partridges*, I took out their Stings,

found

" found them an Inch and a half long, and as
" fharp as Needles. I carefully preferved them
" all, and having fince fhewn them in feveral
" Parts of *Europe*; upon my Return to *England*,
" I depofited three of them in *Grefham-College*,
" and kept the fourth for myfelf."

Now Sir, this Capt. *Lemuel Gulliver* did by his
laft Will and Teftament bearing Date *July* 24,
One Thoufand Seven Hundred and Eighteen,
(a Copy of which you may procure from the
Commons) give and bequeath unto me, all
and every the Curiofities which he brought from
*Lilliput, Brobdingnag, Laputa, Balnibarbi, Lugg-
nagg, Glubdubribb* and *Japan*; together with what
he procured in the Country of the *Honyhnhnms*;
as you will fee by the following.

An *Extract from the Will of Capt.* Le-muel Gulliver.

" And I alfo give and bequeath to my dear
" Friend Mrs. *Mary Midnight*, all and every the
" Curiofities which I brought with me from *Lil-*
" *liput, Brobdingnag, Laputa, Balnibarbi, Glub-*
" *dubrib*, and *Japan*, and the County of the
" *Honibnhnms* to her and her Heirs for ever. And
" as I have never in all my Travels found any
" Perfon fo wife and learned as that Gentle-
" woman, I do alfo give her and her Heirs for
" ever the Property and Copy-right of all my
" Voyages, which fhe fhall think proper to write
" Notes

" Notes or Comments upon, well knowing that
" there is no Person in this World so capable of
" doing Justice to my Works, to my Memory,
" and to the Publick, &c. &c.

Now notwithstanding the Care of the Testator,
and of his Executors, I am informed that there
are certain Persons have laid a Scheme to deprive me of this my Property in Defiance of Law,
Equity, and the Will of the Deceased. I hope
none of your Society are in the Combination, yet
if they should I shall be able to disconcert their
Projects. That the Stings of these Wasps were
lodg'd in your Repository, no Body, I presume,
will have the Face to deny it. 'Twas publickly af-
serted by the Testator in his Life-time, and that
in Print, and as none of your Society have said
any thing to the contrary, or ever offered to dis-
prove it, their Silence will be considered by all
wise and just Men as a tacit Acknowledgement of
the Receipt of those Goods.

Besides the above, Mr. *Jonathan Gulliver,* a
Relation of the Captain's, assures me, that some of
your Society borrowed of him the said Captain, a
Snail's Horn brought from *Lilliput,* which was so
small that it could not be perceived even with a
Microscope; and another from *Brobdingnag* as
big as the Whale's Rib in *St. James's* Palace
Court. He farther affirms that he also lent your Society the Comb that was made of the King of *Brobdingnag's* Beard, the Eye of a worsted Needle, and the
Back-side of a Bee; all which you are desired immediately

mediately to fend me. 'Tis to no Purpofe to equi-
vocate, as the Fafhion is, and deny the Receipt
of them, for I am ready to prove it by the Mouths
of twenty-fix Evidences, and Mr. *Buftle-about*,
the Witnefs-monger, a Gentleman who attends
many of his Majefty's Courts of Judicature, and
underftands all Sorts of thefe Sort of Affairs, has
promifed to procure me fifty more if through your
Obftinacy my Caufe fhould require it. But I hope
you will weigh and confider thefe Things, and do
immediate Juftice to,

   S I R,

      Your humble Servant,

       MARY MIDNIGHT.

In Imitation of Horace, *by my Lord* O—,

  Eheu fugaces Pofthume, Pofthume, &c.

I.

HOW fwift alas, the rolling Years
  Hafte to devour their deftin'd Prey!
A Moth each winged Minute bears,
Which ftill in vain the Stationers
 From the dead Authors fweep away;
And Troops of Canker-worms with fecret Pride,
Thro' gay vermillion Leaves and gilded glide.

II.

Great *Bavius*, fhould thy critic Vein
  Each Day fupply the teeming Prefs,

           Of

Of Ink fhould'ft thou whole Rivers drain,
Not one Octavo fhall remain
 To fhew thy Learning and Addrefs:
Oblivion drags them to her filent Cell,
Where brave King *Arthur* and his Nobles dwell.
III.
Authors of every Size and Name,
 Knights, 'Squires, and Doctors of all Colours,
From the Purfuit of lafting Fame,
Retiring there a Manfion claim;
 Behold the Fate of modern Scholars!
Why will you then with Hope delufive led,
For various Readings toil, which never will be read.
IV.
With Silver Clafp, and corner Plate,
 You fortify the favourite Book.
Fear not from Worms nor Time thy Fate:
More cruel Foes thy Works await.
 The Butler, with the impatient Cook,
And paftry Nymphs with Trunk-makers combine
To eafe the groaning Shelves, and fpoil the fair
  Defign.

The Humble Petition *of* A N Y - B O D Y,

MAY it pleafe your Ladyfhip, out of your tender and compaffionate Regard for the whole Race of Mankind, to take into your Confideration the lamentable Circumftances of your poor Petitioner, which are as follows.

That

That he is deny'd even the Power as well as Benefit of Exiſtence. An Aſſertion however it may ſeem incredible, yet it is no leſs poſitive than true: When ſome charitable Perſon is inclinable to do an Act of Benevolence, which is deſigned with a liberal Intention and laudable Spirit, for ANY-BODY, *who thoroughly deſerves it,* I am not only deprived of the Donation, but denied even my Exiſtence, with an Anſwer that ANYBODY is NOBODY. Hence it is, that many Things, which are agreed on all Hands to be capable of making ANYBODY happy, are given to NOBODY. Yet what is more common than the Queſtion, is ANY-BODY within? ANYBODY there? which very Queſtions prove my *Exiſtence.*

What greater Indignities can be impoſed on any Being than are daily inflicted on me. Do not I ſee them that are mere Non-Entities given the Right of Precedence and Poſſeſſion before me? How many Times is it ſaid, NOBODY ſhall have it, NOBODY ſhall take it, when at the ſame Time ANYBODY would be glad of it; and at other Times when NOBODY will refuſe it, ANYBODY may take it.

Yet this I may boaſt of, that I am as keen in the Purſuit and Reward of Merit, as ANYBODY is or can be, and that tho' NOBODY diſlikes, yet ANYBODY who has common Senſe, (which an Encourager of Merit muſt have) will always ap-prove your Lucubrations. Conſider then, Madam, of thefe my Complaints, or you will fhortly hear from SOMEBODY whom you little fufpect.

Yours,

ANY-BODY. ·

---

* *From the* R A M B L E R.

——*Fatis accede deifque,*
Et cole felices, miferos fuge. Sidera cœlo
Ut diftant, & flamma mari, fic utile recto.

LUCAN.

THERE is fcarcely any Sentiment in which, amidft the innumerable Varieties of Inclination that Nature or Accident have fcattered in the World, we find greater Numbers concurring than in the Wifh for Riches; a Wifh indeed fo prevalent, that it may be confidered as univerfal and tranfcendental, as the Defire in which all other Defires are included, and of which the various Purpofes that actuate Mankind, are only fubordinate Species, and different Modifications.

Wealth is indeed the general Center of Inclination, the Point to which all Minds preferve an invariable Tendency, and from which they afterwards diverge in numberlefs Directions. Whatever is the remote or ultimate Defign, the immediate Care is to be rich; and in whatever Enjoyment we intend finally to acquiefce, we feldom confider it as attainable but by the Means of

---

* A Paper publifh'd every *Tuefday* and *Saturday*, price 2*d*.

Money,

Money, of which all therefore confefs the Value;
nor is there any Difagreement but about the Ufe.

There is fcarcely any Paffion which Riches do
not affift us to gratify. He that places his Happinefs in full Chefts or numerous Dependents, in
refined Praife or popular Acclamation, in the Ac-
cumulation of Curiofities or the Revels of Luxury,
in fplendid Edifices or wide Plantations, muft ftill
either by Birth or Acquifition poffefs Riches. They
may be confidered as the elemental Principles of
Pleafure, which may be combined with endlefs Di-
verfity; as the effential and neceffary Subftance, of
which the Form only is to be adjufted by Choice.

The Neceffity of Riches being thus apparent, it
is not wonderful that almoft every Mind has been
employed in Endeavours to acquire them; that
Multitudes have vied with each other in Arts by
which Life is furnifhed with Accommodations, and
which therefore Mankind may reafonably be expected to reward.

It had indeed been happy had this predominant
Appetite operated only in Concurrence with Virtue, and influenced none but thofe who were
zealous to deferve what they were eager to poffefs,
and had Abilities to improve their own Fortunes,
by contributing to the Eafe or Happinefs of others.
To have Riches and to have Virtue would then
have been the fame, and Succefs might reafonably
have been confidered as a Proof of Merit.

But we do not find that any of the Defires of
Men keep a ftated Proportion to their Powers of

N 2   At-

Attainment. Many envy and defire Wealth, who can never procure it by honeft Induftry, or ufeful Knowledge. They therefore turn their Eyes about to examine what other Methods can be found of gaining what none, however impotent, or worthlefs, can be content to want.

A little Enquiry will difcover that there are nearer Ways to Profit than through the Intricacies of Art, or up the Steeps of Labour; that what Wifdom and Virtue fcarcely receive at the Clofe of Life, as the Recompence of long Toil and repeated Efforts, is brought within the Reach of Subtilty and Difhonefty, by more expeditious and compendious Meafures : That the Wealth of Credulity is an open Prey to Falfhood, and that the Poffeffions of Ignorance and Imbecillity are eafily withdrawn by the fecret Conveyances of Artifice, or feized by the Gripe of unrefifted Violence.

It is likewife not hard to difcover, that Riches always procure Protection for themfelves, that they dazzle the Eyes of Enquiry, divert the Celerity of Purfuit, or appeafe the Ferofity of Vengeance; that when any Man is inconteftibly known to have large Poffeffions, very few think it requifite to enquire by what Practices they were obtained ; that the Refentment of Mankind rages only againft the Struggles of feeble and timorous Corruption ; but that when it has furmounted the firft Oppofition, it is afterwards fupported by Favour, and animated by Applaufe.

The

The Profpect of gaining fpeedily what is ardently defired, and the Certainty of obtaining by every Acceffion of Advantage an Addition of Security, have fo far prevailed upon the Paffions of Mankind, that the Peace of Life is deftroyed by a general and inceffant Struggle for Riches. It is obferved of Gold, by an old Epigrammatift, that *to have it is to be in Fear, and to want it is to be in Sorrow.* There is no Condition which is not difquieted either with the Care of gaining or of keeping Money; and the Race of Man may be divided in a political Eftimate between thofe who are practifing Fraud, and thofe who are repelling it.

If we confider the prefent State of the World, it will be found, that all Confidence is loft among Mankind; that no Man ventures to act, where Money can be endangered, upon the Faith of another. It is impoffible to fee the long Scrolls in which every Contract is included, with all their Appendages of Seals and Atteftation, without wondering at the Depravity of thofe Beings, who muft be reftrained from Violation of Promife by fuch formal and publick Evidences, and precluded from Equivocation and Subterfuge by fuch punctilious Minutenefs. Among the Satires to which Folly and Wickednefs have given Occafion, none is equally fevere with a Bond, or a Settlement.

Among the various Arts by which Riches may be obtained, the greater Part are at the firft View irreconcileable with the Laws of Virtue; fome are openly flagitious, and practifed not only in

N 3   Neglect,

Neglect, but in Defiance of Faith and Juſtice, and the reſt are on every Side ſo entangled with dubious Tendencies, and ſo beſet with perpetual Temptations, that very few, even of thoſe who are not yet abandoned, are able to preſerve their Innocence, or can produce any other Claim to Regard, than that they have deviated from the Right leſs than others, and have ſooner and more diligently endeavoured to return.

One of the chief Characteriſticks of the golden Age, of the Age in which neither Care nor Danger had intruded on Mankind, is the Community of Poſſeſſions, by which Strife and Fraud were excluded, and every turbulent Paſſion was ſtilled by Plenty and Equality. Such were indeed happy Times, but ſuch Times can return no more. Community of Poſſeſſion muſt always include Spontaneity of Production; for what is only to be obtained by Labour muſt be of right the Property of him by whoſe Labour it is gained. And while a rightful Claim to Pleaſure or to Affluence muſt be procured either by ſlow Induſtry or uncertain Hazard, there will always be Multitudes whom Cowardice or Impatience will incite to more ſafe and more ſpeedy Methods, who will ſtudy to pluck the Fruit without cultivating the Tree, and to ſhare the Advantages of Victory without partaking the Danger of the Battle.

In later Ages, the Conviction of the Danger to which Virtue is expoſed, while the Mind continues open to the influence of Riches, has determined

many

many to Vows of perpetual Poverty; they have suppreffed Defire by cutting off the Poffibility of Gratification, and fecured their Peace by deftroying the Enemy whom they had no Hope of reducing to quiet Subjection. But by debarring themfelves from Evil, they have refcinded many Opportunities of Good; they have funk into Inactivity and Ufeleffnefs, and if they have foreborn to injure Society, they cannot be confidered as Contributors to its Felicity.

While Riches are fo neceffary to prefent Convenience, and fo much more eafily obtained by Crimes than Virtues, the Mind can only be fecured from yielding to the continual Impulfe of Covetoufnefs by the Preponderation of other Motives. Gold will generally turn the intellectual Balance, when weighed only againft Reputation, but will be light and ineffectual when the oppofite Scale is charged with Juftice, Veracity, and Piety.

To Mrs. MARY MIDNIGHT.

MADAM,

I Read the Letter from Mr. *Robinfon* to Mr. *Smyth*, inferted in your laft Number, with incredible Satisfaction, as, I think, there breathes thro' the whole, a truly fenfible, manly, and (what is beft of all) a *Chriftian* Spirit. Nothing in Nature can be more unreasonable or more nonfenfical, than ranging the giving of a Challenge amongft the

Acts

Acts of Bravery, or the refusing one amongst those of Cowardice. The *Romans* were allowed by all the World to be the bravest People in it. And yet from the Foundation of that State to its Destruction, I defy the most learned of our modern Bravoes to produce an Instance of one Duel fought, or one Challenge given. I sincerely, Madam, congratulate you on the Success of your Work, and am glad to see that your Magazine is not (as I at first imagined) a Matter of meer Mirth—— But is ——

With a moral View design'd
To please and to reform Mankind.

Yours *affectionately,*

ISABELLA.

---

‡‡‡ As none of our pretended Poets or Criticks have ever translated the first Ode of my good Friend HORACE, according to the genuine Reading, I shall present them with the following Translation by my Neice *Nelly,* which she undertook for the Benefit of the Gentlemen of both Universities.

Me doctarum hederæ præmia frontium
Diis miscent superis : (for so the Herd of Writers have it) *Nelly* tells me should be :

Te doctarum hederæ præmia frontium
Diis miscent superis, for HORACE had not the Vanity to apply it to himself, and assume a Character

racter that so justly belong'd to Mecænas: Nor could he be so mean-spirited, after he had asserted his Right to quaff Nectar with the Gods, as to condescend to ask his Patron to number him among the Lyric Poets and Ballad-makers.

To M E C Æ N A S.

THY noble Birth, *Mecænas* springs
　　From an illustrious Race of Kings,
　　　That in *Etruria* reign'd ;
Thy kind Protection is my Boast,
My all without Thee, had been lost,
　　　My Patron and my Friend.

Some in Olympick Games delight,
Where Clouds of Dust obscure the Sight,
　　　And darken all the Skies ;
Striving who first shall reach the Goal,
Their kindling Wheels around to roll,
　　　And gain the glorious Prize.

The Palm obtain'd, so great the Odds,
It ranks the Victors with the Gods,
　　　That rule the World below :
Others by low Intrigues elate,
To shine a Minister of State,
　　　All less Pursuits forego.

Some

Some lur'd with Hopes of ample Gain,
Their Garners fill with *Lybian* Grain,
    Awaiting Times of Dearth:
Some wedded to paternal Fields,
Admire the Store that Labour yields,
    Employ'd to till the Earth.

Offer to thefe *Peruvian* Mines,
Or all the glitt'ring Wealth that fhines,
    On *India*'s diftant Shore ;
They would not tempt the ftormy Main,
Where Winds unequal War maintain,
    And Waves inceffant roar.

The Merchant views, with Fear aghaft,
The Fury of the *Northern* Blaft,
    When lofty Billows foam ;
Praifes the Country's calm Retreats,
Yet foon his fhatter'd Bark refits,
    In tracklefs Paths to roam.

Some cheer the Hours with racy Wine,
The Product of the Maffick Vine,
    Reclin'd beneath a Shade ;
Or near a Moffy facred Source,
Where Streams begin their filent Courfe,
    Their liftlefs Limbs are laid.

Others are pleas'd when Monarchs jarr,
Admiring all the Pomp of War,
    And ev'ry warlike Air ;
                    When

When Trumpets fainting Hearts infpire,
And Clarions kindle martial Fire,
    Detefted by the Fair.

The Sportfman bent to chace the Hind,
To all Delights befides is blind,
    His Spoufe entreats in vain;
Defpifing wint'ry Skies he bounds,
Attended by fagacious Hounds,
    O'er Hill, and Dale, and Plain.

Politer Arts, *Mecænas,* fhare,
Thy calmer Hours and banifh Care,
    Th' Employment of the Wife;
An Ivy Wreath thy Temples binds,
An Honour due t'exalted Minds,
    The Kindred of the Skies.

I love to fing the cooling Grove,
Where Nymphs and Fawns in Meafures move;
    And if the Mufes aid:
Euterpe fhall the Flute infpire,
And *Polyhymnia* touch the Lyre,
    Deep in a facred Shade.

Thus rais'd above the vulgar Throng,
To noble Themes I'll fuit my Song,
    And if you rank my Name;
Among the tuneful Lyrick Train,
My Works fhall envious Time difdain;
    Secure of deathlefs Fame.

The

The S I L E N T F A I R;
A S O N G.

I.

FROM all her fair loquacious Kind,
    So different is my *Rosalind*;
That not one Accent can I gain,
To crown my Hopes, or sooth my Pain.

II.

Ye Lovers who can conftrue Sighs,
    And are the Interpreters of Eyes;
To Language all her Looks tranflate,
    And in her Geftures read my Fate.

III.

And if in them you chance to find,
    Ought that is gentle, ought that's kind;
Adieu mean Hopes of being Great,
    And all the Littlenefs of State.

IV.

All Thoughts of Grandeur I'll defpife,
    That from Dependance take their Rife;
To ferve her fhall be my Employ,
    And Love's fweet Agony my Joy.

See the Contraft to the above in Page 85. *Vol.* 1.

By

By Mr. P O P E.

WHAT is Prudery?
                    'Tis a Beldam,
Seen with Wit and Beauty seldom.
'Tis a Fear that starts at Shadows.
'Tis (no 'tis'nt) like Miss. *Meadows.*
'Tis a Virgin hard of Feature,
Old, and void of all Good-nature:
Lean and fretful, would seem wise;
Yet plays the Fool before she dies.
'Tis an ugly envious Shrew,
That rails at dear *Lepel* and you.

These Verses are inserted in the new Edition of
Mr. *Pope's* Works, and (if they are his) I will
venture to say, the much-ridicul'd Mr. *Cibber*
never wrote any half so bad. Quære, 1st. What
are we to think of the Editor? and 2dly, What
are we to think of the Edition!

As I have often given Specimens of Pieces of Poetry, in which I conceived there was Merit, I
am sorry to have so long neglected the *Horatian-*
Canons of Friendship, publish'd by my good
Friend Mr. *Newbery,* in St. *Paul's* Church-yard.
—The Reader will find in the subsequent Extract,
several good and facetious Rules for making and
confirming Friendships, which I heartily recom-
                    O   mend

mend to the Perufal and the Practice of all thofe
who chufe to call themfelves my Friends.

MARY MIDNIGHT.

LET's be like Lover's glorioufly deceiv'd,
And each good Man a better ftill believ'd;
E'en Celia's Wart Strephon will not neglect,
But praifes, kiffes, loves the dear Defect.
Oh! that in Friendfhip we were thus to blame
And ermin'd Candour, tender of our Fame,
Wou'd cloath the honeft Error with an honeft
    Name;
Be we then ftill to thofe we hold moft dear,
Fatherly fond, and tenderly fevere.
The Sire, whofe Son fquints forty thoufand Ways,
Finds in his Features mighty Room for Praife:
Ah! born (he cries) to make the Ladies figh,
Jacky, thou haft an am'rous Caft o' the Eye.
Another's Child's abortive --- he believes
Nature moft perfect in Diminutives;
And Men of ev'ry Rank, with one Accord
Salute each crooked Brachet with My Lord.
(For bandy Legs, hump Back, and knocking Knee,
Are all exceffive Signs of Q----ty.)
Thus let us judge our Friends--- if Scrub fubfift
Too meanly, Scrub is an Œconomift;
And if Tom Tinkle is full loud and pert,
He aims at Wit, and does it to divert.
Largus is apt to blufter, but you'll find
'Tis owing to his Magnitude of Mind:

                          Lollius

Lollius is paffionate, and loves a Whore,
Spirit and Conftitution ! --- nothing more ---
Ned to a bullying Peer is ty'd for Life,
And in commendam holds a fcolding Wife ;
Slave to a Fool's Caprice, and Woman's Will ;
But Patience, Patience is a Virtue ftill !
Afk of Chamont a Kingdom for a Fifh,
He'll give you three rather than fpoil a Difh ;
Nor Pride, nor Luxury, is in the Cafe,
But Hofpitality --- an't pleafe your Grace.
Should a great Gen'ral give a Drab a Penfion ---
Meannefs !---the Devil---'tis perfect Condefcenfion.
Such Ways make many Friends, and make Friends
        long,
Or elfe my good Friend Horace reafons wrong.

A S O N G.

I.

GAY *Florimel* of noble Birth,
    The moft engaging Fair on Earth
        To pleafe a blithe Gallant,
Has much of Wit and much of Worth,
And much of Tongue to fet it forth,
        But then fhe has an Aunt.

II.

How oft, alas ! in vain I've try'd
To tempt her from her Guardian's Side,
        And trap her on Love's Hook ;

O 2

She's

She's like a little wanton Lamb
That frifks about the careful Dam,
    And fhuns the Shepherd's Crook.
          III.
Like wretched *Dives* am I plac'd
To fee the Joys I cannot tafte,
    Of all my Hopes bereaven ;
Her Aunt's the difmal Gulph betwixt,
By all the Powers of Malice fixt,
    To cheat me of my Heav'n.

Some Account of a new Mill to Grind old People Young.

IT is very ftrange that we are ever ready to believe all that is incredible, and to doubt of every
thing that is demonftrable ; yet as much a Miracle
as it is, it is neverthelefs a Truth. Any Perfon
that has been at Mr. *Overton*'s Shop, or indeed at
any Pot-houfe in this Kingdom, has feen depicted
in black and white, the Figure of a Mill to grind
old Folks young ; yet there are many who are
hardy enough to believe there can be no fuch Mill
really exifting, notwithftanding they fee it in Print.
In order therefore to fatisfy the Incredulous, I have
inferted an Account of fome Miracles effected by
a new Mill lately built near *Guildford*.

                                The

The Case of Mrs. Martha Spriggings.

Whereas I *Martha Spriggings*, was violently afflicted with that inevitable Disease old Age, attended
with Blindness, Lameness, Deafness, Numbness and
Dumbness ; I do declare that I am perfectly cured by
being ground in Mr. *Whacum's* Mill near *Guildford*,
and whereas a Year ago I was upwards of Ninety-
nine, I am at this present writing, not quite Eighteen Years Old.

Witness,   MARTHA SPRIGGINGS.
Simon Luck,
Peter Pringle.

The Case of Mrs. Richard Fumbletext, *D. D.* *F. R. S. and Head of* *** *College, in the* *University of* ****.

Whereas I Mrs. *Richard Fumbletext*, was vehe-
mently afflicted with the Weight of Seventy Years
and upwards, by the means of which I became
extremely peevish, froward, absurd and disorder'd,
in the few Senses that were left me : I do assert,
that by being ground in the *Guildford* Mill, I am
perfectly recovered and restored to Youth, inso-
much that I am as much a Child as ever I was.

Witness,   , RICHARD FUMBLETEXT.
Mrs. *George Trinket, D. D. F. R. S.*
Mrs. *Godina Wilking, D. D. F. R. S.*

The

The Case of Mrs. William Capevi, Doctor of Physick.

Whereas I Mrs. *William Capevi*, Dr. of Physic, lately aged Eighty-three; was so immoderately disordered with a Course of Years, that I could not cure myself with any of my infallible Medicines: This is to certify those whom it may concern, that I am no more than twenty-five, being ground so down to that Age precisely, in the *Guildford* Mill, which I sincerely recommend to the old Women of all Faculties.

N. B. The Mill is adapted for Females only, so no Gentleman who does not make it appear that he has been an old Woman, can possibly be ground.

To the Criticks and the Poets.

GENTLEMEN,

IN some of my former Papers I pointed out the Excellency and true characteristical Beauties of Pastoral and Elegiac Poetry, and I shall now, for your Instruction and Entertainment, give you my Sentiments on the Ode and the Song; two Species of Poesy that are of all others my peculiar Favourites. I call them two Species of Poesy, and I think with the greatest poetical and critical Justice; for there is as much Difference between an

Ode

Ode and a Song, as between a high-heel'd and a
low-heel'd Shoe, or indeed as there is between a
Whig and a *Tory*. The Ode-writer mounts *Pegasus* upon the Withers, and for Fear of falling
holds fast by the Mane; but the Ballad-monger
gets up behind, sits a Degree lower, and to save
himself, clings close to the Tail. There are some
Poets indeed, who are a Sort of Mules in Verse,
and are endow'd with such excellent Qualities,
that they can intimately mix these two Species
together, and make of them a true and poetical
Hermaphrodite. A most animated and extraordinary Instance of this Sort we have in one of our
Poets of the last Century, who through his excessive Modesty and abundant Wealth (two Qualities inherent to Poetry and Poets) has endeavour'd
to conceal his Merit, and avoid the Praises he so
eminently deserved. He has by many of our
Criticks been compared to *Horace*, and by others
mounted with *Pindar*; but I think he deserves a
more exalted Class than either, and I am per-
suaded you will be of my Opinion, Gentlemen,
when you have read over the following Stanzas.

On JOLLITY: *An* Ode, *or* Song, *or both.*

I.

There was a jovial Butcher,
He liv'd at *Northern-fall-gate*,
    He kept a Stall
    At *Leadenhall*,
And got drunk at the Boy at *Aldgate.*

II.

II.

He ran down *Houndsditch* reeling,
At *Bedlam* he was frighted,
 He in *Moorfields*
  Be sh--t his Heels
And at *Hoxton* he was wiped.

Now, Gentlemen, for the Dignity of your Science, (which I hold in the higheft Eftimation) I fhall endeavour to point out critically, and according to the Rules of Art, the Beauties, the Graces, and elevated Sentiments in this much admired Piece.

Our incomparable Author, agreeable to the Laws prefcribed by *Ariftotle, Dionyfius, Longinus,* and *Quintilian,* and purfuant to the great Examples of *Homer, Virgil,* and *Milton,* begins his Exordium in a fimple Manner, for here he wifely faw, that the plain Stile would be moft prevalent. Nothing can be more eafy,

 There was a jovial Butcher,

One would think from the Simplicity, natural Eafe, and Elegance of that Line, that the Author intended only the Hiftory of his Hero in Manner of *Thucidydes, Livy,* or any other trifling Hiftorian; for no one from thefe Words would expect a *Pindaric* Ode any more than an *Epic* Poem. But in the next Line he artfully rifes upon you:

 He liv'd at Northern-fall-gate.

How expreffive is this! —— Here you learn in one Line, not only that the Man liv'd, but the
         Place

Place where he liv'd, *viz.* at *Northern-fall-gate.*
Hitherto we are peaceable enough, for *Pegasus*
only trots; but now the Poet is all on Fire, and
his Steed foams at Mouth:

He kept a Stall
At Leaden-hall,
And got drunk at the Boy *at Aldgate.*

And got drunk! —— ay, got drunk! why
that's an Atchievement we little expected: It sur-
prizes us, and therefore is extremely agreeable;
for the Business of Poetry is to *instruct,* to *elevate,*
and *surprize.* And how amply is this effected?
We are *instructed,* and that in few Words, that,

He kept a Stall
At Leaden-hall;

We are *elevated* with the Thoughts of his getting
drunk, and extreamly *surprized* that it was *at the*
Boy at Aldgate; for who the Devil would have
thought of his getting drunk there; Besides, at
the Time this Ode was wrote, 'twas not customary
for People to get drunk; and therefore the Surprize was greater. Drunkenness was then consider'd as the Province only of the Nobleman, the
Knight, the 'Squire, the Lord of the Manor, or
the Justice of Peace; but now we have Ladies of
such elevated Spirits, that they can get drunk as
well as the best Butcher of them all, which ren-
ders that Incident in these our Days less wonderful.

Our Author's Method is also much to be admired; for after he has perfected his first Stanza,
he

he proceeds to the fecond; and pray what can be
more natural than for the fecond to fucceed the
firft ?

He ran down Houndfditch *reeling.*

Homer is not more admired for the *Copiofity* of
his Invention, the Force of his Imagination, the
Beauty of his Similies, the Harmony of his Numbers, or the Dignity of his Diction, than for his
extenfive Knowledge in Nature, and the feveral Arts
and Sciences; He was a Philofopher, a Divine, a
Mathematician, an Hiftorian, a Geographer, and
a Warrior as well as a Poet. He underftood
every thing he has defcribed, and therefore all his
Defcriptions are animated and beautiful, juft and
rational, correfpondent to the Precepts of Art and
to the Laws of Nature. But our Author vaftly
exceeds *Homer* in his Knowledge of Nature and
the mechanic Laws, as may be demonftrated from
this Line :

He ran down Houndfditch *reeling,*

Any Woman who has a Sot to her Hufband can
tell you, that a drunken Man will run up Stairs
when he can't walk even on a fmooth Pavement.
A ftaggering Man, like a reeling Top, is fecured
from falling by encreafing the Velocity of his Motion, and this is alfo illuftrated and proved by a
ftumbling Horfe, who will always travel with moft
Safety when kept up to a good Pace, as our Gentlemen that ride Poft can teftify. But I appeal

from

from the Poſt-Boy to Mr. *Pope*, who in his Eſſay on our Science, has the two following Lines :

Falſe Steps but help them to renew the Race ;
As, after ſtumbling, Jades will mend their Pace.

'Tis therefore with great poetical Juſtice and Judgment that our Author precipitates his Hero down *Houndſditch*, and brings him to *Bedlam*.

Here now is Matter enough to have employed your little modern Verſifyers a Month, who run into long Common-places, and lay hold of every Hint that preſents itſelf. But *ſeaſonable Silence has its Emphaſis*; our Author only informs us in a plain ſimple Manner, that

At Bedlam *he was frighted.*

He would probably have given a Deſcription of that horrid Place, where ſo many of his Fraternity had made their miſerable Exits, but the Cataſtrophe of his Piece was at Hand ; the Fate of this Hero was determin'd, and a long Suſpenſion of it by any Epiſode whatſoever, wou'd have been unnatural and offenſive. He therefore in Imitation of VIR-GIL, *Geor*. IV. 457, *&c.* declines all Allurements of that ſort, for the ſake of Uniformity and Order, without which he knew his Work might be an Heap of ſhining Materials, but not a beautiful and permanent Edifice.

The Cataſtrophe is preceded by the Affright, and is made the Conſequence or Effect of that Cauſe, as you will perceive.

At

At Bedlam *he was frighted,*
He in Moorfields,
Be sh—t his Heels,
And at Hoxton *he was wiped.*

The Geography of the Places where the Action happen'd, is strictly obferv'd and arrang'd in their natural Order; *Hounfditch* is the direct Road from *Aldgate* to *Bedlam,* which is built in *Moorfields*; and as *Hoxton* is not more than half a Mile to the right, it was very natural for him, and very prudent of him to close the Scene there. And to prevent any Disturbances by the Contests of Places, for the Birth of this great Poet, we will, if you please, Gentlemen, assign that Honour to *Hoxton*; This I think we may do with the greatest Propriety and Justice, for every Man is partially prone to favour the Place of his Nativity, and his excessive Fondness of his native Place *Hoxton,* made him without doubt bring the Jovial Butcher from *Northern-Falgate* to enrich it with his Burthen.

I am Gentlemen,

Your faithful Friend, &c.

MARY MIDNIGHT.

Epigram

Epigram of Martial, *Lib.* VIII. *Ep.* 69.
Imitated by Mrs. Midnight.

Miráris veteres, Vacerra, *folos,*
Nec laudas, nifi mortuos poetas ;
Ignofcas, petimus, Vacerra ; *tanti*
Non eft ut placeam tibi, perire.

NO Praife the grutching *Rofalinda* yields
To Bards, till they are in th' *Elyfian Fields.*
She fays that every Modern is a Dunce,
Forgetting *Homer* was a Modern once.
Die—die— fhe cries— and then I'll deign a Smile,
Your Servant, Ma'm, — but 'tis not worth my
while.

A few Thoughts on FAMILY.

By Mrs. Midnight.

THERE are many People in the World,
that are fo proud of their being of a good
Family, that they never feek after any other Excellence, tho' in fact, this is no Excellence at all,
but a meer Matter of Chance. The following
Extract from *Bufbequius* is fo much to my prefent
Purpofe, that I cannot avoid giving a Tranflation of
it for the Benefit of the unlearned Reader. " Qui
" rerum primas a principe tenent ferè funt pafto-
" rum et bubulcorum filii, de quo tantum abeft

P " ut

" ut eos pudeat, etiam inter fe gloriantur ; eoque
" fibi plus tribuunt, quo minùs majoribus aut for-
" tunæ natalium debent. Neque aut nafci, aut
" propagari, traducive virtutem putant. Sed
" partem a Deo dari, partem bona difciplina, mul-
" toque labore & ftudio comparari: utque pa-
" ternam artem nullam, non muficam, non arith-
" meticam, non geometriam ; fic nec virtutem
" ad filium aut hæredem tranfire credunt." In
Englifh thus :

*Thofe who are at the Head of Affairs amongft
the* Turks, *are generally the Sons of Shepherds or
Graziers; of which they are fo far from being
afhamed, that they make a Matter of Boaft of it;
and they attribute to themfelves the more Praife, the
lefs they owe to their Progenitors and the Chance of
Birth ; for 'tis their Opinion that Virtue can neither
be born, propagated, or transferr'd : But that partly
'tis the Gift of God, and partly to be acquired by a
good Education with much Labour and Study : And
as no paternal Art, fuch as Mufick, Arithmetick,
and Geometry devolves to the Son or Heir, the fame
alfo do they believe of Virtue.*

Much to the fame Purpofe fings Sir *William
D'Avenant*, in his GONDIBERT, where fpeaking
of the Manner of a certain Prince's difpofing of
Preferment, he has the following moft excellent
Lines ——

He

He Wealth nor Birth preferr'd to Council's Place ;
  For Council is for Use not Ornament;
Souls are alike of rich and antient Race ;
  Tho' Bodies claim Diftinction by Defcent.

Gondibert, Book II. Canto 2.

Read, meditate, and digeft, my dear Neighbours of St. *James*'s.

Yours,

MARY MIDNIGHT.

To Mrs. MARY MIDNIGHT.

MADAM,

IT is very odd I think that you can't let People
alone to mind their Bufinefs in their own Way.
What have the Tradefmen done to you, you old
Gypfy you, that they muft be lugg'd in Head and
Shoulders, like a Vat of Dowlas among your Maxims in the Index to Mankind as you call it ; you
are an impudent Jade, and deferve to be punifh'd
for your fcandalous Behaviour to your Betters in
this Manner, and when I am Lord-Mayor, which
I hope I fhall be before it be long, I will pack all
fuch old Strumpets out of Town ; know that,
Huffey, and correct and alter your Manners for the
future, or you fhall feel the Weight of my Re-

P 2
fent-

sentment, ye old cock-ey'd Jezebel, you shall so;
and this is all the needful from

"*Yours,*

B. Ballance-beam.

To my Readers.

Gentle Gentlemen,

I Am now going to ballance Accounts with the
great Mr. *Benjamin Ballance-beam,* of *Cheap-
side,* in the City of *London, Middlesex,* and I hope
you will all bear Witness, that I give him a Receipt in full. The said *Benjamin Ballance-beam*
chargeth me with being impudent, and for what?
Why truly, for introducing into my *Index of Mankind* the following *Axioms,* or *Maxims,* or *Postulatas,*
Terms unknown to him in Point of Signification,
but yet such as he has taken into his Head to be
angry with.

These are the Words complain'd of,

A Tradesman's Principle is too often his Interest,
and his Interest his Principle.

He that keeps his Accounts will keep his Family, but he that keeps no Account, may be kept
by the Parish.

A Knave may get more than an honest Man for
a Day, but the honest Man will get most by the
Year.

A Defence of *and Commentary* on *these Maxims,*
the Reader may expect *in a future Number.*

The MIDWIFE's POLITICKS: Or, *Goſſip's Chro-nicle of the Affairs of Europe.*

PORTUGAL *and* SPAIN.

THE Portugueſe Dominions enjoy all the Bleſſings of that profound Tranquility, which augmented their Commerce, and increaſed their Opulence, during the late War; while their Neighbours of Spain were hurried by a Spirit of Quixotiſm to dig themſelves a fatal Grave in the Bowels of Italy.

While the Britiſh Ambaſſador at Madrid, is employing all the Strain of Oratory, which he has ſo frequently, and ſo ineffectually aſſerted, to mollify the Haughtineſs of the turbulent Spaniards; the Miniſtry of Madrid, not only refuſe to hearken to any humble Supplications for a free Navigation in America; but have lately ordered Don Franciſ Buccarelli y Urſua, the Commandant of the Spaniſh Troops poſted in the Diſtrict of Gibraltar, to ſee that the tenth Article of the Treaty of Utrecht be punctually obſerved. By that Article Gibraltar was ceded to the Crown of Great Britain, without any terri-torial Juriſdiction, nor any open Communication by Land, in order to prevent the Abuſes and Frauds that might be committed under Colour of Trafficking. But as it was agreed by the ſaid Article that it ſhould be lawful to purchaſe with ready Money, in the Spaniſh Territory adjacent, Proviſions and other Neceſſaries for the Uſe of the Garriſon, the Inhabitants and the Veſſels lying in the Bay; this Commandant is likewiſe charged to take particular Care that this Stipulation be literally obſerved; and not to ſuffer, upon any Pretext what-ſoever, the bartering of any Merchandize for thoſe Pro-

P 3   viſions,

vifions; it being the Intention of his Catholic Majefty, that the Delinquents, befides the Penalty of Confifcation, fhall be profecuted with the utmoft Rigour of the Law. —— However, this Reftriction is not fo bad for the Englifh as a Siege; though, under this political Difguife, the Spaniards can greatly diftrefs the Garrifon, by allowing them to trade only for a very fmall Quantity of Provifions, which they have frequently done, and obliged the poor Englifh to feek for a Supply from the Coafts of Barbary. —— Surely the Britifh Nation is to be no longer liable to the Infults of Spain! My old Blood glows with Refentment when I recollect their former Depredations; and I, *Mary Midnight*, take upon me to affure the old Lady at St. Ildefonfo, that the Subjects of her late Hufband, have no exclufive Right to the Navigation of the American Seas. Was not it this important Matter that raifed the Voice of every old Woman in England, both in and out of Minifterial Employment, to arm againft the infolent Spaniard? It was; but what have we done? To our Shame, Nothing! —— The Spaniards ftill give Interruption to our Trade; while foreign Politicians cannot refrain from fneering at our tedious Negociations at Madrid, and feem to wonder how Britons can be fo patient, while a mutinous Spirit in the Spanifh Weft Indies, and the enterprifing Humour of the States of Barbary, put it in our Power to bring that Court to reafonable Terms: but, for this falutary Purpofe, we muft recal Don Benjamin from his pacific Overtures; and fend the brave honeft Admiral Vernon to re-demolifh their Porto Bello.

ITALI.

ITALY.

The Barbary Corfairs renew their piratical Excurfions on the Italian Powers, who, roufed by the Sufferings of the Merchants, are, in proportionate Contingents to form a naval Force effectually to fupprefs thefe barbarous Invaders; thefe Confederates are faid to be the Pope, the King of the two Sicilies, with the Republics of Venice and Genoa; who are in Expectation that Spain and Portugal will accede to the League, and furnifh powerful Contingents, becaufe thefe two Nations are equally concerned in the Deftruction of thofe Pirates. —— The Bankers in moft of the principal Cities in Italy have had confiderable Failures, efpecially at Turin and Bologna, which has affected feveral other Cities, and together with the great and fudden Fall in the Price of Silk, occafions frequent Bankrupcies at Naples, Leghorn, Florence, Genoa, Modena, Bergamo, and Novi. —— However; the poor Genoefe are in the moft calamitous Condition; becaufe they have difgufted the French at Corfica, who are evacuating the Ifland, having reftored the Town of St. Fiorenza to the Malecontents. But I apprehend this to be a Sort of a Stratagem, to make the Genoefe relinquifh their Right to that troublefome Ifland, and introduce the unprovided Infant Don Lewis of Spain to the Throne of Corfica.

FRANCE.

The French continue to fill their Magazines in Alface, where they intend to form a Camp of 40,000 Men: But for what Purpofe? Ha! Old as I am, my Eyes, or my Head, are yet good enough to difcover that the Intentions of France can only be to awe the Election

Election of a King of the Romans, as they did of an
Emperor in 1742. As Cardinal Tencin has quitted the
Ministry, and retired to his Archbishoprick of Lyons, I
would advise him to consider that he is an Ecclesiastick,
and should consequently be a Promoter of Peace, which
he was the Cause of banishing from the Plains of Europe
for eight Years together: let him think how many
thousands of Lives he has wantonly sacrificed, and surely
he must expect that the Manes of Bernclau, the Prince
of Prussia, Clayton, Belleisle, Grammont, Ponsonby,
and the rebel Lords of Scotland, will perpetually disturb
his Quiet, if his Crimes are not properly expiated by a
due and seasonable Contrition; let him remember that
Saxe is gone to find out Fleury the Lord knows where;
that Lowendahl may soon go in Quest of the coadjutor
Tencin, but the Lord knows when. His most Christian
Majesty has nominated M. de Rouille, late Secretary for
the Department of the Marine, to be Secretary of State
with the Count de St. Florentin: M. Rouille is become
the Darling of the Court and People, for his great
Vigilance and Industry in restoring their Marine, which
is now almost in as good a Condition as it was before
the great Sea-fight off La Hogue, in the Year 1692.
A sorry Truth for Old England! —— The French Clergy
begin to lower their Crests, and submit to their dictatorial
Power, with regard to their Payment of the twentieth
Penny, and the Declaration of their ecclesiastical Re-
venues —— Though the French have reported that M.
Bompart, Governour of Martinico, had caused the Islands
of Tobago, St. Lucia, and Dominico, to be evacuated; I
have receiv'd private Intelligence to the contrary; though
I should be glad to find it true, because then the French
would

would give us one Proof of their Sincerity among those daily exhibited of their Politenefs.

GERMANY.

It has at laft appeared that the Elector of Cologne deferted the maritime Powers for the Sake of obtaining a Debt of 160,000 Crowns from France; fo that now I fhall call him an Old Mifer, inftead of an Old Woman. —— The Empire is ftill in the fame uncertain Condition about the Election of a King of the Romans : but the Emiffaries of France give Reafon to imagine, that their Court has a greater Share, than it would have the World believe, in the Oppofition made to fuch an Election, by a Faction having at its Head an Elector pleading for the pretended Rights of the Princes; againft the indifputable Rights which the electoral College has enjoyed ever fince the Extinction of the Emperors of the Race of the Carlivingienne, and which has been confirmed by the whole Body of the Empire, in its Approbation, and accepting of the Golden Bull. However, let France take what Pains fhe will, it is to be hoped that there is ftill a Majority in the Electoral College to maintain and defend the Rights of that Conftitution.

DENMARK.

Mr. Titley, the Britifh Minifter at Copenhagen, is reported to have made fome Propofitions for a Marriage between his Royal Highnefs George Prince of Wales, and the Princefs Wilhelmina Carolina, fecond Daughter of their Danifh Majefties, born 10th of June 1747; but I entirely difapprove of fuch nuptial Contracts, becaufe, not to mention they are firft Coufins, I think Princes are

born

born to fhare an equal Felicity with other Men; and we had an Inftance of the bad Effects of fuch Engagements, in that between his prefent Majefty of France, and the young Infant of Spain; befides, I fhould not like to fee our DARLING HOPEFUL PRINCE, efpoufe a Lady, born on the 10th of June; for the Jacobites may then have a feafonable Opportunity of commemorating the Anniverfary of the Pretender, even under a Cloak of Loyalty.

S W E D E N.

While the Swedes feemed to be happy in the peaceable Declarations of Ruffia, they have fuffer'd a great Devaftation in their Capital City, by a Fire which broke out on the 19th of June, in the Church of St. Claire, in the Norder Malm, and burnt with fo much Violence, that this fine Building was foon reduced to Afhes, together with feveral Houfes adjoining, befides, the Wind being very high, the Flames communicated to fome Houfes at a Diftance, which were likewife confumed. About an Hour after, the fame Day, another Fire broke out in the Suder-Malm, which did a great deal of Damage; and, about Nine o'Clock in the Evening, a Brewer's Houfe took Fire, and was burnt to the Ground; as were feveral adjacent Houfes. The King being informed of thefe Fires, came to Stockholm from Ulrichdahl, and went in Perfon to the Places where there was the greateft Danger. His Majefty gave fuch Orders for ftopping the Progrefs of the Flames, that the Fire was extinguifhed the next Day; after which his Majefty returned to Ulrichdahl. The 21ft, a frefh Fire broke out in the Market in the Suburb of Ladugarfland, and the Day following another in the fame Diftrict, near

the

the Packer Market. The Number of Houfes confumed amounts to near 1000; among which are the fine Houfe of the Senator Count Thuro-Bielcke; another magnificent Edifice belonging to Baron Palftierna, the fuperb Church of St. Clara, the Hotel of the late Prefident Rolam, and many other confiderable Edifices both in the North and South Quarters. The Ships and Gallies, as alfo the Arfenals and the Granaries, which lie in thofe Quarters, were in great Danger, but happily received no Damage, the King's Directions, for preventing the Flames fpreading towards them, having been extremely well executed. —— It is pretended that combuftible Materials have been found in divers Parts of the Town, and fome fufpicious Perfons have been taken up: A Reward of 2000 Ducats is alfo offered to fuch as may difcover any of the Incendiaries, with a free Pardon to any one that fhall impeach his Accomplices; who, I dare fay, were no other Sort of Old Women than fuch as are ufually difcover'd under jefuitical Habits.

R U S S I A.

The moft pacific Intentions are apparently prevalent among the Northern Powers; but Peace has more refplendently fhewn her Countenance at the Court of Peterfburgh, where a Declaration, concerning the Affairs of Sweden, has been delivered to the Maritime, and other allied Powers, wherein the Czarina declares her perfect Satisfaction in regard to the Conduct of his Swedifh Majefty, fince his Acceffion to the Throne. — As a Proof of the Inftability of human Happinefs, the Czarina, while the Gates of Janus are clofed in her Capital, fees her poor Subjects of the Ukraine, invaded and plundered by a lawlefs Body of the Crim Tartars, who lately made an Invafion, and rifled feveral Villages; but were met and engaged, and difperfed by a

D

Detachment of Coffacks in the Neighbourhood of Precop.

PERSIA.

This Country is in a more deplorable Condition than ever, having at prefent no lefs than five Competitors for the Throne. The ancient Lores, or Bactrians, who plundered Spahan, have made a great Progrefs in their Conquefts; and the young Man they have nominated for King, being of the old Race, induced the People of Shyrafs to deliver their City into his Hands without Refiftance; notwithftanding which, the People were carried into Slavery. It was imagined Jaroom, Doroob, and Ireffau, would have made a bold and refolute Stand; but they all fubmitted themfelves to Slavery; the Lores making no Diftinction between Force or voluntary Submiffion. As the ill Treatment the Englifh Gentlemen met with at Spahan, left them no Expectation for Favour or Mercy, both they and the Dutch came to a firm Refolution to leave Gombroon, and it is not doubted but they have put it into Execution; fo that the grand Scheme of plundering the two European Factories, where they imagined half the Wealth of Perfia was contained, will prove abortive.

TURKEY.

The Ottoman Miniftry feem to poftpone every military Preparation on the Borders of Europe; and it is furprifing that they have, at this Time, fuch a regard to their fiducial Engagements, as to neglect making an Incurfion into the Heart of Perfia, while that diftracted Country is too much incapacitated by its inteftine Commotions, from making any Refiftance.

POLAND.

Affurances have been received from Warfaw, that the eldeft Son of the Pretender to the Britifh Throne, has been lately married very privately to the Princefs Radzivil, reputed the moft opulent Heirefs in Poland.

The MIDWIFE.

NUMBER V.

VOL. II.

A Letter to Mrs. Mary Midnight *from the* Guildford *Miller, intreating her to be ground forthwith; together with some fresh Cases.*

Most incomparable MADAM,

IT has been dogmatically laid down, and creduloufly received, as a Maxim, that no Perfon can give any thing, of which he himfelf is not poffeft. — In fome Inftances indeed this is true, but by no means fo with regard to the Poet and Hiftorian; for they can beftow Immortality, though they are but frail Flefh and Blood; and the Works of fome perifhable Hands are calculated to furvive the Univerfe. — In this Light, Madam, I confider both you, and your Works — and the Bufinefs of this Epiftle is not fo much out of a lucrative View of bringing more Grifts to my Mill, as to do an eminent Piece of Service to the whole World. If you are difpofed to be ground, or (to ufe your Publifher's Language) you intend to have a new Edition of your felf, I declare in the firft Place, that it fhall not coft you a Penny — the Popularity which I fhall acquire by reftoring fuch an amiable and ufeful old Lady to Youth, will be more than an adequate Recompence for my Trouble.—I affure you, Madam, there is no fort of Pain attending the Operation, but you grow *back again* (if I may be allow'd the Expreffion) in the fame gradual imperceptible Manner, only in a much leffer Time, as you grow old. But as you may be curious to know the Nature and Mechanifm of this Mill, I have fent you a Tranfcript of an Account taken by a Fellow of the Royal Society.

A Mathematical Defcription of the Guildford *Mill.*

By NEHEMIAH NICKNACK, F. R. S.

The *perpendicular Altitude* of this Mill is about thirty Feet, and the *horizontal Aperture*, or *Dilatation* of the *Hopper*, is about ten. There are nine *principal* or *cardinal* Wheels, fo *judgematically contrived*, that in them all the *Squares* of the *periodical Times* are equal to the *Cubes* of the *Diftances.* The Sails (for it is a Wind-Mill) are feven, *numerically* confider'd, but *proportionally* they

they are in a *reciprocal subduplicate Ratio* of the *Diameters* of the Wheels.

The Trough, which is the Receptacle of the Perfons ground, is a *Parallellogram,* the *Diagonal* of which is about two Yards and an half. Between the Trough and the Hopper are twelve Tubes feal'd *hermetically,* of different Sizes, for the Squares of their Diameters rife in an *Arithmetical Progreffion.* Diametrically oppofite to the Tubes are four Ropes fufpended *funicularly,* at the *Extremities* of which are four Levers of the third Kind, namely, fuch as have the *Pow'r* between the *Fulchrum* and the Weight. Befides which, there are Abundance of *inclined Planes, Axes in Peritrochio,* Polyfpafts, Cylinders, together with the *Trochlea, Cuneus,* and *Cochlea,* and in fhort all the *mechanical* and *mathematical Powers.*

Such is the Defcription of my Mill, which is fo admirable for it's PERSPICUITY, that a Child fix Years old may underftand it; fo I fhall not any further explain it, for that would be to give a Defcription of a Defcription, in the Manner of modern Commentators. I fhall therefore add a Cafe or two, and for the prefent take my Leave of you.

The Cafe of the Honourable Mrs. PHILIP HUG-BRIBE.

Whereas I *the Honourable Mrs. Philip Hugbribe* was lately fo fuperannuated, that I flob-

Q 2   ber'd

ber'd in Company, and could by no Means give a rational Anſwer to any Queſtion propoſed; and whereas I drivelled to ſuch a Degree, that I miſtook Negatives for Affirmatives, and Affirmatives for Negatives, and in a certain Place of publick Buſineſs ſaid aye, when I ſhould have ſaid no ; which had like to have carried a Point for the Good of my Country, contrary both to my Inſtructions and Inclination ; this is to aſſure the World, that by being ground in the *Guildford* Mill, I am perfectly cured, and I am as wiſe and as upright as heretofore.

Signed

Witneſs   Mrs. *Philip Hug-bribe.*

The Right Hon. Mrs. *Charles Courtly.*
The Right Hon. Mrs. *Peter Penſion.*

The Caſe of the Right Honourable Mrs. Simon Sharper.

Whereas I *the Right Honourable Mrs. Simon Sharper* was ſome Time ſince ſo very old and infirm, that I could not play at Hazard without Spectacles, and ſo very paralytic, that I was obliged to quit both Billiards and Tennis ; this is to certify all old Women of Quality, that by being ground in the *Guildford* Mill, I am reinſtated in my former Health and Youth, and will be bold to ſay, that I can now cheat at Cards, or cog the

Dice

Dice, as well as any Perſon of HONOUR in the three Kingdoms.

Signed,

Witneſs,   Mrs. *Simon Sharper.*

The Right Hon. Mrs. *Ben. Bragwell.*

The Right Hon. Mrs. *Roger Rout.*

I am, dear Madam,

Your faithful Servant,

and ſincere Admirer,

Guildford, July 24, 1751.

Walter Whacum.

The little Lighterman, *or the diſſembling* Waterman, *(which was ſung at the Corner of* Blow Bladder Street *on the 10th of* June *laſt, to the Tune of the Rolling Hornpipe) Chirurgically diſſected.*

I.

PRAY did you never hear of a ſad Diſaſter —
  'Twas but t'other Day that he ran away from
  his Maſter.
Oh the little little Lighterman, and the diſſembling
  Waterman ;
Molly's a Girl that will dye, if ſhe has not a Kiſs
  from the Lighterman.

Q 3

2.

2.

With his black Shammy Pumps and his rolling
   Eye, Sir,
He did kiſs ev'ry Girl that he did come nigh, Sir.
   Oh the little, little, &c.

3.

But when his Maſter he found him he put him into
   Bridewell;
Molly ſhe loved him ſo well that ſhe gave him a
   Pot of Porter.
   Oh the little, &c.

I am ſorry to inform my Readers that this Ballad is
the reputed Bantling of a Gentleman of great E-
minence and Diſtinction, becauſe I am fully perſuaded that upon a candid and impartial Examination, we ſhall find it fraught with Principles deſtructive to the Community, derogatory from the
Dignity of the Crown, and repugnant to that Integrity and Honour which every *Briton* ought to
bear in his Breaſt.

Allegories have been always ſuſpected of evil
Tendency, and diſcouraged by the wiſe Legiſlators
of every Nation. PLATO, who had as much
Prudence, Wiſdom and Learning as any Man a-
mong us, baniſh'd *Homer* out of his Common
Wealth for this very Conſideration; SOLON ex-
pelled CHILOSA for the ſame Reaſon, and MOR-
TOLO was exiled by LYCURGUS for entituling
                                          his

his Poem Χραμβοφαγ⊙ *(i. e.* the *Cabbage Eater)* in which that great Lawgiver thought himſelf affronted, as his Father had for ſome Years before his Advancement praƈtiſed the Art of a Taylor.

That HOMER's *Iliad* was a Satire upon the ſeveral States and Princes of *Greece.* I make no doubt, and was it at all to my Purpoſe I could prove it; for thoſe high Encomiums with which that Poem is interlarded, could never be aſcribed but by way of ſneer or ſarcaſm to Princes, who, for ten Years together, had beat their Subjeƈts Brains out againſt the Stone Walls of *Illium,* and that for a Woman who had not half the Beauty, Modeſty, or Virtue that I have. No — one might as well ſuppoſe that Mr. ***, or any of our modern Poets, wou'd write a ſerious Epic Poem on King *Richard's* frantic Expedition to *Damaſcus.*

The Author of the above Song had doubtleſs ſtudied *Homer,* for, together with his Art of *ſecretly diſpenſing invidious Satire,* he has tranſlated ſome of his poetical Flights, and retain'd in a great Meaſure the Struƈture of his Verſification. But let us leave the Poets to themſelves, as a Pack of poor paultry People unworthy our Conſideration, and examine this wicked Piece of Work to the Bottom, in order to diſcover the ſecret Deſigns and Villanies of its audacious Author, and endeavour as much as poſſible to conviƈt and bring him to condign Puniſhment for his attrocious Crimes.

Pray

Pray did you never hear of a sad Disaster.

No Man that is possest of a Grain of common Sense, can doubt but that the Author by this *sad Disaster* means the Pretender's landing in *Scotland*, and especially when he comes to weigh and consider the Purport of the following Line,

'Twas but the other Day he ran away from his Master.

Not only the *French* King but the whole Court of *France* pretended such Ignorance at the Time he left that Kingdom, of his Destination and Enterprize, that the following Advertisement was printed in some of their Papers.

Stolen or Stray'd,

A living Creature five Foot eight Inches high, that talks rationally and walks erect; whoever shall bring him to (I forget the Name of the Place) *shall receive* 30,000l. *Reward.*

This not only strengthens and corroborates what I advanced before, but evidently proves that the Author in this Song makes the *French* King his Master or Employer, for stolen or stray'd signifies being forced away, seduced away, led away, or going or running away, voluntarily and wilfully, or by Accident and without Design; and the Crime in this Case must depend on *Volition*, as Mr. LOCK very justly observes; for a Servant who loses his Way in a Wood by Accident and against his Will,

is

is not culpable or anfwerable to his Mafter for the Time that has been fo mifemploy'd or loft.——— But leaving this to the Cafuifts, let us return to our Poet.—The next Line ftill ftrengthens my Argument.

Oh the little little Lighterman, and the diffembling Waterman.

Here he calls his Hero the little Lighterman, which Name or Appellation is drawn from that Circum-ftance of his running away, for *Lighterman* is only a Corruption of the Phrafe *Lighter-Man*, i. e. a Man that is lighter, or fwifter on foot, and can run fafter.

By the diffembling Waterman, the Author un-doubtedly means the *Dutch*, for you muft remember, gentle Reader, that thofe high and mighty People did not come up to their Contract with us at that Time, to fay no worfe of it ; which I think will account for the Epithet or adjective *diffembling*, and when to the adjective diffembling we join the fubftantive *Waterman*, you will plainly fee the Force of the Argument ; for, as the *Dutch* are bred among the Fens and the Frogs, and are am-phibious Creatures that live fometimes on Land and fometimes in the Water, which cannot be faid of any other People in the World, the Term *Water-man* muft appertain unto them and them only, for *Waterman* is a Corruption of *Water-Man*, i. e. a Man that can live in the Water. But if you ex-clude this Argument (which is as felf evident as any

Axiom

Axiom in EUCLID) and confider thofe People-
without having regard to their Country and Manner
of Life, you will find that no Man hath fo much
of Water in his Compofition as your *Dutchman.*

The bearing of the Author's Song is too audacious
to be pafs'd filently over, and deferves the Confideration of the Magiftracy as much as any Part of it.

Molly's a Girl that will die if fhe has not a Kifs
from the Lighterman.

This was wrote to warm and animate the Hearts
of our *Britifh* Amazons in behalf of the young Pretender, and I believe in my Confcience was the
Caufe of the mad and unaccountable Healths that
were drank, the party colour'd Ribbands they
wore, and the Dancings, Clubs, Songs and Revel-
lings of that Time; which I fuppofe will be talk'd
on with Wonder and Amazement, when my little
Grand-Child is a Grand-Mother. But to proceed ——

With his black fhammy Pumps, and his rolling
Eye, Sir,
He did kifs every Girl that he did come nigh, Sir.

This Verfe alludes to a private Ball given by
the Cardinal TENCIN, juft before the little Lighterman's Expedition, where it was particularly obferv'd that he danced in black fhammy Pumps,
gave a wanton Liberty to his Eyes, and, what is
not ufual in polite Affemblies, kifs'd all the Ladies in Company, as foon as the Ball was over;
which

which Circumftance this wicked Poet has improved to the Pretender's Advantage, with a palpable Defign of promoting his Caufe, by rendering his Perfon and Behaviour the more agreeable to our *Englifh* Ladies.—We come now to the third and laft Verfe of this Virulent and Treafonable Performance, in which the Poifon is fo artfully and deeply conceal'd, that 'twill coft us fome Pains to difcover and expel it:

But when his Mafter he found him he put him into
  Bridewell;
Molly *fhe loved him fo well, fhe gave him a Pot*
  of Porter.

That the young Adventurer, upon his Return to *France,* was feized by Order of the *French* King, is a Circumftance too well known to be longer infifted on; and that during this Confinement, Application was made for his Enlargement by *Molly,* which all Decypherers allow means *Molly Britaina,* or *our Britifh Ladies,* is altogether as notorious, who are here faid to have given him a *Pot of Porter,* that is, procured him a *free Paffage*; for Porter, in this Place, means no more than the Perfon who has the Care of the Portal of the Goal; and confequently the Phrafe, *gave him a Pot of Porter,* fignifies *paid the Porter,* or *gave him his free Liberty:* And in this Senfe it is taken by GRONOVIOUS, CAMBLITARO, and ELMILLIUS.

And here I muft beg Leave to obferve, that *Molly,* or *Molly Britannia,* is indifferently ufed by

             our

our Author, either for the Daughters of *Britannia*, or a Moiety of the *English* Ladies ; and of Confequence this Line,

Molly's *a Girl that will die if fhe has not a Kifs*
    from the Lighterman,

was not only wrote for the Purpofe I have already mentioned, but alfo to infinuate, that the Daughters of *Britannia* are in a languifhing State for the Lofs of this Lighterman. This is, I muft own, too grofs to be mentioned but in polite Company, and too bad to be farther explain'd in any ; but it plainly fhews what this wicked Author would be at, and fufficiently indicates the Neceffity of placing him in a State of *Durance.* — But I have done — no, I have not done — Creatures of this Complexion, Monfters of this Magnitude, Serpents of fuch Subtility, can never be enough expofed.

This *Janus-headed* Author (for I hate a Man that has a double Face) has fo artfully contrived this Piece, that if it be fung on any other Day of the Year except the 10th of *June,* and to the Tune of *Jack in the Green,* or any other Tune but the *Rolling Hornpipe,* the Words will have a quite different Signification ; but the Virulence remains, 'tis only Poifon differently prepared, in order to anfwer different wicked Purpofes ; and this laft is a Circumftance that could not have been difcover'd, but by my extraordinary Knowledge in the Art of *Decypheration.*

M. Midnight.

On the *Practice* of *Gaming* among *Ladies* of *Quality*.

WOman was intended by the great Creator, as the moſt amiable of terreſtrial Beings; with Beauty little inferior to that of Angels; with Senſation equal to the brighteſt Son of Reaſon, and inveſted with the Robe of Modeſty to give an additional Luſtre to all her Actions. Without the Poſſeſſion of this delectable Aſſociate, Man had roved comfortleſs even through the perennial Groves of Paradiſe; without the Solace and pleaſing Endearments of Woman, he had been no more than a rational Brute, unconſcious of Love, inſenſible of Joy: but for the Promotion of his Felicity, Woman was created; for his Comfort, the divine Author of Nature formed Woman from the Loins of Man, and infuſed into her Noſtrils the Breath of Life, principally to contribute to his Happineſs.

Upon this Conſideration it has been aſſerted, that if Providence intended Women only for the Service of Man, that the ſame Providence ought to ſecure her from Danger and Temptation; becauſe,

—— if weak Women go aſtray,
Their Stars are more in fault than they.

But I think this one Inſtance of the refin'd Impiety of the modern Age; for, unleſs we deny

R　　　　　　　Woman

Woman the Faculty of Reaſon, ſhe can never be more peculiarly exempted from acting according to her own Judgment than Man is allow'd to do; and this is one of thoſe Privileges which no Woman will eaſily be brought to relinquiſh.

If the firſt Woman deprived her Huſband of Paradiſe by her Indiſcretion, her Deſcendants are not more inculpable in other Reſpects, which I could prove by innumerable Examples from the Days of *Helen,* and *Dalilah* to thoſe of *Catherine de Medicis* and *Iſabella* of *Farneſe*; but as this would be altogether immaterial to my preſent Deſign, I ſhall confine myſelf to the prevailing Folly and Vice of the preſent Day, ſo ardently purſued by the *Britiſh* Ladies at Routs, Drums, Maſquerades and Aſſemblies; all tending to the Abolition of connubial Happineſs, the Miſery of every indulgent Huſband, and the Deſtruction of whole Families.

Gaming, as it is now encouraged, is productive of every Calamity that can involve Ladies into thoſe inextricable Snares, which are perpetually ambuſhed for the Captivity of Virtue; and when that is gone farewel Pleaſure, farewel Joy; Content is fled, Tranquillity is baniſhed. What an unamiable Sight it is to be a Spectator at a Gaming-Table, ſurrounded by Ladies of Quality, in Company with Profligates and Sharpers! where the Smile of Beauty is waſted upon an inanimate Card, or diſtorted into all the hideous Features of a Fury. When the Deciſion of a Stake of four or five Hundred Guineas is dependant upon a ſingle

Card,

Card, furely it muſt be attended with the utmoſt Anxiety. If the Event is fortunate, it is only the Parent of Extravagance; but if unſuccefsful, the Mother of Neceſſity.

I am acquainted in a very illuſtrious Family, where the Lady of the Houſe has loſt more in Gaming in leſs than a Week, than would have maintained a Coach and ſix for a Twelvemonth. As I had the Honour to attend this Lady in my maternal Capacity, I frequently found her out of Humour, and generally in a diſconſolate Diſpoſition; though, perhaps, the ſame Day, I have ſeen her paying a Viſit to my Lady *Whiſt-away*, with all the Raptures of inexpreſſible Joy and Jollity. I thought this Variation of Temper very extraordinary, and began to entertain ſome ſhrewd Suſpicions tending to the Impeachment of her Virtue: but on reflecting that her Huſband had every amiable Quality that could charm her Sex or dignify his own, my Suſpicions vaniſhed; and I was ſoon afterwards convinced of the Reality of this ſtrange Viciſſitude in the Temper of a Woman, who was univerſally allowed to be a Lady of extraordinary Senſe and Delicacy; which indeed, though a Daughter of a very worthy Gentleman, was the only Fortune ſhe brought to her noble Conſort, or, at leaſt, was the only one he admitted to his Arms. As her Ladyſhip was pretty far advanced in her Pregnancy, I paid her an early Viſit in the Morning; but, to my great Surprize, was informed by her Lord, that ſhe was diſcarded

from

from his Houfe, till her Vanity was diminifhed, and her Prudence increafed. I was aftonifhed at fuch an Information; but as I was fenfible his Lordfhip had a particular Regard for me, I humbly entreated him to confider the Confequence of fuch a Refolution; I reprefented to him the Malevolence of the World, both from his own Enemies, and thofe of her Ladyfhip; and defir'd he would prevent the ever-flowing Tide of Cenfure and Scandal from approaching his Refidence. His Lordfhip declared, that he valued his own private Happinefs and Peace of Mind, more than all the Cenfures of an ill-natur'd World; he allowed that he had banifhed a Woman from his Breaft, whom he had once fondly repofited there as a fweet tender Dove; but as fhe was now altered to a Viper, and infected the Heart fhe had once moulded to her Pleafure, he was of Opinion that he fhould ftand readily aequitted in the Eye of God, and in the Light of Reafon. "For, Mrs. *Midnight*, continued he, Heaven alone knows the Diftraction of my Mind." He paufed here, and in fpite of his manly Pride, gave way to the fofter Power of Nature, though he attempted to conceal it, I perceived a large Drop of Anguifh tremble in his Eye. He defired me to fit down by him; then told me, he knew his Lady had a great Opinion of my Underftanding; that he had a Regard for me; and therefore fhould readily difclofe to me the Affliction of his Heart; hoping I would endeavour to alleviate his Sorrows. "Madam, continued

he,

" he, it is now more than three Years fince I en-
" tered into the State of Matrimony. My For-
" tune and Patrimony were too noble to lead my
" Inclinations to Wealth ; I therefore fought only
" to illuftrate my Line by intermarrying into a
" worthy tho' not opulent Family ; and I foon
" fixed my Affections on an Object every Way
" adequate to my Wifhes. She foon made me
" the happy Father of a beautiful Child ; I was
" all Indulgence, fhe was all Love and Compla-
" cency ; but, in fome unhappy Hour furely her
" Reafon was extinguifhed, her domeftic Fide-
" lity eradicated. I had little of her Company ;
" fhe came home generally difconcerted in Tem-
" per ; and was either extremely angry to all
" about her at Night, or very liberal to her Ser-
" vants in the Morning. Inftead of indulging me
" in her ufual Careffes, or fhewing her maternal
" Fondnefs to her little Babe, fhe endeavour'd to
" fhun my Company, and feem'd offended at the
" fweet Innocence of her Child. This continued
" for fome Time, before I difcover'd that all her
" Uneafinefs proceeded from a Fondnefs to Gaming;
" I found fhe had fquandered away more Money
" than her Fortune would have amounted to had
" I receiv'd it ; and I ftrongly remonftrated to her
" the Folly and Danger of her Continuance in
" fuch a Scene of Extravagance. But this was all
" ineffectual ; fhe redoubled her Purfuit of Gaming;
" augmented her former Lofs with feveral Thou-
" fands ; and though I laid before her the Train

" of

" of Poverty and Misfortunes confequential to
" fuch a Behaviour, fhe ftill perfifted in her riotous
" Excefs, till the Neceffity that furrounded me,
" convinced me that I was to confult the Prefer-
" vation and Honour of my Family, rather than
" tamely fubmit to the Folly and Vanity of a de-
" luded Woman. With this Refolution, I yefter-
" day informed her how greatly fhe had impove-
" rifhed my Eftate, and infifted upon an Affurance
" that fhe would immediately confult the Honour
" of our Family, and relinquifh all the Pleafures
" to be found in a Society of Gamefters. But fhe
" threw up her Head with an unaccuftom'd Shew
" of Infolence, affuring me that fhe was then en-
" gaged to fpend the Evening at Lady *Swabb*'s on
" a Party of Whift, and could not poffibly forfeit
" her Honour. I endeavour'd to diffuade her
" from her Defign, exerting all the Force of En-
" treaty, with all the Declarations of Authority :
" but in vain ; fhe was determin'd to go, though
" I vowed by every Thing folemn that if fhe went,
" fhe fhould have no Admiffion on her Return.
" And yet, Mrs. *Midnight*, fo ftrongly is fhe ad-
" dicted to her Pleafures, that fhe difcharged her
" Affignation, nor did fhe deign to return till
" Day-light waited upon her Home, where, by
" my Orders, fhe was refufed Admiffion, and I
" am unacquainted with what is come of her
" fince." Juft as his Lordfhip had ended this melancholy Relation, we were alarm'd with the loud

ring-

ringing at the Gate; when a Servant came up and acquainted his Lordſhip that his Lady's Mother deſired Admiſſion ; which was immediately granted, and I retired : but I was ſoon inform'd that the Mother acquainted his Lordſhip that her Daughter had been with her, and gave her an Account of what had happen'd ; that the Mother told her ſhe ſhould have no Encouragement in her Folly from her ; and had compelled her to return to his Lordſhip to acknowledge her Error, implore his Pardon, and ſincerely promiſe a total Amendment : which ſhe was now deſirous of doing, and only waited below for his Lordſhip's Order to fall at his Knees, and give him the moſt abſolute Aſſurance of Obedience. Overjoy'd with this unexpected Declaration, his Lordſhip ſprang to the Arms of his penitential Lady with all the Raptures of an eager Lover. Since which happy Minute, their Lives have been one interrupted Scene of domeſtic Pleaſure and Tranquillity : The Lady, truly ſenſible of her Errors, ſtrives to make an ample Attonement, by all the winning Ways that Love and Prudence can invent ; while her happy Lord confineś all his Deſires to the Promotion of her Felicity.

I wiſh Heaven would ſo turn the Thoughts of ſeveral other Ladies of Diſtinction, whoſe Love and Purſuit of Gaming muſt be deſtructive to their Families, and perhaps the Means of ſacrificing their Virtue. Debts of Gaming, are called Debts

of

of Honour, and they muſt be ſatisfied : a Gaming
Huſband indeed may do it by mortgaging his Eſtate,
but a Wife, when her Pin-money is exhauſted,
may be obliged to gratify an importunate Dun with
ſomething more valuable than Pelf.   I would have
Ladies to conſider, that Gaming is not only deſtructive to the Eſtate of their Huſbands, but is
equally ſo to their own Beauty ; which cannot
continue long, under the Diſadvantages of thoſe
hollow Eyes, haggard Looks, and pale Com-
plexions, perpetually attendant on the intemperate
Hours of Female Gameſters ; and what a Race of
Warriors, Patriots, and Stateſmen, is poor *Britain* to expect I ſhall bring into the World from
the Wombs of ſuch diſſolute Mothers?

---

*A Diſſertation on the following moſt excellent
old* Engliſh *Rules,* videlicet,

COME WHEN YOU ARE CALLED,
Do as you are bid, and
SHUT THE DOOR AFTER YOU.

Notwithſtanding theſe Rules are ſo obvious and
intelligible, that any Ruſtic may underſtand them,
yet the perpetual Breach of them makes it neceſſary for me to preach them into Practice at this
Juncture.   I ſhall conſider them in their proper
Order,

Order, and endeavour to set them in a proper Light.—And first,

Come when you are called.

I had a violent Hoarsness upon me for three Months with calling my *Woman*, who was so wilfully Deaf, that neither the jingling of the Bell, the stamping of my Foot, nor my own Voice (which Heaven be praised is pretty distinguishable) could ever make her approach, when I wanted her.—I have recommended this Precept with the more Vehemence, because I have always enforced it by my Example, and if I had not punctually *came* when *I was called* in my maternal Profession, half the Women of Quality in this Kingdom wou'd have dy'd before their Time.

And now for the second Rule,

Do as you are bid.

This I look upon to be one of the most capital Rules in the World, *in* this are included, and *by* this are inculcated the Duty of a Child to his Parents, of a Soldier to his General, of a Subject to his Prince, with an Hundred and Fifty *& cæteras*. I was credibly inform'd by the Ghost of Sir *Thomas More*, which appeared to me a few Nights ago, that no Bishoprick, or indeed any Post of Honour, Dignity or Profit whatsoever, was disposed of in the Kingdom of Utopia, without the Persons preferr'd previously giving Security to observe this

truly

truly GOLDEN Rule —and I defire all my Readers would ftrictly adhere to this Injunction of DOING AS THEY ARE BID, when I command them to buy up all the odd Numbers of my Magazine, and compleat their Sets immediately.

And now I come to the moft important Article of all.

SHUT THE DOOR AFTER YOU.

About two Years before my Marriage with my dear Mr. *Midnight*, I took the grand Tour of *Europe*, I vifited all the Iflands in *Archipelago* — I went to *Turky* and *Grand Cairo*, but never could find one fingle Perfon in all my Travels that had Wit enough to obferve this Rule. I had a Dog indeed whofe Name was *Whifky* (tho' he was but a ftupid Dog I promife you) that never fail'd fhutting the Door if he cou'd; but if it was fo fituated that he cou'd not manage it, he bark'd at it, in order to fhew his Indignation, and that he was convinc'd in his own Mind, that it was very wrong the Door fhould remain open. As trifling an Affair as this may feem to fome Criticafters, there has many a Life been loft by this ridiculous Piece of Negligence: Colds have been catch'd, Thieves and Murderers have had Admiffion into the Houfes of honeft Men, Virgins have been deflower'd merely by a Contempt of this Rule: And if I had a Voice ten Thoufand Times louder than *Stentor*, or even Thunder itfelf, I would get upon

the

the Top of St. *Paul*'s and bellow out,

    COME WHEN YOU ARE CALL'D,

    DO AS YOU ARE BID, and

    SHUT THE DOOR AFTER YOU.

A Proposal for expelling all Party, Party People, and Party Principles, out of our two Universities; and all our Churches and Religious Assemblies. By Mrs. SUSANNAH COXETER. *In a Letter to Mrs.* Midnight.

Dear Mary,

MR. *Williams* tells me, that your *Magazine* is read by all the great People, and that you get a great deal of Money by it, which is a great Satisfaction to me and all your Friends in this Country. The Success you have met with, almost encourages me to try my Skill at Writing, for Money is very scarce here, and if one cou'd only make Eighty, or Ninety, or a Hundred Pounds a Year of it, 'twou'd be a great Help to one, now the Interest of Money is so fallen; and Mr. *Williams* says, you get more than that every Year by writing of Manuscript Sermons for your Acquaintance. If so, you can recommend one a little; and I know, dear *Mary*, if it is in your Power you will do it. My Son *Tommy* does not do so well as I would have him; and I find that

the

the Learning I have given him is almost thrown away.

When he first came from College, it was thought neceſſary that he ſhould be examin'd, which *Tom* was terribly afraid of, for he had been examin'd ſeveral Times by his School-maſter before he went to the *Verſity*, as we call it, and flog'd for not being perfect; and as he had improved himſelf there in little elſe but puffing his Pipe, he had great Reaſon to apprehend himſelf in Danger. Wherefore I took him to myſelf, as the Saying is, for eight or ten Days, and retaught him his *Latin*, and *Greek*, and *Engliſh*, together with as much of *Logic*, *Rhetoric*, *Geography*, *Aſtronomy*, *Mathematicks* and *Morality*, as learned Men generally know, and more of *Divinity* than they practiſe, and carried him to the ſage old Gentleman to be initiated. When we firſt came in (it makes me laugh to think on't) my old Gums chatter'd for Fear, and the Lad's Hair ſtood ſo an End, that his Head ſeem'd bigger than I had ever known it. The grave Doctor, however, did not appear ſo formidable as I expected. When I courteſy'd to the Ground, and told him my Buſineſs. *Madam,* ſays he, *you have in your Time been a very handſom Woman; ſit down Madam, and as to your Son there — why I ſhall examine him preſently —Here, bring a Bottle, and my long Pipe, and the Cuſhion* — and then ſwabbing himſelf down in an eaſy Chair — *You muſt know young Man,* ſays he, *our*

Neigh-

Neighbourhood is divided into two Parties; but you, I am told in this Letter, take the Part of my Lord **** and so here's my Service to you — All his Lordship's Friends come well qualified; he was my Patron, and a farther Examination would be unnecessary: but as for the People of the other Side of the Question, they are the meerest Dunces in Nature, and plague me sometimes for Hours together. So I got the Busines done here, and he came from College, and I got him a Curacy of 20 *l.* a Year, and had almost got him a Living, but he happen'd to vote of the wrong Side the Question at our Election, and so that deftroy'd all. And now he's marry'd, Madam, (tho' I don't blame him for that, for a Man had better marry than do worfe) and he has fix Children, and no more than 20 *l.* a Year to maintain them. I wifh I could have foretold this fifteen Years ago, I am fure I would not have beftow'd Five Hundred Pounds on his Education, for with that Money, Mr. *Williams* fays, I could have bought him an Annuity of 50 *l.* a Year for his Life, and he might have follow'd other Bufinefs; and now he has only 20 *l.* a Year, and is oblig'd to follow no other Bufinefs, and that 20 *l.* is only for Life. And I don't fee that there is any Likelihood of his advancing himfelf, unlefs he had confider'd better of it before he had given his Vote. But *Tommy* fays, if it was to do again he would do it, for Clergymen ought not to vote againft their Confciences, as other People do, for the Sake of Mo-

S

ney;

ney; and that is true too, fo that I can't be angry
with him. I wifh, dear *Mary*, you cou'd get him a
Living in *London*; I don't mean a Lecturefhip, no,
Tommy once try'd for that, but your People are fo
bold in *London*, and think themfelves fuch Judges,
that a Man is deny'd before he can afk the
Queftion. Even the Cheefemonger where my Son
lodged, when he put up for that Place, told him,
he fhould be for *Voice and Action*, *Voice and Action*, and tofs'd up his Head like a young Squire
at a Country Affizes; fo I had rather you would
get him a Living, your good Word will go a great
Way with the great People, and I am fure there is
not an honefter Man in the World than my Son,
if that is any Recommendation; and you'll hugely
oblige me and him, and his Wife and fix fmall
Children, fo do dear *Mary* remember us.

> *I am,*
>> *Your loving Friend,*
>>> S. COXETER.

P. S. I think all Party, and Party People, and
Party Principles, fhould be excommunicated out of
our Univerfities, and Churches, and Religious Affemblies, and People only promoted for Piety, and
Virtue, and Honefty; and if Things were order'd
fo, the People in our Country would go to Church
oftener than they do, and come away better taught
than they are: Don't you think they wou'd
Mrs. *Midnight?*

I

. *I do highly approve of Mrs.* Coxeter's *Proposal for expelling all Party, party People, and party Principles out of our Univerſities, Churches, and other Religious Aſſemblies; and deſire that the Expurgation may commence before the Alteration of the Style, that with the new Period we may turn over a new Leaf; for while we have Parties in the Church, there can be no Orthodox Religion; and while there are Parties in the State, there can be no true Patriot Policy.*

MARY MIDNIGHT.

A Queſtion to be debated by the Robin Hood Society *at the Requeſt of a very great Man, and the Arguments* pro *and* con *to be ſubmitted to Mrs.* Midnight.

The QUESTION.

WHether HONEY *or* MUSTARD *is the beſt to oil a Man's* WIG?

N. B. The Gentlemen concern'd are deſired to be particularly careful and circumſpect in diſcuſſing this Point, for the whole Debates will be inſerted in the next Number of my Magazine.

MARY MIDNIGHT.

Con-

Continuation of the Adventures of Meſſrs. IN-
CLINATION *and* ABILITY.

*H*Ercules did not remain a Batchelor long after
he went upon the Stage, for a beautiful
young Lady fell in Love with him, who after
ſeveral Years Cohabitation, made him the happy
Father of the following Sons and Daughters, *viz.*
Garrick, *Quin*, *Ryan*, *Woodward*, *Cibber*,
Pritchard, *Clive*, *Berry*, *Bellamy*, and ſome
others. — ISGRIM married alſo, but in leſs
than a Month his Wife obtain'd a Divorce, for
Reaſons that there requires no great Sagacity
to gueſs at. ABILITY having acquired a very
conſiderable Fortune by his truly admirable Performances, quitted the Stage, and (as he was extreamly generous) gave poor INCLINATION a
pretty Competency, with which he always ſup-
ports the APPEARANCE of a Gentleman. Notwithſtanding the Goodneſs of his Brother, ISGRIM
was ſo ungrateful, as to oppoſe him upon all Oc-
caſions ; the firſt Inſtance of this unnatural Behaviour, was at an Election of a Profeſſorſhip in a
certain Univerſity, where *Iſgrim* was choſe, becauſe he did not *underſtand* the Language he was
to teach, and *Hercules* was rejected for being *too
well qualify'd.* After this Diſappointment, *Hercules* was ſomewhat ſower'd in his Temper, and
Application was made in his Behalf to the great
Mæcenas's

Mæcenas's of the Age; who, without knowing and encouraging one Art, has been reckon'd the Patron and Mafter of them all. He told ABI-LITY he was a very good fort of a Perfon, and that he fhould be glad of an Opportunity of fervy ing him; he foon found an Opportunity, and (what is more marvellous) embraced it. And now, gentle Reader, what do you think he pro= pofed to do? — Why by the Intereft of his Friend my Lord *Danglecourt*, he got a Promife that ABI-LITY, now in the *Bloom* of Youth, and the *Hardinefs* of Health, fond of Peace and ftill domeftic Life, fhould be admitted as a lame, old, difabled Soldier into the *Chelfea* Hofpital. ——

Enraged at this Ufage, and impoverifh'd by his boundlefs Generofity, *Hercules* determined to accommodate his Labours more to the Tafte of the Times. He therefore betook himfelf to the Study of Architecture, and foon found fufficient Applaufe, Profit and Encouragement in every Shape from the Extravagance and Vanity of the Times. Our modern great ones (to do them but Juftice) are vaft Patrons of Matter and Mechanifm, and while they defpife and opprefs Genius and Learning; the Toyman, the Gambler, and the Fidler, are always welcome to their Houfes: *Ifgrim*, you may be fure, muft commence *Vitruvius*, in order to ape his Brother, and many and various were his Exploits in the exalted Science of Building. —— He erected a Fabrick in the Fens, after the Model of a Palace in the hotteft Parts of *Africa*.——

S 3

He

He perfuaded a Nobleman to be at ten Thoufand
Pounds Expence to level an Hill which intercepted
the Profpect of a Marfh, and kept off the defira-
ble Breezes of the Eaft-Wind, with many Works
equally laudable and judicious.

[*To be continued.*]

E P I G R A M.

BOLD Bavius, the Bard — by *himfelf* much
   renown'd,
Came up to *Apollo*, and beg'd to be crown'd,
And (he cry'd) *Brother Phœbus*, 'fore George we
   fhall quarrel,
Unlefs you provide me the beft of your Laurel.
The God laught aloud, and he beckon'd to *Momus*,
Who was fmoaking his Pipe, and caroufing with
   Comus :
Th' old *Wag* cry'd, dear *Bavius*, from hence I
   muft drive ye,
But firft pray accept of this Wreath of GROUND
   IVY.

*A Word or two for thofe whom it may
Concern.*

MRS. *Midnight* is perfectly well fatisfied with
   the Alteration that is to be made in the
Stile; 'tis what fhe has long wifh'd for, and en-
                              deavour'd

deavour'd to promote in her Magazine, but as by
such Alteration her Rent becomes due eleven Days
sooner than usual, and she is totally unprovided for
the Discharge of it, she desires the honourable
Gentlemen who were the Promoters of that Scheme
would discharge it for her, and they shall be repaid out of the Profits of her next Magazine,* as
a Security for which, a Note of her Hand in the
following Form will be given.

I promise to pay the ***** or Bearer, three
Hundred and seventy Pounds out of the Profits of
my next Magazine. At my Bank in St. *Paul's
Church Yard*, Aug. 12. 1751.

MARY MIDNIGHT.

* Or if it be more agreeable, Mrs. *Midnight* will attend the Gentleman's Lady in her maternal Capacity,
after the Rate of one Guinea each Time 'till the whole
Money is repaid.

N. B. At Mrs. *Midnight's* Bank abovemention'd,
Annuities are granted on Lives, and Ships insured (but
no Men of War unless she knows the Commanders) for
the Payment of which her whole Magazine is made
liable.

---

*An Attempt to prove that the Fair Sex have
every Qualification necessary for Learning.*

THE Male Sex have perpetually plumed themselves in the vain and ambitious Opinion of being as much superior to Women, in their rational
Facul-

Faculties, as they are in the natural ones of Strength
and Activity; and this has been moſt tenaciouſly
exerted by all Ranks and Conditions of Men,
from the Nobleman lolling in his gilded Chariot,
to the plain Ruſtic labouring at the Plough.　If a
Lady of Quality pretends to the leaſt Appearance
of Wiſdom; if ſhe is allowed to be a Woman of
extraordinary Senſe; and ventures to declare her
Opinion upon any important Matter in which the
national Intereſt is moſt materially concerned;
truly her ſenatorial Conſort replies, 'Madam, theſe
are Affairs above the Reach of a Female Capacity,
we Men are only deſign'd by Nature for Politicians, and the moſt a Woman can pretend to is
Virtue and Diſcretion.　The Merchant will never
permit his Lady to hold the leaſt Converſation on
commercial Affairs; becauſe, ſays he, how can ſhe
be acquainted with the different Intereſts and Con-
nexions of Nations; or how can ſhe tell what
Commodities a *European* Trader muſt barter for
Slaves on the Coaſt of *Africa?* The Lawyer will
not admit his Wife to have any Pretence to Eloquence, though her Tongue is inceſſantly flowing
with the utmoſt Volubility.　The Clergyman will
grant his Lady to be endowed with good Senſe,
and every œconomical Virtue; but deſpiſes her
Underſtanding, becauſe ſhe is unacquainted with
the Beauties of the antient Claſſics.　The Mechanic ſays his Wife is a very prudent Woman, but
rejects her Advice in many material Affairs, becauſe ſhe is ignorant of the Secrets of that Profeſſion

feffion which he had ferv'd a long Apprenticefhip
to learn.   And the Farmer allows that his honeft
Mate may underftand how to manage her Dairy,
but fagacioufly conceives fhe has no Right to tref-
pafs upon the Superiority of Man, who is born to
be abfolute.

That Men are extremely fallacious in thefe Opinions, and erroneous in their Conduct, I think
may be very evidently demonftrated, and is therefore a Tafk which I have undertaken to illuftrate
in Vindication of my Sex.

Women, as reafonable Creatures, are certainly
upon an Equality with Men; and this is a Maxim
univerfally acceded to in every Country of Chriftianity; though if I was to declare my Sentiments
fo freely in the *Ottoman* Empire, I make no doubt
but I fhould be deftroyed for a Magician, among
a People who maintain the heretical Opinion that
a Woman has no Soul.   It is not the Sex, but the
Species, that diftinguifhes fublunary Beings; and if
the Females in all the Animal Creation are equally
eftimable with the Males, why fhould not Woman
be fet upon an equal Comparifon with regard to
Man?

That the Mind of Woman is capable of the
fame Improvements as that of Man, is to be
proved by innumerable Inftances.   Women are
generally allowed to have a fpeedier and more pe-
netrating Apprehenfion than Men; nor are they
lefs retentive in Memory; and as for the peculiar
Grace, Elegance, and Volubility of Speech, it
                                                      woul-

would be next to Impiety for the Men to conteſt it. Why then are not Women capable of diſtinguiſhing themſelves as much as Men in the Acquiſition of Knowledge, the Invention of Arts, and the Refinement of Sciences?—If a *Pythagoras* civilized the rude *Samians* by his ethical Preſents; if a *Lycurgus* reſtrained the Licentiouſneſs of the *Lacedemonians* by his legiſlative Inſtitutions; or if a *Plato*, ſurrounded with the Gloom of *Paganiſm*, could trace the glorious Attributes of the omnipotent Creator, and with his pious Reflections ſtartle the Profeſſors of Chriſtianity; all this ought not to be attributed to any Superiority of Sex; for thoſe venerable Sages as much ſurpaſſed the reſt of Mankind, as the moſt ſtrenuous Votary for the Male Sex eſteems the Inferiority of Women to Men.

Stoical Reſolution, and cynical Pride, have always been held derogatory to the Female Sex; though this was a Stroke of Policy in the Men, which was diſregarded both by *Portia* and *Hipparchia*; the former proving herſelf as ſtanch a Stoic as *Cato* her Father, and the latter deſpiſing Cenſure as much as *Diogenes*. The human Soul is every where the ſame, though Climates and Cuſtoms may implant in it different Paſſions and Senſations: therefore, I make no Doubt, but the Female Inhabitants of *Great Britain*, may, under proper Regulations, appear as illuſtrious as any of the ſame Sex that ever breathed the Air of *Greece* or *Rome*.

How

How greatly is it to be lamented, that the Female Sex fhould be in a Manner difinherited from their Right of common in the Fields of Learning? That we have Capacity for attaining the Height of Wifdom ought not to be denied; and why was the bright Spark of Reafon implanted in our Souls? Surely, not to place us in a State of Subjection. Let our Faculties be improved, and our Abilities tried, we fhall foon convince Men of our Equality. And certainly an Application to Learning among the Female Sex, would be attended with many Advantages to themfelves, their Acquaintance, and the whole Nation in general; and therefore ought to be encouraged. For by the Advantages refulting from a liberal Education, the Ladies might be attending to a Syftem of Ethics, inftead of cenfuring the Conduct of their Neighbours: they might be examining the Beauty and Regularity of the planetary Syftem, inftead of exclaiming againft the Indecency and Intemperance of their Hufbands: they might be admiring the Secrets of the vegetable Creation, inftead of commenting upon the Indifcretion of a celebrated Beauty; and, above all, they might be fcrutinizing into the Tenets of Philofophy, inftead of diftorting their Countenances at a Game at Whift. Befides, there is another extraordinary Advantage that would immediately accrue from the Encouragement of Female Learning, efpecially in thofe of Women of Quality; and this is the Prefervation of Senfe, which is greatly endanger'd in our pre-

fent

fent illuftrious Families, where Hufbands are generally Strangers to every Part of Literature, leaving it now confined as a Mechanical Thing, to Butlers and Footmen, juft able to fpell, and figure out a weekly Bill of domeftic Expences in thofe few Houfes where any Regard is had to Œconomy.

I would not here be underftood to mean, that Ladies of Quality in general are unacquainted with Learning; no, I am confcious to myfelf and muft acknowledge, that her Grace of ****, her Grace of ****, her Grace of ****, her Grace of ***, and about nineteen other Ladies, whom you have had the Honour frequently to drink Tea with, have a greater Share both of Genius and Learning than I am poffeft of, and are abundantly better qualified to write on any Subject than their

Moft obedient humble Servant,

SARAH MARIA SMITH.

Memoirs of a Pamphlet reflecting on the Mifs G——gs.

Written fomewhat in the Manner of *Dean Swift.*

—— *Multum ille & terris jactatus & alto.*

IN fweet *Vaux-hall* I love to ftray;
  But wifh it were completely gay:
In fplendid Scenes we drink and eat;
In fordid Huts ——— evacuate:

Ah!

Ah! why, ye Gods! more Care about
What we put in, than we put out?
Yet I've no Reaſon to complain;
My Off'rings pleaſe in any Fane:
Fair *Cloacina* nods the Head,
While Fumes of Incenſe round her ſpread.

 Beſides, it lately was my Lot
To meet Adventures in her Grot:
Scarce had I oped and ſhut the Door;
And veil'd, in Form, the Common Shore;
When, lo! I ſpy'd a Wretch forlorn,
In hapleſs Plight, all rent and torn;
Vile as the batter'd, dying Whore,
Lie half expiring on the Floor.
This *Being* once a Pamphlet ſhow'd;
An Hundred Leaves together ſow'd:
Now only two from Fate could ſave;
And one of them was in the Grave.

 " I've been (it cry'd) in bloody Wars;
As you ſhall hear: pray, mind my Scars.
I know my Doom —— to kiſs your Br——
My Hour is come—I'll make my Speech.
Fortune nor * Periwig, nor Gooſequill
(Compared to me) did ever uſe Ill.
I've been a Vagabond from firſt,
A luckleſs Fox, though ever curſt.

 In Youth a Stationer, for Pay,
Poor me to Printer pack'd away.

---

* The Midwife has given us the Memoirs of a Tie-
Wig, as the Student has preſented us with thoſe of a
Gooſequill.

     T

           My

My fpotlefs Innocence was ftain'd;
The worft of *Characters* I gain'd.
But, like the Miftrefs of a K——,
Obtain'd a *Title* by my Sin.

At † **'s next my Tent was pitcht,
Where I was folded, prefs'd and ftitcht.
As Cinder-girls, embracing Shoe-men,
No more are Girls, but Cinder-women;
Or Eggs, well batter'd, turn an Amlet;
Thus I, when ftitcht, commenc'd a Pamphlet.
Whence all my Miferies I date;
Whence Gods and Men confpire my Fate.

A new-born Libel flies about;
Quicker than Felon juft broke out:
Thus I, full foon for Six-pence bought,
To G——e's Coffee-houfe was brought.
But know, the Meffenger in fport,
Thrice dropt me fhiv'ring in the Dirt;
And thrice he cry'd, why d——n your Blood,
You've ftrange Propenfity to Mud.

Yet all the Criticks I could fee,
Were more intemperate than he.
They d——n'd me as they read me o'er;
They never read fuch Stuff before.
Thefe twift me when they light their Pipes;
Thofe foul me, tortur'd with the Gripes.
One fwell'd as big as any Porpus,
And fpill'd his Chocolate on Purpofe.
Another flop'd his Bohea Tea,
And two whole Leaves diffolv'd away.

---

† A Publifher.

Coffee

Coffee (the Politicians vext)
Depriv'd me of my Title next.
An honeft *Scotfman* in a Huff,
Begrimed me with *half-fnotty* Snuff.
Hear me, ye Manufcripts of *C*———— !
I interpofed, or he'd bef——t ye.
A——d! where's now your candid Strain?
Good — *very good* — and *good again?*

  *   *   *   *   *   *

  A Beau, who would not for the World,
A Lock of his fhould go uncurl'd ;
Before the Glafs, in raging Vein,
Tore out a Leaf to eafe his Pain :
Befides (my Mufe the Truth relates)
All Folly, but his own, he hates ;
So next Day, at his Breakfaft ftuffing,
Greafed me all over with his Muffin.
To-night he brought me to this Garden ;
Forgetting I belong to † *Hardin :*
But rofe too foon, for ever fickle,
And waddled off in dainty pickle.

  Thus I obtain'd a fhort Reprieve ;
But fhall, alas ! no longer live :
My Courfe of Wickednefs I've run ;
Befides, I fee you've almoft done :
And you will not, right well I ween,
Take your Departure till you're clean.

  For ev'ry Ill my Sire I blame ;
My Sire, who often bore the fame :

---

† He keeps G————e's Coffee-houfe.

     Muft

Muſt I too ſuffer, and attone
For Crimes, that he commits alone ?
Could he his Naſtineſs contain,
Nor void the Ordure of his Brain ;
I might have paſs'd like other Folks,
And unpolluted crack'd my Jokes :
But Excrement long having born,
I muſt to Excrement return.
Brought forth in Folly ! born in Sin !
Happy had Dunces never been ;
Or Scandal were confin'd to Tea ;
No Vengeance then had fall'n on me.
 But from its Riſe my Fate I'll trace :
The Author of each dire Diſgrace,
Would ev'n the Queen of Beauty brave,
Bright *Venus* riſing from the Wave.
Vile as the foul-mouth'd, foul-tail'd Trull ;
Or Heart—and Body—rotten Cull !
For know, the Caitiff, fraught with Spight,
With Pen envenom'd prone to write,
Choſe for his Strumpet-Muſe a Theme,
The heav'nly *G—nn—gs* to blaſpheme.
And I was doom'd to bear about,
The blackeſt Rancour he could ſpout.
Hence all the Evils I have bore ;
My preſent Doom to Common Shore ;
And yet leſs wretched ! ſince my End
In Time of Need can you befriend.
 I've made my Story very ample ;
Take Warning by my ſad Example :

I

I die in Charity with Men,
Who for the G—nn—ngs draw the Pen."
    It ceas'd. I snatch'd the trembling Victim,
Had I the Author I'd have kick'd him.
Whom not the Love-creating Smile
Of either G—nn—ngs could beguile;
Not all their Paradise of Charms,
~~The Rancour of his Soul disarms.~~
But I could bear no more delay;
No other Paper in the Way:
~~Had Painter's Works, like Painter, flood,~~
To suffer for another's Good;
Oh! were there left one Birth-Day Ode,
To grace the lower fam'd Abode;
No! I in vain search'd all around,
For not a Scribble could be found.
    'Twas then the flutt'ring Leaf I spread;
The Sisters bid me cut the Thread:
I gave it first the Honours due;
The Goddess' Robe of Saffron Hue:
The Winds a mistic Murmur bear;
" Where more is meant than meets the Ear."
At length, my Finger stretching wide,
It flounders in the sable Tide.
    So *Square* or *Thwackum*, one or t'other,
When *Tom* at *Molly's* made a pother,
While the Nail holds, in high-tied Rug,
Certes, a yellow one, lies snug;
But when that fails, the Pedant-Sot
Falls Headlong in the Chamber P—.

T 3

Bat

But now fair *Cloacina's* Rites
Perform'd, the Grove once more invites:
And fee the G—*nn*—*ngs* fpread their Charms:
Oh! could I clafp them to my Arms!
But, while each Nymph my Soul bewitches,
Ye Mufes, clofe your Poet's **

The gentle Reader may, if he pleafe, add the
Word *Speeches.*

On the Merit of Brevity; being a Fellow to the * Jackboot.

By Mrs. MIDNIGHT.

SI *non ingenium certè* brevitatem *approba;*
   Quæ commendari tanto debet juftiùs,
Quanto poetæ funt molefti validiùs.

PHÆDRUS.

In *Englifh* thus,

If you think that my Works are too puft up with
   Levity,
Yet at leaft Approbation is due to my Brevity,
The Praifes of which fhou'd be now more egre-
   gious,
As our Bards at this Time are confoundedly te-
   dious.

The *Spartans,* who, by the Bye, for *Brevity's*
fake, were ftyl'd the LACEDÆMONIANS, were

* See Numb. 3. Page 116.

very

very eminent for this Virtue ; they are reported to
have fent a full and fatisfactory Anfwer to the *A-
thenians* upon the Wing of a Fly. *Thucydides* and
Salluft have acquired more Reputation by this Excellence, than by all their other Virtues. *Horace*
however, feems to condemn it as the Parent of
Obfcurity.

——— *Brevis effe laboro* ———
Obfcurus fio.   De Arte Poetica.

And now fince Example goes beyond Precept,
I'll give you an Inftance of Brevity A-la-mode a
Paris. ——— Taken from a merry Doctor.

Change Saddles.

For thus it is exprefs'd in *Englifh* Prolixity.

But in *French* Brevity it runs thus: Do thou get off
from thy Horfe, and I will get off from my Horfe ;
and when thou haft got off from thy Horfe, and I have
got off from my Horfe ; then thou fhalt take the
Saddle off from thy Horfe, and fhall take the Saddle
off from my Horfe ; and when thou haft taken the
Saddle off from thy Horfe, and haft taken the
Saddle off from my Horfe ; thou fhalt take that
Saddle which was upon thy Horfe, and fhall put it
upon my Horfe, and fhall take that Saddle which
was upon my Horfe, and fhall put it upon thy
Horfe ; *& cætera, & cætera, & cætera.*

Mrs.

MRS. *Midnight* thinks it extreamly hard, that she who values herself upon her Attachment to the present happy Establishment both in Church and State, should be accused, or even suspected, of doing any Thing which might render her Writings obnoxious to her Friends in Power; and in order to bring the Author of the malicious Paragraph lately inserted in the publick Papers to Justice, she doth hereby promise a Reward of TEN THOUSAND POUNDS, to any Person or Persons who shall discover the Author, or Authors, Perpetrator, or Perpetrators thereof.

Witness my Hand,

St. *James's Place*, July 24, 1751.

MARY MIDNIGHT.

An EPIGRAM.

MY *Polly*'s most divinely Fair,
    Soft, tender, lovely, sweet and young,
How delicate her Shape and Air?
And what Inchantment arms her Tongue!
Her swimming Eye! her swelling Breast!
From her the Graces ne'er are sunder'd,
This Charm too add, which crowns the rest,
She can be constant ———— to a Hundred.

N. B.

N. B. This *Epigram* was wrote by a Phyfician, and with a Defign to affront the Ladies; in return for which Favour, I fhall prefcribe the Doctor a Dofe of his own Phyfick in one of my fubfequent Magazines.

The MIDWIFE's POLITICKS: Or, *Goffip's Chronicle of the Affairs of Europe.*

PORTUGAL *and* SPAIN.

HIS moft faithful Majefty of Portugal, feems to inherit none of that religious Pufillanimity which was inftilled into his Father by the Artifices of Father Gafpard. This Monarch who is now in the 37th Year of his Age, was brought into the World by the Affiftance of one of my intimate Acquaintance, who deliver'd his Mother the Archdutchefs Mary Anne of Auftria of this lovely Prince, Don Jofeph, on the 6th of June 1714, when fhe acquainted his Mother that fhe could difcover, by her Skill in Metopofcopy, that the young Prince would have more of the Auftrian than of the Braganzan Difpofition; which fhe can now have the Happinefs to fay, was a very faithful Prediction. — His Moft Catholic Majefty feems wholly attentive to the Augmentation of his Marine; having iffued Orders for affembling all the Seamen that can be found in the refpective Ports of Spain: Orders are alfo given for reftoring the Regiment of Miquelets which had been reformed, and for completing with the utmoft Diligence, the Troops of his Catholic Majefty: A Thoufand full
grown

grown Trees are ordered to be felled in the Forests of Catalonia; and the Marquis de la Enfenada, who has the Care of the Navy, has found Means to engage into the Spanish Service, an Englishman, of whose Skill in Ship-building several fine Ships built at Carthagena, are valuable Proofs to the Spanish Monarch, who grants him a Piſtole per Diem.

ITALY.

The Italian States are still prejudiced by the Barbary Corfairs, who have lately taken a Maltese Felucca —— Count Chriſtiani, Chancellor of Milan, has happily adjuſted all the Claims for Money expended by his Sardinian Majeſty during the laſt War, for the Troops of the Empreſs Queen; and also regulated whatever Difficulties ſtill remained in regard to their reſpective Frontiers in Lombardy.—M. Chauvelin was to have a Meeting with the Corſican Chiefs on the 25th of July; for which Purpoſe circular Letters were diſpatched to all the Pieves of the Iſland, inviting them to ſend Deputies to a general Aſſembly that was to be held before the End of that Month, for definitively ſetling the Affairs of their Country; and it is reported that a Spaniſh Emiſſary will be there, to concert Meaſures for facilitating an Agreement to yield up that turbulent Iſland. By Advices from Florence we find, that while England is endeavouring to furniſh the Court of Vienna with a King of the Romans, the Dutchy of Tuſcany is going to furniſh the French with Timber for Ships, to diſpute the Superiority of the Main.

FRANCE.

FRANCE.

The Conteſts between the French Court and the Parliament of Paris, kindle upon the leaſt Occaſion: but his Majeſty has ordered the premier Preſident to acquaint the Parliament, that he expreſly forbad them interfering for the future, in any Thing more than examining into the Conduct of the Sub-Directors; deſiring them to make no more Remonſtrances againſt the Regulations for the good Order of the Hoſpitals; for, as well in this Reſpect as in all others, his Majeſty inſiſted upon being obeyed without Reply. *A fine Inſtance of arbitrary Power; therefore, happy Britain, whoſe Monarch rules only by the Law of Juſtice, and in Concurrence of that Parliament which is the pure repreſentative of Liberty!*—The Breſt Squadron, conſiſting of ten Men of War and two Frigates, ſet ſail the 20th of July to the South-Weſt; and it is generally reported to be deſtined for the American Colonies; however, they have left that Diſcovery to be made by a neighbouring Nation as ſoon as they can.

GERMANY.

The ableſt Heads at Vienna, among the Auſtrian and Britiſh Negociators, are clubbing their Wits to bring about a Reconciliation between the Ruſſian and Pruſſian Courts; being ſenſible that the making Pruſſia eaſy, is an Article that muſt precede the bringing the Election of a King of the Romans on the Tapis: and, in Germany, it is ſincerely wiſhed they may ſucceed, not becauſe of any real Intereſt Britain may have in perpetuating the Imperial Dignity in the Auſtrian Family, but becauſe they apprehend ſhe is not now in Circumſtances to go to War about it.

SWEDEN

S W E D E N *and* R U S S I A.

The Hopes of a thorough Reconciliation between the Courts of Peterſburgh and Stockholm continue, and increaſe ſo much, that the Czarina certainly intends to viſit Moſcow and the Ukraine in October next; and the Court of Vienna has interpoſed its good Offices, to bring about an amicable Underſtanding between the Courts of Peterſburgh and Berlin. This Tranquillity is ſo much the more fortunate at Stockholm, as the Attention of the King and Miniſtry can be employed, without Avocations, on the beſt Means for retrieving the Damages of the Fires, and procuring to every one, as far as poſſible, what they may have loſt in the Confuſion. Poor Swedes! while their new Monarch was healing the Wounds given them by the Temerity of Charles XII, how great a Calamity has fallen upon them.

P E R S I A.

The laſt Letters from Conſtantinople make mention of a bloody Battle fought in the Neighbourhood of Iſpahan, between the two Competitors for the Perſian Throne, in which upwards of 30,000 Men were killed on the Spot. They had not as yet any Particulars of this Action, but only knew in general, that Fortune followed the Standard of the Shah, whom the Majority of the Nation had already acknowledged in Quality of Sophi; that his Victory was complete, and that his Rival had been wounded in the Battle, but had nevertheleſs the good Fortune to eſcape with a ſmall Part of his Army. Peace, and Felicity, when are you again to reviſit the Plains of Perſia! Plenty, when art thou again to ſmile in the Vallies watered by the Streams of Araxes! while the Sect of Omar wear the Turban in Tranquillity; the Followers of Hali have their ſilken Mandils ſtrewed over the Soil among an Hecatomb of ſlain: ſuch is the Rapacity of contending Tyrants, ſuch the Devaſtation of inteſtine War!

The MIDWIFE.

NUMBER VI.

VOL. II.

A Letter from the Whispering-Gallery *in St.* Paul's, *to Mrs.* MARY MIDNIGHT.

Madam,

AS I have the Honour to be the Confidante of almost every Individual in this great Metropolis, I imagine my Correspondence may be of some Service to your Magazine ; I therefore promise it you unask'd, and as a Specimen both of my Intelligence and Abilities, I have inclosed a Copy of a Letter, which I beg you'd publish or suppress, according as you approve or dislike it. I assure you Madam, there's not a Day passes over my Head, but I hear something *whisf-*

pered to your Advantage; in Consequence of which, I muft profefs myfelf,

Your Friend, Servant, and Admirer,

The WHISPERING GALLERY.

A genuine Copy of a moſt ſurpriſing Epiſtle ſent by the Whiſpering Gallery *in St.* Paul's, *to a certain* Chocolate-Houſe *at the other End of the Town.*

Calumniari ſiquis autem voluexit,
Quod ARBORES *loquantur, non tantum feræ,*
Ficitis jocari nos meminerit fabulis.

PHÆDRUS.

Thou Place of Infamy!

Didſt thou think, that. I, who am acquainted with all the Proceedings of the two moſt opulent Cities in the World, cou'd be long ignorant of the enormous Pranks to which thou art Witneſs : Didſt thou think, that I, who am privy to the tender Sighs of the wiſhing Maiden, the profound Secrets of the unfathomable Politician, the lamentable Groans of the grutching Mifer, and grievous Grumblings of the difcontented Tradefman, cou'd be a Stranger to thofe CRIMES which are publifhed by the COM- MITTERS, and to that NONSENSE which is pro- pagated by NOISE. There were two worthy Al- dermen *whiſpering* in my Precincts the other Day;

that

that a *little* Society of Men that frequent *Thee*, have made feveral *Bye-Laws* againft Gaming, which is not fo much a Vice itfelf, as it is the Parent of all others.—Notwithftanding which *Bye-Laws* (they ftill perfifted to *whifper*) that the *little* Society aforefaid, did meet on purpofe to break the Statutes they themfelves promulged, and *this* more particularly on *that Day*, when every thing about me in the fober City, is dedicated to the moft facred Purpofes. When fuch Things as thefe are tranfacted in thee, how dareft thou remain upon thy Foundations, why doft thou not fhake at every Oath, or rather, why doft thou not tumble down and crufh the horrible Blafphemers ?

Much more I have to fay to thee, and much more I *will* fay to thee, if I do not fhortly hear it *whifper'd* that thou mendeft thy Manners. Thy Vanity, thy Pride, thy Folly, Ignorance and Gluttony, will afford an ample Field for *Whifperers*, and what they *whifper* I will divulge, for Secrecy, when fhe works for the wicked, revolts from her fair Miftrefs Prudence, and becomes a Vice inftead of a Virtue.

Thine, as thou behaveft,

The WHISPERING GALLERY.

N. B. Mrs. *Midnight* hereby gives Notice, that fhe has now made a League, and eftablifhed a Correfpondence with the *Whifpering Gallery :* So People of all Ranks and Degrees, are particularly ad-

monifh'd

monifh'd to be careful in their Conduct, or they will certainly be detected and expofed.—'Tis high time to do fomething for the Caufe of Virtue, when the very *Stocks* and *Stones* cry out againft us.

To Mrs. SARAH ROWDEN, *Senior Organift of St.* Paul'*s Church,* LONDON.

Madam,

IN the following Account of the Difpute between you and your Brother Muficians, I hope I have done you the Juftice you expected. I have prevailed on my Bookfeller, who is alfo a Genius, to undertake the Infpection of the Work you are about to publifh, and if I can be otherways ferviceable to you, 'twill be a great Satisfaction to,

Madam,
Your Friend and Admirer,
M. MIDNIGHT.

A GENIUS *reftor'd; Or the Matter fet in a clear Light.*

MODESTY has been generally efteemed the true Characteriftic, and conftant Concomitant of Merit. And as the Fraternity of Muficians have been as famous for the one as the other; that is to fay, for *Merit* as for *Modefty,* I am not a little furpriz'd at their Treatment of my Sifter *Sarah Rowden.*

Rowden. As the Difpute between that old Gentlewoman and the other Organifts and Muficians,
has of late ran very high, I fhall lay the Matter
open, that every Body may fee who has the better
of the Argument, and of Confequence where the
moft Merit is center'd.

That Mrs. *Rowden* is a prodigious Genius, her
very Enemies muft and do allow: It will be fufficient therefore if I only fet forth how I became acquainted with that extraordinary Woman, and give
a true Hiftory of the Cafe, without enforcing any
Arguments to the Advantage or Difadvantage of
either Party. Truth is beft when naked——And
here follows the naked Truth.

As I was walking the other Day in one of the
Ifles of St. *Paul*'s Church, I perceiv'd an old Woman in a dark Hole under the Organ Loft, preffing
down feveral large Pieces of Timber, one of which
arofe before the other was well nigh down, fo that
fhe was oblig'd to move backward and forward
with great Celerity, without the leaft Refpite or
Relaxation, and her Labour (if you will make Al-
lowance for preffing down inftead of heaving up)
appear'd to me not unlike that of old *Syfiphus*
mention'd in my Edition of *Ovid*'s *Metamor-
phofes.* Upon my enquiring what fhe was about, fhe
ftarted with Surprize, that I fhou'd afk fuch a Queftion. *Don't you hear,* fays fhe, *that I am playing
the Organ; this is the* 104*th Pfalm, and by and by
I fhall play you one of Dr.* Boyce's *Anthems. Ay,*

U 3   fays

says another good Woman that stood by ; *'Tis very
true, Dr.* Green *is the reputed Organist, and re-
ceives the Salary, but* Goody Rowden *plays the
Organ for Forty Shillings a Year.* Here I began to
reflect on the ill Treatment the Aged of our Sex
meet with, and the Difficulties we labour under.
We are undoubtedly the wisest of all the human Species, and so essential in Life, that you see a Boy
can't well be born, or an Organ play'd, without
our Aid ; and yet we are despised and contemn'd
by those who are our Inferiors and Dependants.—
But to return to my Subject—I was determin'd to
go, as we say in my Country, to the Bottom of
this Affair ; and seeing a Gentleman come out of
the Organ-Loft, that I knew, ask'd him who had
play'd the Organ: *Madam,* says he, *I play'd it
myself, and I hope I had the Honour to please you.*
As this was confirm'd by two of the Vergers, who
stood by, I was still more embarrassed ; and returning to *Goody Rowden,* told her I had been informed that Mr. *** had play'd the Service. *Ay,* says
she, *The Clapper rings the Bell, but who pulls the
Rope ? 'Tis here as in a Puppet Show ; you apprehend that Punch speaks, but 'tis we behind the Cur-
tain that move his wooden Limbs, and articulate the
Sounds. In short we do the Business, and they gain
the Applause.*—Nor is this to be wonder'd at, for
all the World seems to detract from the Merit of us
old Women ; and my Printer had the Assurance
t'other Day, to tell me, that the extraordinary

Sale

Sale of my Magazine, was entirely owing to his Manner of printing it.

As I have taken on me the Guardianſhip and Defence of my Sex, I thought it my Duty to vindicate this poor Woman; accordingly I ſummon'd all the great muſical Maſters to attend. The Conteſt lay between Mr. *Handel* and Mrs. *Rowden*; and juſt as he was playing his Coronation Anthem, and for the Sake of Pre-eminence, jiging his Fingers upon the Keys, a total Suſpenſion of all Sound enſued; upon which the old Woman peeps out of her Hole, *Where are ye now? Out*, ſays the Artiſt above. *Out, ay*, ſays ſhe, *you can't play your own Muſic without my Aſſiſtance.* Upon this a Truce was drawn, and under my Mediation it was agreed, that the Reputation acquired, or to be acquired, by the free Uſe and Exerciſe of that Organ, ſhould be divided into two equal Parts; one whereof to be given in the firſt Place to *Goody Rowden*, as the Senior Performer on the Bellows, and the remaining Part to the other Organiſt, who ſhou'd jig the Jacks above Stairs.

It gives me a two-fold Satisfaction, that I have been abled to get this Affair ſettled upon ſo amicable a Footing; in the firſt Place becauſe it is doing Juſtice to Genius, and aſſigning to my old Friend *Goody Rowden* her Right; and ſecondly, becauſe it will be a Means of preventing Diſputes of this Nature for the future; and keep my Brother Organiſts in proper Order.

I re-

I remember an Affair of this Sort once at *Windfor*: A particular Friend of mine was playing on that Organ one of Dr. *Blow*'s Anthems, and juft as he had finifh'd the Verfe Part and begun the full Chorus the Organ ceas'd; upon which he call'd to *Dick Hoar*, the Organift beneath, to know what was the Matter, *The Matter*, fays Dick, *I have play'd the Anthem below : Ay*, fays the other, *but I have not play'd it above. No Matter*, quoth Dick, *you might have made more Hafte then, I know how many Puffs go to one of* Dr. Blow*'s Anthems as well as you do; I have not play'd the Organ fo many Years for nothing.*

But as all Difputes of this Sort are now entirely fettled, and accommodated to the Satisfaction of both Parties; I have only to inform my Readers, that *Goody Rowden* the Organift, is a very induftrious Woman, tho' very poor, and to defire all Gentlemen and Ladies to call at her Office under the Organ Loft, and leave fomething towards her Subfiftence before they go into the Choir, which will greatly oblige their

Moft obedient humble Servant,

M. Midnight.

The

The Queſtion, " Whether 'tis beſt to oil a Man's Wig with Honey or Muſtard," *being propoſed to the moſt numerous Aſſembly that ever met at the* ROBIN-HOOD,

The celebrated Mr. WHIPPER SNAPPER *ſtood up, and ſpoke in Subſtance as follows.*

Mr. PRESIDENT,

AS the Queſtion propoſed is of the utmoſt Dignity, and the laſt Importance, I hope I ſhall be favour'd with a patient, candid, and judicious Audience. — Hope? do I ſay? I am perſuaded I ſhall be ſo, and therefore ſhall proceed upon the Debate modeſtly, moderately, and methodically. In order, Gentlemen, to form any tolerable Judgment of the Affair in Hand, it will be highly requiſite to conſider the Nature, Genius, and Extent of the four cardinal Virtues; that is, JUSTICE, PRUDENCE, TEMPERANCE, and FORTITUDE: I don't know, Gentlemen, whether I arrange theſe Virtues in their proper Order, but that is neither here nor there, neither on one Side nor t'other. — *Magna eſt veritas & prævalebit.* And now let us examine what Juſtice has to ſay, — Why Juſtice ſays, before you precipitately give your Opinion, you ought to conſider the Conſtitution and Conſequence of a Wig. — Well then, what is a Wig? — Why, what do you think it is?

Well

Well I'll tell you what it is. — I define a Wig to
be a certain Quantity of Hair, artificially combined and connected together by a Mechanic, who
in the vulgar Tongue is ſtyled, call'd, and deno-
minated a Barber. Now every Man that wears a
Wig, is under a triple Obligation, or (if I may
be allow'd the Expreſſion) under an Indenture
tripartite, between himſelf in the firſt Place, the
Barber in the ſecond, and the Wig in the third : He
is in Fact obliged to do Juſtice to all three Parties.
— If it therefore can be proved, that oiling with
Muſtard is more for the Credit of the Barber,
the Dignity of the Wearer, and the Ornament
and Preſervation of that inanimate Piece of Hair,
which is entitled and call'd a Wig ; I ſay, Gentlemen, that we are obliged Gentlemen, in *Juſtice*,
Gentlemen, to prefer Muſtard to Honey, or any
other unctious Subſtance whatſoever. — And now
let us weigh this momentous Affair in the Scales
of *Prudence*, which is another cardinal Virtue, —
What then ſays Prudence ? Why, what do you
think ſhe ſays ? Well I'll tell you what ſhe ſays.
She ſays that if it be cheaper (as undoubtedly it is)
to oil your Wig with Muſtard, why in point of
Oeconomy you are to diſcard Honey, and uſe the
leſs expenſive Lotion. —— And what ſays *Temperance ?* Why ſhe ſpeaks according to Cuſtom,
with great Coolneſs and Candour, and begs Leave
to ſtand Neuter, being equally averſe to all Honey or all Muſtard. — And now for *Fortitude*,
and what ſays Fortitude ? Why Fortitude ſwears
ſhe'll

fhe'll fight of our Side, if fhe lofes her Commif-
fion for it. Forbid it *Cæfar*, forbid it *Marlbro*,
forbid it *Eugene*, forbid it ***d*, and you, ye illuftrious Shades of *Shovell* and *Gorgon*, that Honey,
the Delight of pufillanimous Milk-fops, and the
Compofition of paltry Infects, fhou'd be prefer'd to
Muftard; that draws Tears from the Eyes of Barbarians, that bites the Tongues of the Eloquent,
and braces the Nerves of the Magnanimous. ——
And now wou'd I add (but I fee the * uplifted
Hammer) much more to as much Purpofe, but I
fhall conclude Mr. *Prefident*, by humbly prefum-
ing, Mr. *Prefident*, that what I have faid, Mr.
Prefident, is fufficient Mr. *Prefident*; and pray
Mr. *Jenkinfon* be fo good as to pufh the Porter a
little this Way.

This was anfwer'd by Mr. WILLIAM HONYCOMB,
in the following Manner.

Mr. PRESIDENT,

I MUST for once ftart out of my Turn, and
I hope all the Gentlemen will excufe me, to
anfwer the Gentleman that fpoke laft, for no Man
that has any common Senfe, and common Honefty, and common Truth, and common Juftice,

---

* We are allow'd in our Society to fpeak five Minutes and no more, which Time is determined by a
Watch, Mr. *Prefident* and a Hammer.

can any longer fit ftill and ftand to hear fuch Stuff. For a Man for to come, for to go, for to fay, that Muftard is better to oil a Man's Wig than Honey, is monftrous, and ftupid, and ridiculous, and abfurd, and filly. Am I warm? I am,—the Caufe deferves it. That Honey is better both for the Hair, for the Wig, for the Wearer of the Wig, and for the Nation and Conftitution in general, every Gentleman here does believe, and no Man that is not a Friend to the Pope and to the Pretender, and an Enemy to the true Intereft of Wigs in general, wou'd attempt to prove the contrary. Mr. *Prefident*, this Queftion, Mr. *Prefident*, is of more Confequence, Mr. *Prefident*, than is generally fuppofed and believed, Mr. *Prefident*. As to my Part, I can without any Pretence to Prophecy, fee Popery, Jacobitifm and Toryifm lurking at the Bottom of it; and I hope every Gentleman here will exert himfelf in Favour of his King and Country, and the Church and the State. This Queftion, Gentlemen, is of the utmoft Importance to us, and not to us only but to our Pofterity; ay to our Pofterity both prefent, paft and to come; and were we to give into it what wou'd be the Confequence? or rather what wou'd not be the Confequence?—What wou'd our paft Pofterity fay to us? Why I'll tell you what they wou'd fay; they wou'd never forgive us; our prefent Pofterity wou'd be fill'd with Indignation, and our future Pofterity wou'd be out of all Manner of Patience.

Befides

Befides, Gentlemen, a Practice of this Sort wou'd be of the utmoft ill Confequence to our Politicks. *Plato*, that great Politician, always prefcribed Honey to oil Wigs, and why did he do it? Why I will tell you why: He knew that the Bees had in themfelves a Commonwealth, a State that was managed with Prudence, and without Bribery and Corruption, and he wifely forefaw that by oiling his Pupils Wigs with Honey, the political Effluvia thereof wou'd afcend to their Heads, and ftrengthen and corroborate their Pofteriors. And pray what has been done, or rather what has not been done by thofe who have oil'd their Wigs in this Manner? Every Beau about Town at this Time, if I am rightly inform'd, oils his Wig with Honey, and all of them that are arrived to Manhood, oil their Beards with it alfo. Hence the Honey gets into the Lips, hence fweet Kiffing; — hence the Honey gets into the Tongue, hence fine fpeaking; ay and fweet Smelling; and I can venture to fay, that all the Ladies of Fortune who have been married to Gallants without a Penny in Poffeffion, or even in Expectation, have been obtain'd and procured by this Means: That is to fay, by the invincible Power of the Honey which oil'd their Wigs. And none but a *Durham* Man cou'd, contrary to all Honour and Confcience, have had the Face to have faid fo much in Favour of Muftard.

X   Mr.

Mr. CHARLES CHATTER-MUCH *then arofe, and defired the Queftion might be read, and finding it to ftand thus,* viz.

" *Whether Honey or Muftard was beft to oil a Man's Wig,*" *be proceeded in the following Manner.*

MR. PRESIDENT, and you Gentlemen of the Club, here is a Queftion propofed to us of a very extraordinary, a very uncommon, and a very fingular Nature. I'll tell you what it is, Gentlemen: It is whether Honey or Muftard be beft to oil a Man's Wig; one Gentleman has already fpoken very learnedly in Favour of Muftard, and another has deliver'd himfelf very lycoantriptically in Behalf of Honey, and fo which is in the Right of it, he that fpoke for Honey, or he that fpoke for Muftard, I leave you to confider; and if Honey be beft, you'll vote for Muftard, and if Muftard be beft, you'll vote for Honey. I can't help obferving likewife, that it wou'd be better to add a little Milk to the Honey, and fo Mr. *Prefident* my Service to you.

N. B. There were in all forty-five Speeches made on this Subject, but thefe three I have inferted are the moft confiderable.

A LET-

A LETTER *from a Surgeon of great Practice and Experience.*

Mrs. MIDNIGHT,

" IF you look into the Daily Papers of *Wed-*
" *nefday* the 28th of *Auguft* laft, you will find
" the following Paragraphs which are worthy your
" Perufal, *viz.*

On *Monday* Might there was the greateft Concourfe of People of both Sexes (or rather Mob) at
Bartholomew Fair, ever known to any Inhabitant
in that Place, which occafion'd great Riots and
Diforders : The rude and infolent Mob began firft
with kicking down the Saufage and Fritter-Fry
Stalls ; they afterwards proceeded to greater Extremities, by throwing of Stones, Dirt, &c. by
which they wounded a great Number of Perfons,
which occafioned a general Confufion, in which
the Pick-pockets had no fmall Share : Three were
carried to the Hofpital, having their Legs broke,
and very much bruifed. —— Such are the Confequences of publick Fairs in and near fo populous
a City as *London*, efpecially where the common
People are fo audacious, infolent and ungovernable.
— And laft Night the Fair ended, to the general
Satisfaction of all who wifh well to the Peace,
Order, Sobriety and Induftry of this City.

Monday Night about Five o'Clock, as a Toll-
Man in *Smithfield* was endeavouring to ftop a
Hackney-Coachman, with a Box in the Boot for

Toll, and he refuſing to pay, the Toll-Gatherer fell down, and the Wheel of the Coach unfortunately went over his Thigh and broke it to Pieces: He likewiſe had his Arm broke. He was immediately carried to St. *Bartholomew*'s Hoſpital, when the Surgeon ſet his Arm, but yeſterday Morning his Leg and Thigh were oblig'd to be cut off.

The ſame Day an ancient Man was run over by a Coach at the End of *Long-Lane*, *Weſt-Smithfield*; whereby one of his Legs was broke, and his Skull fractured. He was carried to St. *Bartholomew*'s Hoſpital.

" From hence you will perceive, Madam, how
" our Buſineſs daily encreaſes, thro' the wiſe and
" good Government of this great and opulent City.
" If one Fair, and that in ſo large a Space, pro-
" duces ſuch Emolument to the Craft, what Ad-
" vantages might we not expect from many of
" them, and eſpecially if they were held in Places
" more cloſely circumſcrib'd? For as our Mob
" have now gain'd the Point of becoming maſter-
" leſs, great Havock wou'd be made on every ſlight
" Occaſion, and a Surgeon might then hope to live
" without the Aid of the *Lues Venerea*. You are
" therefore deſired, dear Mrs. *Midnight*, to make
" uſe of your Intereſt (which we know is great)
" to procure a monthly Puppet-Show Fair to be
" erected at the *Royal-Exchange*, which would
" anſwer all our Purpoſes. I know there are thoſe
" who will object to it, and ſay it wou'd interrupt
" our Trade—— But what have we to do with
                                                    " Trade?

" Trade? Only let the *French* have our Wool, our
" Factories, our Plantations, our Shipping, and
" they will do the Bufinefs for us, and fave us the
" Fatigue. Let them know that Mrs. *Midnight,*
" and tell them I had it from very good Hands, for
" the Offer was made to me by the Manufacturers
" of *Abbe Ville.* In fhort, Trade is a troublefome
" Thing, and as we can now get rid of it, and
" have People to do the Bufinefs for us, I don't fee
" why we fhou'd not lay hold of the golden Oppor-
" tunity.

I am, Madam,

Your moft humble Servant,

New Surgeons-Hall, Old-
Baily, *Aug.* 28, 1751.　　V A L E N T I N E   V E R T E B R A.

Mrs. MIDNIGHT'S *Reflections on the above Letter.*

This Subject is too ferious to be laugh'd at, and
yet no other Method will be found effectual to this
abandoned Race ; among whom the *Satyrift* will
always do more good than the *Sage.* How much
muft Foreigners admire our Prudence and Policy,
our Wifdom and Œconomy, that for the Sake of
one Man's Emolument, will permit a Fair, or rather a Riot to be kept in fo large a City, and let
loofe a turbulent headlefs Mob, to facrifice annually the Lives of many innocent People ? I might
here take Notice alfo of the Diftrefs this muft bring
to many fmall Families, who, perhaps are ftarving
at Home, while their Parents are fquandering away
their little Subftance Abroad.—The Lofs too which

X 3

Trade

Trade muft fuftain, wou'd deferve our Confideration; but Trade, fays my Letter Writer, is become a troublefome Thing! Aye, and fo is Religion too in this refined Age, I doubt not, and on that Account is fo little regarded. But mark this ye wife Ones—when Trade declines, Riches will take their Flight; when Religion dies, Morality will make it's Exit, and Government fink into the Grave. Peace and Plenty, Virtue and Induftry, will drop down together; Regularity will give Place to Confufion, and Tyranny feize the Seat of Juftice.

An EPIGRAM *by Sir* Thomas More.

De Tyndaro.

NON minimo infignem nafo dum forte puellam
   Bafiat, en ! voluit Tyndarus effe dicax.
Fruftra, ait, ergo tuis mea profero labra labellis,
   Noftra procul nafus diftinet ora tuus.
Protinus erubuit, tacitaq; excanduit irâ,
   Nempe parum falfo tacta puella fale.
Nafus ab ore meus tua fi tenet ofcula, dixit,
   Quà nafus non eft, hâc dare parte potes.——

Imitated by Mafter Chriftopher Midnight, *my Great Grandfon.*

The Long-Nose'd F A I R.

ONCE on a time I fair *Dorinda* kifs'd,
Whofe *Nofe* was too diftinguifh'd to be mifs'd :
                    My

My Dear, fays I, I fain wou'd kifs you clofer,
But tho' your Lips fay *Aye*—your Nofe fays *No,*
   Sir—
The Maid was equally to Fun inclin'd,
And plac'd her lovely Lilly-Hand BEHIND :
Here, Swain, fhe cry'd, may'ft thou fecurely kifs ;
Where there's no Nofe to interrupt thy Blifs.

A DISSERTATION *on* Apparitions, Ghofts,
Spirits, &c. &c. *By* MARY MIDNIGHT.

AS many able Men have employ'd their learned
Pens on this Subject, and talked as elaborate-
ly on *Non-Entities,* as if they had really a *Subftance*
under their Confideration ; one would imagine that
the World might have been fatisfied in this Particular, without peftering me with their idle Interroga-
tions. But fuch is my Reputation among the *Lit-*
terati ; fo much I am efteemed by the Members of
every Faculty ; and fuch Deference is paid to my
Judgment by all Nations, all People, all Languages,
and all Religions ; that no Determination but mine
can be decifive.—Pray read the following Tranflation of a Copy of a Letter from *Paris.*

   Madam,
   " Whether SPIRITS, or APPARITIONS can
" be *feen, felt, heard,* or *underftood,* has been a
" Matter of Difpute between the learned Doctors
" of the *Sorbonne,* and fome Members of the Royal
                " Academy

" Academy of Sciences, and of the Belles-Lettres;
" who being unable themfelves to fettle a Matter
" of fuch mighty Moment, moft humbly crave
" your Determination, which they all agree fhall
" be abfolute and final. We congratulate you on
" the great Succefs of your learned Labours, and
" I have the Honour to fubfcribe myfelf, moft
" magnanimous Madam,

Your moft Oordient, moft Obfequious,

Votre tres humble Serviteur.

DE TRELEVOUS.

P. S. " Our Grand Monarch would be oblig'd
" to you for your Company and Counfel. Your
" Acquaintance the Cardinal *de Fleury* is dead;
" your Coufin, the Cardinal *Tencin,* is about to die
" by and by, and another good Old Woman's Opi-
" nion will be wanted. Our Grand King's politi-
" cal Scheme is the *Univerfal*; and if you by your
" Art and Skill in Negociation, will make him the
" *Univerfal Grand Monarch,* you will be the Uni-
" verfal Grand Madame."

From hence it is plain, that the *French* want to
poffefs themfelves of our Wit and Learning, as well
as of our Trade and Money; but I hope I fhall have
more Grace than to go over to them, or affift them
in any thing that may be prejudicial to my King
and my Country. As neither can be affected however by my folving this Queftion refpecting *Appa-*
ritions,

ritions, I fhall in point of good Manners anfwer that Part of the Letter.

A Monfieur a Monfieur DE TRELEVOUS à *Paris.*

`Monfieur,`

BY the manner of ftating your Queftion, *Whe-ther a Spirit or Apparition, can be feen, felt, heard, or underftood?* I apprehend, you want to know, whether an Apparition be a Noun-Subftantive, or in other Words, whether it can ftand by itfelf? Which is a Queftion not very eafily anfwered, at leaft it is not very prudent for me to anfwer it. As moft Men judge and determine in Matters of this Sort, not from Evidence and Conviction, but in Imitation of the Learned; People of great Abilities fhould be very circumfpect and cautious, as well in thei Writings as Examples. Was I to anfwer in t' _ Affirmative, and give Countenance to this Doc.. ine of Apparitions, my Authority would be quoted as a Sanction for the moft flagrant Abfurdities: Every Church-yard, Grove, and fhady Place wou'd be filled with Goblins and Spectres, and all the antiquated, and once hofpitable, Seats in the Country abandoned.——On the other Hand, fhou'd I anfwer this Queftion in the Negative, in this fceptical Age, in which Infidelity fo much abounds, Atheifts and Deifts would apply it to their wicked Purpofes, and my Authority wou'd be wrefted as a fort of Argument for Doctrines and Opinions, that have not the leaft Foundation in the

Nature

Nature and Fitness of Things. That the Almighty
has permitted and made use of such supernatural
Means to answer the wise Purposes of his Providence, I make no doubt: We have all the Evidence
for it that the *Nature of the Thing* requires, or that
Beings in our State can expect; namely, *The concurrent Testimony of the inspired and profane Writers*; and any Person who from the Testimony of
profane Historians, will believe there were such Men
existed as *Alexander the Great, Julius Cæsar, Henry
the Fifth*, or *William the Conqueror*, may, I think,
from the Evidence before-mention'd, very well believe, that there has been such Phœnomena permitted as Apparitions. But because Providence,
for certain wise Purposes, beyond the Reach of our
shallow Comprehension, has suffer'd four Instances
of this Kind, in the space of Six-thousand Years;
are we to conclude that every idle Tale we hear of
this Sort, is any thing more than the effect of a crude
Imagination, or a distemper'd Brain? No—It happens in this Case as in most others: Artful, crafty,
and designing Men taking Notice of the Terrors
these Notions have produced in the ignorant and
superstitious part of Mankind, have propagated the
general Belief thereof, and applied it to their
own particular Occasions, as will appear from the
following Story, publish'd by the CHEVALIER de
MAINVILLERS, in his Travels and Adventures.

" The illustrious House of *Hohenloe* has many
" Branches, each of which are Sovereigns in their
" own

" own Eftates. A young Count of that Family,
" being fent by his Father to *Paris*, with a View
" of giving him an Opportunity of improving his
" Manners by obtaining the Polifh of *France*, ar-
" rived there with a Number of Domefticks. He
" had a Bill of Credit for ten thoufand Crowns
" drawn on a Banker, who had enrich'd himfelf in
" the Service of that Houfe, probably in the Poft
" of a Steward. This complaifant and refpectful
" Perfon being informed by Letter of the Arrival
" of the Son of his old Mafter, waited with Impa-
" tience to give him an Apartment in his own
" Houfe, which was a very magnificent Edifice.
" But the young Count, knowing that he was old,
" and from thence judging that his Difpofition
" could not be very agreeable to one of his Age,
" did not think proper to alight at the Banker's ;
" but took a furnifh'd Apartment, as a Place in
" which without minding any Body, he might
" freely enjoy his Liberty in the moft agreeable
" Manner. A young Officer of a noble Family
" had alfo taken Lodgings in the fame Houfe ; but
" his ordinary Refidence was in any Part of the
" Town where he knew there were pretty Girls.
" He was brifk, fprightly, and had an inexhauftible
" Source of Humour, and in one Word, filled up
" with great Dignity the Station of a Mufqueteer.
" He foon took Notice of our *German* Count, and
" remarking he had ftill the Ruft of his ancient
" *Teutonic* Caftle, he refolved to give him fome
" Leffons of Debauchery.

" The

" The young *Hohenloe* on becoming the Muf-
" queteer's Pupil, made a rapid Progrefs in a little
" Time. What an edifying School! The Muf-
" queteer initiated him into the Myfteries of what
" he called true Science, by teaching him the Man-
" ner of anfwering to fome Purpofe the Calls of
" indulgent Nature. Mufick, Shews, Plays, ex-
" cellent Wine, handfome Women, could not fail
" of rendering thefe Calls more frequent and more
" agreeable to Perfons of fuch exalted Intellects.
" The young Count, who admired the Mufqueteer
" as one of the greateft Men that had ever appeared
" upon Earth, (for the *Germans* are in Love with
" thofe of an exalted Genius :) the young Count,
" I fay, who advanced in the Courfe which his
" Mafter had fet before him with the Strides of a
" Giant, had no other than the fame Taftes and
" the fame Inclinations. The Preceptor, af-
" ter a ferious Application on the Thefes of what
" is effentially beautiful, invented a Coat in a new
" Tafte, and the Difciple had like to have thrown
" his Taylor out of the Window, becaufe he
" brought home one which was not exactly like that
" of his illuftrious Pedagogue. The Mufqueteer
" had a Miftrefs of about nineteen Years old,
" brown, of a fmall Stature, brifk and lively. The
" *German* preparing himfelf to love with all his
" Might, fearch'd the Middle and all the four
" Corners of *Paris*, to obtain a Miftrefs who per-
" fectly refembled her ; but not being able to find
" one,

" one, his Regard for his Mafter encreafed to fuch
" a Degree, as render'd them infeparable. But
" alas! it became neceffary for them to part; he
" died, and the Mufqueteer had not the leaft In-
" clination to follow him.

" The Count *Hohenloe* on his Death-bed, gave
" the Mufqueteer his Letter-cafe, and the Keys of
" his Chefts to deliver them to his Banker, whom
" the Infatuation of his Pleafures had prevented
" him from feeing. He had made no Ufe of his
" Bills of Credit, as Death had not given him Time
" to fpend the ready Money he had brought with
" him. The poor young Man having given his
" laft Sigh, the Mufqueteer made the neceffary
" Preparations for his Funeral. While Things
" were in this Situation, there arrived two *Englifh*
" Noblemen at the fame Houfe. They were pla-
" ced in a Chamber adjoining to that in which the
" dead Body was laid, and out of which it had been
" removed. They could only allow one Bed for
" them both, all the others being engaged; but as
" the Weather was cold, and they were Friends,
" they made no Difficulty of lying together.

" In the middle of the Night, one of the two
" not being able to fleep, and growing weary of
" his Bed, arofe in order to amufe himfelf in the
" Kitchen, where he heard fome People talking.
" He had diverted himfelf there for fome Time,
" when being willing to return from whence he
" came, he again went up Stairs, but inftead of
" entering his own Chamber, went into that of the

Y

" de-

" deceafed Count, over whofe Face they had only
" thrown a Cloth.   There is not fo much Cere-
" mony ufed in *France* in the Management of
" their Dead as in *England* and *Germany*; for
" they are there fatisfied with fhewing their Af-
" fection to the Living.   The *Englifh* Noble-
" man having put out his Candle, laid down
" boldly by the Defunct: When creeping as clofe
" to him as poffible, in order to warm himfelf,
" and finding his Bedfellow colder than he, he
" began to mutter, What the Devil's the Matter,
" my Friend, faid he, you are as cold as Ice?
" I'll lay a Wager, numb'd as you are, you
" would have been warm enough if you had but
" feen the pretty Girl that is below Stairs. Come,
" you may take my Word for it, added he, pull-
" ing him by the Arm; come, Zounds ftir, I'll
" engage you fhall have her for a Guinea. While
" he was holding this fine Converfation with the
" Dead, who, detached from the Things of this
" World, did not even give himfelf the Trouble
" of making him a Reply; his Chamber Door
" was opened, which made him raife his Head
" from the Pillow to fee who was coming in.
" But judge what muft be his Surprife, when he
" faw a Servant lighting in a Joiner, who car-
" ried a Coffin on his Shoulders ! He thought at
" firft that he had been in a Dream; but look-
" ing about him, and feeing the Vifage of one
" who had not fpoke a Word, a Vifage over-
" fpread with a mortal Palenefs, he made but one
" Jump from the Bed into the middle of the
                                        " Cham-

" Chamber. The Joiner and the Maid were
" immediately perſuaded that it was the Corpſe,
" who being unwilling to be ſhut up in the Cof-
" fin, was now playing its Gambols. Their Legs
" were unable to move with a Swiftneſs pro-
" portionable to their Fear; and the Joiner,
" Maid, Coffin, and Candleſtick, roll'd one
" over another, from the Top of the Stairs down
" into the Kitchen. Zoons, What are you all
" about? cried the Landlord: What is the De-
" vil flying away with the dead Man? Mercy on
" us! cry'd the Maid, quite Chap-fallen, it is
" rather the dead Man that would run away with
" us. I am the Son of a Bitch, ſaid the Joiner,
" if that dead Man there, has any more Occa-
" ſion for a Coffin than I have; why he is got
" into the middle of the Room, and has juſt
" ſtruck up a Hornpipe. The Devil he has! cry'd
" the Landlord, taking a Light, faith we'll ſoon
" ſee that.

" While all the Family were trembling and get-
" ting ready to follow the Maſter of the Houſe,
" the *Engliſh* Nobleman, who had found again
" his Chamber, had ſlipt into Bed, quite out of
" Breath: And his Friend having aſk'd him
" where he had been, he told him that he had
" juſt been lying with a dead Body. 'Sblood! a
" dead Body! it had perhaps the Plague, cried
" he, jumping in his Turn out of Bed, and run-
" ning to the Door to call for a Light. The

" Land-

" Landlord, the Lady, and Servants, who were
" paffing thro' the Gallery, no fooner faw him,
" than they imagined that it was the Dead who ap-
" peared again. What Confufion! What Shrieks!
" What Clamours! The *Englifhman* terrified at
" the hideous Noife, run into his Room and flip'd
" into Bed to his Companion, without the leaft
" Fear of catching the Plague. In the mean
" Time an honeft Country Prieft, who lodged in
" the Inn, got up, and appeared armed with
" Holy Water, and a long Broom inftead of a
" little Brufh. He made his Afperfions, and the
" Conjurations prefcribed by the *Romifh* Church,
" and conducted, by Way of Proceffion, the
" terrified trembling People into the Chamber of
" the Defunct, who, thinking no Harm, lay
" quietly in Bed. The Prieft was inftantly re-
" garded as a Saint, who had bound the Corpfe
" to its good Behaviour, and prevented its being
" refractory.

" The Mufqueteer arrived at the Time appoint-
" ed for the Funeral. Twenty Voices at a Time
" related to him the dead Man's Behaviour in the
" Night. And he was of too humorous a Difpo-
" fition not to ftrengthen ftill more the frightful
" Ideas they had imbibed.

" The Funeral being performed, and the Prieft,
" Sexton, Servants, and Landlord paid, the Muf-
" queteer went two Days after to pay a Vifit to
" the Banker. He fent in Word that he came
                                        " by

" by Defire of the Count *de Hobenloe*, as it was
" natural he fhould, to deliver up his Effects;
" but the good Man underftood that this was that
" young Lord himfelf. He had been extremely
" impatient to fee him, and we may eafily imagine
" with what tender Eagernefs he ran to the Per-
" fon he took for him, as well as the Aftonifh-
" ment of the Mufqueteer, to find himfelf ftifled
" in the Arms of the old Man, whom he fufpected
" of being arrived at his Years of Dotage. What
" a ftrange Incident! He at laft difcovered the
" Banker was under a Miftake, and had taken
" him for the Count: On which he refolved to
" perfonate him, and to form his Behaviour on the
" Error of the People of the Inn, as to his Re-
" turn from the other World. Quick, cried the
" Banker, a Seat for my Lord the Count. Adfbud!
" how old you make me, added he; when I left
" my Lord your Father's Court, you was but
" juft fo high. Pray, dear my Lord, fit in that eafy
" Chair. It is no Matter, faid the Mufqueteer,
" for I muft return back into the other World.
" What do you mean? faid the good Man, have
" you a Mind to joke with me? My Dear, have
" you given Orders for their bringing a Bottle of
" Champaign, for us to be drinking while we
" wait for Supper? Sir, faid the Mufqueteer, in-
" terrupting him in a dejected Air, the Dead
" don't drink, and I have drank fo much while
" I was alive, that I am to fuffer the Penance of
" not drinking now I am dead! Odfheart! cried
Y 3   " the

" the good Man, I fee very well that my Lord
" the Count is a Wag, for he has a Mind to
" perfuade me that he is dead, and then to rally
" me for believing it. Come, come, continued
" he, let me fhew you the Appartment I have
" prepared for you. Alas! Sir, replied the pre-
" tended Count, I have one in St. *Euftache*'s
" Churchyard, where I am buried. But really
" now, faid the Banker, What is the Meaning
" of all this? Pray put an End to this difagreeable
" Rallery, and tafte the Wine. Upon my Con-
" fcience I cannot, replied the falfe *Hohenloe*, the
" Dead, as I have told you, have loft all Relifh
" for' it.

" The Banker's Wife, who had laid by her
" Work, and thro' her Spectacles was examining
" with Fear and Trembling the pretended Spirit,
" faid in a low Voice, I have heard a great deal about
" Apparitions, if this fhould be one! My Dear,
" I know better, replied the old Man, with a
" good deal of Confufion. Yes, Sir, refumed
" the Mufqueteer, I died in the City of *Rouen*,
" at a Houfe near the New Bridge, and am bu-
" ried in St. *Euftache*'s Churchyard. If you de-
" fire a fuller Proof of it, here is my Letter-Cafe,
" which I have brought with me, with a Bill of
" Credit for ten thoufand Crowns. Here is alfo
" a Purfe, in which there are thirty Louis d'Ors.
" You muft be fenfible that a young Man, if he
" was not dead, would not tender you this Mo-
" ney, fince that is a Thing he can never hav

" to

" too much of: But at prefent, inftead of Mo-
" ney, Wine and Women, (who are very hand-
" fome at *Paris*) I have occafion for nothing but
" Prayers.

" At thefe Words the pretended Deceafed made
" his Efcape from the Banker, who almoft refolv-
" ed to run after him, and was left in very great
" Aftonifhment at fuch a Vifit. As to the Wife,
" fhe was extremely terrified, fhe maintained that
" they had been talking with a Spirit, and con-
" firmed this Opinion by afferting, that when he
" went out, he had Eyes of Fire. The Banker,
" on his Side, infifted upon it that his Wife was
" a Fool; and that by fome Accident or other,
" unknown to him, the Count had loft his Senfes:
" And therefore to fatisfy himfelf in this Point,
" went to get better Information at the City of
" *Rouen.*

" As foon as he arrived at the Place, he afked the
" Miftrefs of the Houfe to tell him where he might
" fee the Count *de Hohenloe.* Alas! replied fhe, in a
" doleful Tone, he is dead, and is buried at St. *Eu-*
" *ftache.* At the Word *Euftache,* the Banker ftarted,
" and continued fhrunk all of a Heap; but at laft
" recovering himfelf, he followed the good Woman
" into the Chamber where the Deceafed had been
" laid, when the firft Thing that ftruck his Sight,
" was a Coat like that in which the Mufqueteer
" had appear'd at his Houfe, and which the young
" Count had ordered to be made in Imitation of
" it. There needed no more to convince the
　　　　　　　　　　　　　　　　　　　" Ban-

" Banker that the Count was really dead. Bless
" me! Madam, said he to the Landlady, look!
" see! there's the Coat he had on when he came
" to bring me this Letter-Case and these Keys.
" O Lord ha'Mercy! cry'd she, joining her
" Hands, he walks still then. The poor young
" Man suffers sorely, ay, and I'll warrant has
" great Need of Prayers. It is these cursed Ladies
" of *Paris* that have thrust him into Purgatory.
" Explain yourself, Madam, said the old Man,
" Did he appear in your House as well as in mine?
" Appear! ay marry did he, replied the Ho-
" stess; why we really thought that the Evening
" before he was buried, he would have turned
" the House upside down, and that we should ne-
" ver be able to get him into his Grave.

" The Banker no sooner returned home, than
" sinking into an armed Chair, he continued look-
" ing wildly at his Wife. She was terrified, and
" did not cease importuning him with her Que-
" stions. At last he cried out, There is nothing
" more true than that he is dead, and walks about
" every where. I have seen the Coat he had on
" when he came here. Oh! Oh! cried the
" Banker's Wife, seeking for her Gloves and her
" Muff, no longer will I stay in this House. I!
" I stay in a House that is haunted by dead Ghosts!
" No, Sir, don't think any such Matter: These
" are the Visits that your fine Acquaintance with
" the Lords of *Hohenloe* have brought upon you.
                                          " This

" This faid, fhe ran to communicate her Fears
" and Apprehenfions to a Neighbour. The Mi-
" ftrefs of the Lodging, on her Side, fet up her
" Throat againft her Hufband, telling him that
" fhe would ftay no longer in a Houfe where fhe
" was expofed to the Infults of the Dead, and that
" all their Cuftomers would go and lodge elfe-
" where; for as how, they would not care to
" have a Ghoft live amongft them, or make a
" Jeft of them by his Frolics. As to the Muf-
" queteer he hugg'd himfelf, and it was comical
" enough to fee him enquire coolly into the Cir-
" cumftances of an Affair of which he was the
" Hero; taking Care, however, not to appear
" before the Banker."

This Story, Sir, you will do me the Favour to
read to the learned Doctors of the *Sorbonne*, and
to the Members of all your Academies; and fignify to them at the fame Time, that, as I take
Pleafure in cultivating the Sciences, and propagat-
ing Learning in general, I fhall be always ready to
move the Rubs out of their Road, and folve any
Difficulties they meet with in the Courfe of their
Studies. But they need not fend over a Courier
on Purpofe, as they have done in this Cafe, for I
can as well tranfmit my Opinion by the Poft.

 I am, Sir,
   Your humble Servant in a modeft Way,
    MARY MIDNIGHT.

To

To *Mrs.* MARY MIDNIGHT.

MADAM,

I HAVE fent you a Specimen of a Poem in Praife of *Hackney*, which is the Work of an eminent Pen-man in *Shore-ditch*. I efteem the whole Piece to be a great Honour to the Language, and a fingular Inftance to what ftupendous Heights unaffifted Genius can foar. I will not abfolutely affirm, that the four following Lines are better than any in *Shakefpear*, but I am pofitive they are as good; pleafe to obferve ————

Hackney, thy Glory thy own Lips fhall tell;
Witnefs a *Dalftone* and a *Shacklewell*,
And *Hummerton*, and *Clapton* DO declare,
The many Country-Seats that THERE are THERE.

I muft beg Leave to point out the Beauties of thefe Verfes one by one, for taken collectively they fhine with fuch a refulgent Glare, that they actually dazzle the Imagination:—And firft, not to mention a Word of the *Numerofity* of the Lines, the Mufick of which is fo delectable, we have a bolder Figure, than has yet been known in Rhetoric; *Dalftone* and *Shacklewell* are elegantly call'd the Lips of *Hackney*, whofe Glories they are naturally employ'd in celebrating.

Hackney, thy Glory thy own Lips fhall tell,
Witnefs a *Dalftone* and a *Shacklewell*.

What

What is this but to equal, or rather excel both *Orpheus* and *Amphion*, who indeed made Stocks and Stones dance Hornpipes, but never cou'd arrive to the Perfection of making them speak, as our inimitable Bard has done in this exquisite Couplet; but let us proceed to the third Line, in which there are such a Posse of Excellencies, that they really confound the Understanding,

    And *Hummerton* and *Clapton* DO declare,

Delectus verborum origo est Eloquentiæ (says *Cæsar*) a judicious Choice of Words is the Origin of Eloquence. If the Author had searched the whole Globe, he cou'd not have found out a more sonorous Word for the Name of a Place than *Hummerton*; a Word that ought to be set to Musick, and is worthier to be sung than said. The *Greeks* valued themselves, upon the Sweetness, Fullness and (to use *Horace*'s Word) the *Rotundity* of their Language————

————— *Graios dedit ore Rotundo Musa loqui.* —————

    And yet what is Θηβαι, and what is Αθηναι, the Names of *Thebes* and *Athens*, their two chief Cities in Point of Dignity and Magnificence with the high-sounding *Hummerton?* Much might be said in Behalf of *Clapton*, but we will wave that for the present, and proceed to the conclusive Part of the Verse, —————

        Do *declare.*

                    Now

Now a common Writer wou'd have been contented with the simple Word *declare*, but our
SHOREDITCH GENIUS knew better Things.—*He*
adds the expreffive Energy of the Particle DO, which
gives incredible Force to the Sentiment—*Hummerton* and *Clapton* don't make a fimple unornamented
Declaration, but they really, actually, *ipfo facto &
bonâ fide*, without Equivocation, mental Refervation, or any Evafion whatfoever, DO *declare* pofitively, comparatively, and fuperlatively, that——
what ?

The many Country Seats that THERE are THERE.

—Which being the laft Lines in the Specimen ; I
muft unavoidably conclude with it.—I fhall not infift upon the Merit of the prior Hemiftich in this
Verfe, becaufe what is Self-evident can need no
Expofition—But as for the laft, namely,

That THERE are THERE——

There certainly were never four Monofyllables affembled together to fuch admirable and expreffive
Purpofes. Here we have the Rhime like a two-
edged Sword in *utrumque paratus*, backwards or
forwards—upwards or downwards : THERE on
this Side, and THERE on t'other Side—The Twin
Rivals, or the happy Pair !—Amafing Dexterity !
Inconceivable Elegance ! Bring me Oceans of
Ink—bring me Reams of Paper ! Or rather bring
me Two-pence to purchafe the Whole of this admirable Performance, for that is all the modeft Author

thor requires for it, tho' its intrinfic Value be in-
eftimable.———

I am, Dear Madam,
your moft humble Servant,
GEORGE PILKINTON.

Deputy—Vice—Affiftant to the Under-Sexton of
Shore-ditch.

CARE *and* GENEROSITY;

A F A B L E.

By *Mrs.* MIDNIGHT.

OLD Care with Induftry and Art,
 At length fo well had play'd his Part;
He heap'd up fuch an ample Store,
That Av'rice cou'd not figh for more:
Ten thoufand Flocks his Shepherd told,
His Coffers overflow'd with Gold;
The Land all round him was his own,
With Corn his crouded Granaries groan.
In fhort fo vaft his Charge and Gain,
That to poffefs them was a Pain;
With Happinefs opprefs'd he lies,
And much too prudent to be wife.
Near him there liv'd a beauteous Maid,
With all the Charms of Youth array'd;
Good, amiable, fincere and free,
Her Name was *Generofity.*
'Twas hers the Largefs to beftow
On Rich and Poor, on Friend and Foe.
Her Doors to all were open'd wide,
The Pilgrim there might fafe abide:

Z

For

For th' hungry and the thirſty Crew,
The Bread ſhe broke, the Drink ſhe drew;
There Sickneſs laid her aching Head,
And there Diſtreſs cou'd find a Bed.—
Each Hour with an all-bounteous Hand,
Diffuſed ſhe Bleſſings round the Land:
Her Gifts and Glory laſted long,
And numerous was th' accepting Throng.
At length pale Penury ſeiz'd the Dame,
And Fortune fled, and Ruin came;
She found her Riches at an End,
And that ſhe had not made one Friend.—
All curſed her for not giving more,
Nor thought on what ſhe'd done before;
She wept, ſhe rav'd, ſhe tore her Hair,
When lo! to comfort her came *Care.*—
And cry'd, my dear, if you will join,
Your Hand in nuptial Bonds with mine;
All will be well—you ſhall have Store,
And I be plagu'd with Wealth no more.—
Tho' I reſtrain your bounteous Heart,
You ſtill ſhall act the generous Part.—
The Bridal came—great was the Feaſt,
And good the Pudding and the Prieſt;
The Bride in nine Moon's brought him forth:
A little Maid of matchleſs Worth:
Her Face was mixt of *Care* and *Glee,*
They Chriſten'd her *Oeconomy*;
And ſtyl'd her fair Diſcretion's Queen,
The Miſtreſs of the golden Mean.
Now *Generoſity* confin'd,
Is perfect eaſy in her Mind;
She loves to give, yet knows to ſpare,
Nor wiſhes to be free from *Care.*

Con-

Conclusion of the ADVENTURES *of Messrs.* INCLINATION *and* ABILITY.

HERCULES having again obtain'd a great Fortune, retired into the Country, where he bought a very fine Estate, and where, for his own Amusement, and for the Benefit of his poor Neighbours, he studied Physic, with great Diligence, and practised it with a Success which was adequate to that Diligence.—*Isgrim*, you may be sure, must be dabbling, and so turn'd Mountebank, to the Emolument of the Undertakers, the Increase of the Weekly Bills, and Destruction of Mankind.—— *Isgrim* had puff'd himself into some Reputation, before he began to practise; and the very first Patient he had was a Person of great Eminence, which was the Occasion of a good Repartee made to him one Day in the *Temple Exchange Coffee-House.*——*Isgrim* was glorying that he got Fifty Guineas by his first Patient; Mr. Critic *Catchup* cry'd out, Sir, you got a great deal more——Not a Jot more, I assure you, says *Isgrim*, I scorn to brag——Aye but you did, replies *Catchup*,—— *You got a Hatband, a Ring, a Pair of Gloves and a Scarf.*

The next Character in Life *Ability* chose to assume was that of a Painter, and an admirable one he was, for all *Frank Hayman's* Pictures were of his doing —— *Inclination*, of Course, became a

Dauber,

Dauber, and the following Story which has been told of others is only true of him.

A certain Nobleman, having built a Chapel, had a Mind the Stair-case leading to it fhou'd be or-namented with fome Scripture-hiftory, — which he at laft determined fhould be the Children of If-rael paffing thro' the Red Sea, and the *Egyptians* purfuing them —— *Ifgrim* was employ'd upon this Occafion —— and fell to work immediately; and after he had daub'd the Wall from Top to Bot-tom with red Paint, he call'd to his Lordfhip, and told him the Work was done —— Done! quoth the Peer — What's done? Where are the Children of *Ifrael?* My Lord, they are all gone over, re-plies *Ifgrim* — " But, Zounds, where are the E-" gyptians then!" They are drown'd, rejoin'd *Ifgrim*, to a Man.——Thefe are all the Adven-tures of the two Brothers communicable at prefent —— for *Ability* is gone abroad upon his Travels, but has promifed me his Correfpondence——As for *Ifgrim*, he is to be met with at any time at Mr. *Woudbe's*, a Gold-beater, at the *Cork* and *Feather*, in *Blowbladder-ftreet*.

M. MIDNIGHT.

The

The MIDWIFE's POLITICKS: Or, *Gossip's Chronicle of the Affairs of Europe.*

SPAIN.

ONE of the Points discussing between Mr. Keene and the Spanish Ministry, is the Right the English claim to cut Logwood in the Bay of Campeachy; which will be difficult to adjust: For Don Ensenada is not such an old Woman as to give us any favourable Concession in this Respect, at a Time when he is fortifying the Island of Rattan, where our brave Admiral Vernon made a Settlement for Englishmen, who it seems have left it for the Spaniards.

ITALY.

The poor Genoese continue in a very bad Situation, for though the Valley of Polsevera could boast of having 18,000 Inhabitants before the Austrian Invasion in 1746, at present they are reduced to 4000; the Republic is extremely poor, and may be at last tempted to alienate Corsica for another Regality to the House of Bourbon. A terrible Earthquake has happened in several Parts of Italy; particularly at Gualdo in the Ecclesiastical State, where two thirds of the City are destroyed; and at Palermo in Sicily, where the Damage is computed at upwards of 150,000 Crowns.

FRANCE.

It is whispered in the Coffee houses of Paris, and some make no Scruple to talk openly, of a Destination of the Brest Squadron, which was little thought of. M. du Perrier, say they, when he comes off Lisbon, is to make directly for the Azores, where he is to open his Orders, and join fifteen Ships ready built at Canada; whom he is to man with his Complements, which, for that Rea-

son

fon have been doubled : From thence he is to fail to the Coaft of Coromandel, and there eftablifh a decifive Superiority of Strength, fuch as, upon a Rupture with the Englifh, will carry the Settlements of that Nation before them : *All which may be too true.*

GERMANY.

According to Advices from Hanover they feem to be pretty pofitive that his Britannic Majefty will go over early next Spring, in order to accelerate by his Prefence the Election of the Archduke Jofeph, to the Dignity of King of the Romans : Indeed, England cannot afford to continue her Scenes of Liberality on the Continent ; but if this falutary Work can be effected, it will be well worth the laying out a Million in oppofition to France.

SWEDEN *and* RUSSIA.

The Ruffian Army confifts of 200,090 effective Men, ready to take the Field ; 160,000 of which are Foot, and 40,090 Horfe, befides Calmucks, Coffacks, and the Militia of the Country : The Fleet alfo confifts of 80 Man of War and Frigates, exclufive of Gallies and leffer Veffels, which are returned into Port ; and every Thing tending to the Continuance of a Pacification with Sweden, is to be mutually difcovered at the Courts of Peterfburgh and Stockholm.

TURKY.

Above 70,000 People have been already deftroyed by the Plague in Conftantinople, and the neighbouring Iflands : They have alfo fuffered a dreadful Conflagration at the Porte, by which 4000 Houfes were laid in Afhes ; and their Commerce muft be interrupted by the Orders for all Ships coming from the Levant, performing Quarantine in Great-Britain and Holland.

For

A Penny fav'd is a Penny got : Or, a Word of Advice to the Oeconomifts.

NOtwithftanding Oeconomy is often a fofter Term only for *Littlenefs of Soul*, yet taken in its true and genuine Sènfe it is an admirable Virtue, as I have fhewn in my Fable of *Care* and *Generofity* ; the Moral of which, I hope, will be duly attended to by all Gentlemen who are inclined to keep within Compafs, and all Ladies who wou'd be good Houfewives. To fuch then Be it Known, that 'till the Fourteenth of October next enfuing, any Number of the fecond Volume of my Magazine may be had for the trivial Expence of Three-Pence : — But after that Time, no Number either of the firft or fecond Volume, can be purchafed under our-Pence ; and this by the Defire of feveral Thoufands of my Friends, who have done me the Honour to. remark, THAT MINE IS THE ONLY BOOK EVER PUBLISHED WHICH ALL THE PURCHASERS COMPLAIN'D WAS TOO CHEAP.

—— *Nullum numen abeft, fi fit Prudentia,*

MARY MIDNIGHT.

For the Benefit of MANKIND.

Advertifement.

WHEREAS the *Carpenters* and *Joiners* of a Book lately publifh'd, Entituled, *The* QUARTERLY BEE, have made free with Mrs. *Midnight*'s Property, and very injudicioufly mix'd her Honey with their Muftard ; this is to inform the Publick, That fpeedily will be publifh'd a Work of the fame Nature with theirs, which for the Sake of Propriety, and in Imitation of them, I fhall entitle and call, *The* QUARTERLY OX. Gentlemen and Ladies who are willing to fubfcribe, are defired to fend their Names to *Francis Fleece*, at the Sign of the *Bull*, in *Blunderhall Street*, and they fhall be *taken in*.

SUSANNAH SERIOUS.

AN INDEX

TO THE

SECOND VOLUME.

An INDEX to the SECOND VOLUME.

An INDEX to the SECOND VOLUME.

CPSIA information can be obtained at www.ICGtesting.com
Printed in the USA
LVOW131507291211

261605LV00013B/94/P

9 781175 269065